OPERATION VULTURE

JOHN PRADOS received his B.A. and his Ph.D. from Columbia University. He is the editor of *America Confronts Terrorism: Understanding the Danger and How to Think about It*, and the author of *Combined Fleet Decoded: The Secret History of American Intelligence and the Japanese Navy in World War II; The Hidden History of Vietnam; Valley of Decision: The Siege of Khe Sanh; The Blood Road: The Ho Chi Minh Trail and the Vietnam War; The Soviet Estimate: U.S. Intelligence Analysis and Russian Military Strength; Presidents' Secret Wars: CIA and Pentagon Covert Operations from World War II Through the Persian Gulf War*; as well as the creator of several simulation games. Prados is a senior fellow of the National Security Archives in Washington, D.C. and a contributing editor to *MHQ: The Quarterly Journal of Military History*. He currently lives near Washington, D.C.

AVAILABLE NOW

Helmet for My Pillow
The General
The March to Glory
By Robert Leckie

Samurai!
By Saburo Sakai with Martin Caidin
and Fred Saito

Thunderbolt!
By Robert S. Johnson and Martin Caidin

Fork-Tailed Devil: The P-38
The B-17: The Flying Forts
By Martin Caidin

When Hell Froze Over
By E.M. Halliday

The World War II Reader
By the Editors of *World War II* magazine

Vietnam: A Reader
By the Editors of *Vietnam* magazine

The Civil War Reader: 1862
By the Editors of
Civil War Times Illustrated and
America's Civil War

The Lost History of Gettysburg
By Colonel James K. P. Scott

OPERATION VULTURE

By John Prados

ibooks
new york
www.ibooks.net

DISTRIBUTED BY SIMON & SCHUSTER, INC

An Original Publication of ibooks, inc.

An ibooks, inc. Book

Ibooks, inc.
24 West 25th Street
New York, NY 10010

The ibooks World Wide Web Site address is:
http://www.ibooks.net

Photographs by Russell De Somer, Thomas A. Julian, and Jack McDonald

Editor: Dwight Jon Zimmerman
Cover Art: Robert Zohrab
Cover Design: J. Vita

ISBN: 0-7434-4490-6
First ibooks printing August 2002
10 9 8 7 6 5 4 3 2 1

Share your thoughts about *Operation Vulture* and other ibooks titles in the
new ibooks virtual reading group at www.ibooksinc.com

For Davida, who was present at the inception

"Nothing can be precluded in a military thing. Remember this: when you resort to force as the arbiter of human difficulty, you don't know where you are going; but, generally speaking, if you get deeper and deeper, there is just no limit except what is imposed by the limitations of force itself."

–President Dwight D. Eisenhower,
January 12, 1955

Contents

CONTENTS

Preface

A lost artifact of the history of America in Vietnam, *Operation Vulture* represents the restoration of a study that can almost be said never to have appeared. The present book is also far different from the one that almost wasn't. In 1983 The Dial Press, the original publisher, was reorganized and liquidated by its parent company, Doubleday. That action took place seven days *before* the publication date of this book. As a result the work received even less support than usual, and for long has been virtually unknown. In addition, the original version suffered from differences in editorial viewpoint between author and editor. The latter thought the details of French actions at the battle of Dien Bien Phu would be the primary attraction for an American audience. The author maintained that it was the *American* actions in the Dien Bien Phu crisis that were unknown, in particular that putting together American diplomatic maneuvers with U.S. military actions illuminated the real U.S. purposes of the time in a startling new way. The book published in 1983 represented the editor's point of view more than the author's. I struggled to preserve as much of the relevant detail as possible, and in many cases settled for the compromise of short summary passages that furnished the merest whiff of the original material. Among the material that suffered as a consequence were important details of Washington's deliberations on intervention and bombing at Dien Bien Phu and after, accounts of the U.S. naval operations involved, important passages on United States Air Force activities, and the story of the first American prisoners of war taken in Vietnam. I have always wanted to restore this book to its original form and full evidentiary value.

In addition the process of research did not end with publication. A number of documents that were in declassification

PREFACE

review at the time only became available later. The author also interviewed even more witnesses of the original events in the months and years afterwards. *Operation Vulture* also presents their stories, ranging them alongside the restored material, which reflects interviews as well. The combination adds immeasurably to the first edition, perhaps not enough to say this is an entirely new work, but certainly sufficiently to argue that the book now has depth and nuance not available previously.

The new evidence in the author's view adds even more to the argument made in 1983 that at Dien Bien Phu the Eisenhower administration stood ready to go to war, ten years ahead of the Vietnam war with which Americans are familiar. Avoiding war in 1954 was not a matter of the president just saying now, as many conventional accounts of these events paint them, or of a certain United States senator (Lyndon B. Johnson) rejecting the proposals of John Foster Dulles and military chief Arthur Radford. Nor was the intervention project simply the personal agenda of Secretary of State Dulles as other versions portray it. Nor would America be saved from war merely because allies refused to enlist in the enterprise, which is the theme in yet other pictures of Dien Bien Phu. Rather, President Eisenhower would be central to intervention, souring on it only much later and slower than believed earlier; Johnson privately favored intervention, with typical retellings of this story reflecting the way the original leak occurred; and while allied (especially British) lack of enthusiasm would be important to the outcome, equally vital would be dawning realization of the danger of general war with China and Russia. Read when, where, how, and why in the pages that follow.

To provide consistency in the text, the forms "Viet-Nam" and "Indochina" are used throughout, even in quoted material, in place of "Vietnam" and Indo-China." However, in quotes where the originator has used such forms as capitalizing words ["Communist," "Red China"], these forms have been retained in the excerpt even though the text consistently uses the lower case.

John Prados
Washington, DC
December 2001

Acknowledgments

This study would have been impossible without the assistance of many persons, most particularly the helpful and hardworking staffs of a number of libraries and research facilities. The author wishes to thank especially the staffs of the Library of Congress, the New York Public Library, Columbia University Library, and the Echols Collection at Cornell University Library. At the Library of congress special thanks to Dr. Bruce Martin. The same goes to Dr. David Humphreys at the Lyndon Baines Johnson Library, Dr. John E. Taylor at the National Archieves, Mr. Herbert Pankratz at the Eisenhower Library, as well as to Dean C. Allard and Barbara A. Gilmore at the Naval Operational Archives. Thanks also to R. Cargill Hall of the Albert F. Simpson Historical Research Center, Maxwell Air Force Base, and to Alfred M. Beck at the Office of the Chief of Military History. For photographs as well as materials from his extensive collection I am indebted to Jack McDonald. Also for photographs I wish to thank French Indochina veterans Thomas A. Julian, Russell De Somer, and Reginald Berube. I am only sorry I could not reproduce all the pictures they cheerfully supplied. I additionally want to thank these and other individuals who agreed to interviews or sent remniscences. Thanks for logistical assistance go to Joseph Prados and to Harlene Hipsh. James Dingeman provided hard-to-find reference works from his extensive collection. Special thanks to Jill Gay, who read and commented upon the manuscript. Much of what is good in what follows is due to the collective and individual efforts of these and other persons.

Like a mighty army moves the church of God
Brothers, we are treading where the saints have trod.
We are not divided, all one body we,
One in hope and doctrine, one in charity.

Onward Christian soldiers, marching as to war,
With the cross of Jesus going on before.

. . . .

At the sign of triumph Satan's host doth flee;
On then, Christian soldiers, on to victory!
Hell's foundations quiver at the shout of praise;
Brothers, lift your voices, loud your anthems raise.

Onward Christian soldiers, marching as to war,
With the cross of Jesus going on before.

—Sabine Baring-Gould, 1864
lyrics to *Onward, Christian Soldiers*

I

THE IDES OF MARCH

March 20, 1954. The mist lifted slowly after dawn. Wisps lay over Jamaica Bay and a light drizzle fell at Idlewild Airport as Trans World Airlines Flight 931 lined up on its final approach for landing. It was half past six in the morning, but the French and American army officers waiting at the airport had already been working for hours. When the plane drew up in front of the terminal, they met short, craggy General Paul Ely, who was on a mission from the French government to the United States.

General Ely was chief of the General Staff for National Defense—the board of senior military advisors to the French government. A certain protocol was observed in meeting this top French general. Major General Sebree was on hand, as was a French officer, Colonel Maurice Chabot. But the greetings were restrained and the party made haste. A private plane was waiting, sent by Admiral Arthur Radford, Chairman of the Joint Chiefs of Staff and Ely's equivalent number in the United States.

Lieutenant Colonel Phillip Cocke led the French party to the shuttle plane, a C-47 military transport. Within less than an hour they were airborne again, this time for Washington, D.C. Ely and his aides, French Air Force Colonel Raymond Brohon and Army

Captain Maral, had no chance to recover from the grueling fourteen-hour transatlantic flight. But the general, who personally prided himself on an ascetic demeanor, would say nothing about exhaustion. Time was of crucial importance.

The C-47 arrived at National Airport in Washington at about ten in the morning. There Ely was met with the full honors accorded to an officer of his high rank. Admiral Radford shook his hand warmly. General Jean Valluy, the French representative to the NATO Standing Group (in fact, Paul Ely's successor in this position), came with Jean Daridan from the French Embassy. The U.S. State Department sent Philip Bonsal.

However, the Americans again were sensitive to the urgency of Ely's mission from the French government, and festivities at National were not prolonged. Radford invited General Ely to dinner at his home, "Quarters A" in the naval compound up Nebraska Avenue, and Ely was bundled into a car for the drive to the French Embassy with Radford. The fourth seat in their car was apparently taken up by a Central Intelligence Agency security man. General Ely spoke very little English and he discovered that Radford's French was equally poor, so conversation between the two officers was rather limited until they arrived at the embassy on Massachusetts Avenue.

Ely was the bearer of frightening news and his visit posed a stark choice for American officials. A major Cold War crisis was brewing in Asia, in Indochina specifically. There the French, with American support, were engaged in a war with Vietnamese nationalists. The French needed more help. For the first time they thought they might lose a big battle, one being fought at Dien Bien Phu in the mountains of northern Indochina, a region called Tonkin. Just before leaving Paris, General Ely had even been called back from Orly Airport because of last-minute news concerning the crisis.

At Dien Bien Phu the French had established an entrenched camp, surrounded by their adversary, the Viet Minh. The position was entirely dependent on aircraft for its supply and reinforcement, for troop rotation, and for a good deal of fire support. The airfield at Dien Bien Phu had had to close down shortly after the battle began, swept by Viet Minh artillery barrages and soon even by direct fire. This meant that the camp had to rely solely on what could be parachuted to it from the outside.

General Ely had come to ask the Americans for more transport aircraft to fly supplies in Indochina and for additional bombers to hit the Viet Minh. Even if these were supplied he still could not assure the Americans that the battle at Dien Bien Phu could be won.

Ely was also concerned about the threat of air intervention from the People's Republic of China. The French considered this the worst possible scenario, since their military effort at Dien Bien Phu depended entirely upon unrestricted use of Indochinese airspace. But the Chinese had jet aircraft. If they wished, they could fill the air over Dien Bien Phu or launch attacks on the air bases used by the French. There was not a plane in the *Forces Aériennes Françaises d'Extrême-Orient* that could match Chinese jets in speed, to say nothing of the aerial combat experience gained by the Chinese in the Korean War of 1950 to 1953. The French did not even have a capable early-warning radar in Tonkin.

Invited to dinner at "Quarters A" that night were General Matthew B. Ridgway, Chief of Staff of the United States Army and a colleague of Radford's on the Joint Chiefs of Staff, Richard M. Nixon, the Vice-President of the United States, and Allen Dulles, the head of the Central Intelligence Agency. At the working dinner Ely, who had been at Dien Bien Phu on an inspection visit in February, described conditions at the entrenched camp.

Ely did not make all his points right away. In particular he did not mention French concern over a possible Chinese air intervention. Perhaps he decided to reserve his most sensitive questions for Radford when formal discussions opened the next day.

For Washington, Paul Ely's presence crystallized the hypothetical contingencies that had been discussed in the administration for more than a year. The situation was real. The emergency was now, and it was named Dien Bien Phu.

Dien Bien Phu. It was not even a real place. The name translates as "large administrative center on the frontier." There was no village called "Dien Bien Phu." Rather, a cluster of villages filled a large valley in northwestern Tonkin, close to the borders of both Laos and China. That this valley should become the scene of the climactic battle of the first Indochina war was the result of daring and desperate decisions by the French High Command. General Henri Navarre, the French commander in chief, was implementing a plan to increase his strength and mobility in order to defeat the Viet Minh in 1955. The plan required avoiding major battles during 1953–1954, yet Navarre deliberately accepted battle at Dien Bien Phu.

The Viet Minh met General Navarre's challenge. They moved the bulk of the main force units in the Viet-Nam People's Army to the upland valley and then spent months amassing supplies and making preparations. The assault was timed for the weekend. On March 13, 1954, they attacked.

In Washington the White House press secretary recorded it as a quiet day at the office. President Dwight David Eisenhower had taken the day off to motor to the lodge at Camp David. On the way he stopped in Maryland country towns to shake the hands of excited constituents. The illustrious war hero was in the second year of his first term as President. There was still a sense of dynamism then and "Ike" exerted powerful personal magnetism over Americans. At Camp David the President relaxed, oblivious to the crisis at Dien Bien Phu.

It is true that Indochina had been for some time on the President's mind. His administration was engaged in protracted interagency discussions to formulate a policy for Indochina, and it had specifically determined to provide extra military aid to France directly in Indochina. As a result, aid to France constituted a third of the entire military aid appropriation request that President Eisenhower was sending to Congress that spring. The dollar amount was over $1.1 billion and France was the largest single recipient of military aid.

United States policy opposed any negotiated settlement in which concessions were made to the Viet Minh. This meant that the French could not be allowed to suffer a military reverse in Indochina and that no negotiated solution should be allowed at the international conference scheduled to take place in Geneva at the end of April. Thus Dien Bien Phu was a delicate problem for the United States.

The Viet Minh captured an important French strongpoint at Dien Bien Phu on the first night of the attack and another two days later. The French lost a third vital hilltop position when its garrison of local tribesmen deserted on March 18. By the time General Ely arrived in Washington on March 20, the situation at Dien Bien Phu indeed seemed catastrophic: it had already been five days since General Navarre reported the prospect of its imminent fall.

What could the United States do to avert this disaster? Would the United States resort to military intervention in the situation?

The policy quagmire on Indochina was a postwar development in American foreign policy. Before World War II, Indochina had been the largest French colony in the Far East. With the early French defeat at the hands of Germany, Japan moved on Indochina and established a protectorate there. During the early years of the war President Franklin D. Roosevelt opposed assistance to any French return to the colony, arguing that this would put the United States in the role of supporting colonialism. Roosevelt's stance was not popular with desk officers in the State Department who saw that it would critically affect relations with the French. There is some evidence that Roosevelt's determination weakened before his death in April 1945.

President Harry S Truman, on the other hand, deferred to his professional diplomats. With a French Expeditionary Corps already en route to the Pacific, and faced with the choice of good relations either with the erstwhile colonial nations of Indochina or with France, Truman chose France: in an official statement on October 20, 1945, the U.S. government stated that it had no thought of opposing the reestablishment of French control over Indochina and, in a complete denial of Roosevelt's policy, maintained that no American statement had ever questioned, even by implication, French sovereignty over Indochina.[1]

Even so the United States initially maintained a position of qualified neutrality on Indochina. As Cold War competition with the Soviet Union sharpened, however, American officials came more and more to identify the Marxist views of many opponents of the French in Indochina with loyalty to a monolithic Soviet communism. In September 1948 the American ambassador to Paris told officials of the French Foreign Ministry, or Quai d'Orsay, that if France so desired, the United States was willing to give public approval of and also consider financial aid for Indochina under the Marshall Plan. The offer was made even more explicit in a State Department cable to the American consul in Saigon on May 10, 1949: "At the proper time and under the proper circumstances, the Department will be prepared to do its part by extending recognition to the [French-supported Vietnamese] government and by expressing the possibility of complying with any request by such a government for US arms and economic assistance."[2] Before the year was out, the United States allowed French sailors to enter the country and make a transcontinental trip. They picked up several naval craft, which had been sold to France, and sailed them from the West Coast to Viet-Nam. This was in direct violation of an embargo on military assistance to France in Viet-Nam that had been in effect since 1947.

In December 1949 high-ranking officers of the United States' Far East Command visited Saigon for talks with the French commander in chief. The discussions coincided with the end of the Chinese civil war when the Kuomintang were driven from the mainland and the People's Liberation Army arrived on the border of Indochina. Certain French authorities encouraged rumors of a secret agreement between Mao Tse-tung and the leader of the anti-French Vietnamese, Ho Chi Minh.

While the anti-French resistance had many communist members, it also had a strong nationalist orientation. In fact the Indochinese Communist Party was "officially" dissolved in 1945, although it maintained a shadowy existence within the Viet Minh united front. The Viet Minh struggle was essentially directed at winning independence from France, a goal that captivated the hearts and minds of many Vietnamese. This was the core of the French political problem: The Viet Minh were highly motivated.

The United States was far from ignorant of this problem. Reports from American diplomats in Viet-Nam had consistently emphasized the support the Viet Minh seemed to enjoy among Vietnamese, while contrasting this with the apathy that prevailed toward the French-created Bao Dai government. A State Department policy paper in July 1948 recognized that "the objectives of United States policy can only be attained by such French action as will satisfy the aspiration of the peoples of Indochina."[3] A split developed among State Department officials, however. The offices dealing with the Far East insisted on the necessity of concessions from France, while the Bureau of West European Affairs held with equal vehemence that any French government that made such concessions would fall.

With the intensification of the Cold War, the disarmament of Germany, and the economic troubles of Britain, France was seen as a principal factor in U.S. European strategy. Pressuring France on the Indochina question could reduce French cooperation with NATO Europe.

So in 1950 the main outlines of American policy were firmly set along lines favored by State's Western European Office. The recommendation of the Asian specialists that recognition of the Bao Dai government be contingent on French agreement to a "timetable" for making Viet-Nam into a truly independent nation was rejected. Just over one week later France submitted a formal request for military assistance in Indochina.

On February 27, President Truman held a meeting of the National Security Council to consider the request. The outcome was a policy paper that concluded "it is important to United States security interests that all practicable measures be taken to prevent further communist expansion in Southeast Asia. Indochina is a key area of Southeast Asia and is under immediate threat."[4] The departments of State and Defense were instructed to prepare a program of "practicable measures" to safeguard U.S. interests. It was agreed that military assistance was the best "practicable measure." After a meeting with the French foreign minister on May 8, Secretary of State Dean Acheson emerged and declared that

> the United States government, convinced that neither national independence nor democratic evolution existed in any area dominated by Soviet imperialism, considers the situation to be such as to warrant its according economic aid and military equipment to the associated states and to France in order to assist them in restoring stability and

> *permitting these states to pursue their peaceful and democratic development.*[5]

The United States was in the war.

The first monies allocated for military assistance to Indochina amounted to $10 million—coming from funds that had previously been appropriated by Congress for countries in the "general area" of China. In the summer of 1950 the Americans formulated a program providing $100 million for Indochina. After high-level talks in the fall, and French military reverses in Tonkin, aid was increased for 1951, and in 1951 it was increased again. In fact the French requested half of the $600 million the war was estimated to cost that year and they received $170 million. By 1952 it was widely known that the Americans were carrying between one third and one half of the financial cost of the Indochina war.

With fiscal involvement came more direct American engagement in Indochina. Military aid generally entailed several activities, among them the responsibility for scheduling the arrival and monitoring the "end use" of aid shipments, for advising the host government on military matters, and for troop training when requested.

In Indochina, however, the French were not interested in these things. This was not apparent from the ostentatious greetings given the first ten U.S. officers assigned to Indochina, on August 2, 1950. But, when those officers tried to move around in the field to monitor "end use" of American equipment, they were accused of getting in the way of French operations. Attempts to advise the French on military strategy were regarded as interference in French conduct of the war. No American role was permitted in training either French troops or the national armies of Viet-Nam, Laos, and Cambodia, ostensibly because the French preferred training the national armies in French-style military techniques. Even though U.S. manpower in Indochina continued to grow, reaching 128 in 1951, the group was increasingly limited to pro forma inspections arranged in advance with the French, and to information for Washington supplied by the French.

Thus the French were careful to guard their prerogatives and were sensitive to any indications of the United States exercising an independent role. In formal talks during October 1950 the French agreed to nothing more than maintaining "full consultative contact." American exasperation with this attitude increased throughout the Truman administration.

Nevertheless, American frustration did not preclude a steady supply of weapons and equipment to Indochina. In 1950 the French got their first bomber and transport aircraft—B-26 Invaders and C-47 Dakotas—as well as F-8F Bearcat fighters. An average of 5,000 tons of equipment arrived monthly until the end of 1951, and the two-hundredth shipload of U.S. equipment docked in July 1952. Between October 1952 and July 1953 the volume of equipment deliveries to Indochina stood at twelve shiploads per month. By the end of 1952 the French had been supplied with 777 armored fighting vehicles, 13,000 transport vehicles, 228 aircraft, and 253 naval vessels in addition to thousands of lesser items.

The major considerations of American policy were again stated in a National Security Council policy review undertaken to assist the incoming Eisenhower administration. The paper was completed on January 19, 1953, and presented a global picture of basic national security policy. In discussing European defense it argued that "the French will not be able to make their full contribution to the security of Europe as long as a substantial portion of their resources is committed to the war in Indochina. The French will continue to try to transfer a growing part of the Indochinese war's cost to the US and to the Associated States."

The policy study's observations on Far Eastern matters also gave a grim prognosis on the situation:

> . . . *without (1) the deployment in Indochina of additional forces from outside the country sufficient to permit the French-Vietnamese forces to take the military initiative, (2) the development of additional Vietnamese forces, and (3) a political offensive by France and the Vietnamese government to enhance the appeal of the government of Viet-Nam and elicit more effective support by nationalist and "neutralist" elements, the military situation in Indochina will probably continue to be stalemated with a resultant deterioration in the political and economic situation. Such a situation would have serious implications for the security of the rest of Southeast Asia.*[6]

Clearly State Department and Pentagon planners felt that the need to support the French outweighed the difficulties of dealing with them over military assistance and the French political approach to Indochina.

Before becoming President, Eisenhower had been briefed periodically by his wartime subordinate Walter Bedell Smith, who served Truman as director of central intelligence. Eisenhower also had had considerable access to information during his tour as general commanding the Supreme Headquarters, Allied Powers in Europe (SHAPE), the central military command under NATO, from 1950 until 1952.

Several times in 1951 Eisenhower corresponded on the subject with the Secretary of Defense in Washington. During March, when the French commander in chief for Indochina, General Jean de Lattre de Tassigny, was on a mission home to urge reinforcements be dispatched to the Expeditionary Corps, De Lattre thought it useful to appeal for Ike's support. The two generals met on March 17. Eisenhower commented in his diary that

> the French have a knotty problem on that one—the cam- paign out there is a draining sore in their side. Yet if they quit and Indochina falls to [the] Commies, it is easily pos- sible that the countries of Southeast Asia and Indonesia would go, soon to be followed by India. That prospect makes the whole problem one of interest to us all. I'd favor heavy reinforcement to get the thing over at once; but I'm convinced that no military victory is possible in that kind of theater. Even if Indochina were completely cleared of communists, right across the border is China with inex- haustible manpower!![7]

General Eisenhower again commented on the Far Eastern problem in a letter to Secretary of Defense Robert Lovett on De- cember 19, 1951. Ike observed that

> occasionally, new evidence becomes available that seems to indicate a gradual buildup of Chinese Communist forces in Southeast Asia. Obviously, if Communist China should extend its aggressive operations to include, soon, a South- east Asia front, it will at some point become impossible for the free world to allow them to continue with the fic- tion that only Chinese "volunteers" are participating. If American interest should become actively involved, we would have a de facto war on our hands, no matter what we might call it in official communiques.[8]

Robert Lovett's reply informed Ike that the French had begun saying they could not continue the fight in Indochina, probably because of their fiscal difficulties. Lovett stressed financial aid and noted that the Joint Chiefs of Staff unanimously opposed any use of American ground troops in Indochina. In answer to Ike's questions about Chinese action in Southeast Asia, Lovett noted "we have done some quiet and unofficial planning as to how we might help the French in case of a catastrophe. But it is not a pretty picture for the moment or for some time to come. We are going to agree to a Southeast Asia conference and I hope will be able to perfect certain additional plans."[9]

At a June 1952 press conference General Eisenhower saw the proper Indochina policy as aiding the French but avoiding American troop commitment. After his election Ike made a famous trip to Korea, from which he returned aboard the Navy cruiser *Helena* accompanied by a company of senior advisors. There were lively discussions on vital issues, among them Indochina. One participant recalls that Eisenhower brought up the Indochina matter himself, indicating that it was not only possible, but probable that a serious problem would emerge there.

As he put it in an interview, "I constantly was saying to the French government, 'Look, you people are making one very bad error. You're letting the world, and particularly the people of Indochina, believe that you're still fighting a colonial war. You've got to make this thing a matter between freedom and communism.' "[10]

II

THE NAVARRE PLAN

At the very end of World War II it was inevitable that the Viet Minh would seize control in Tonkin. Organized by the Indochinese Communist Party as a nationalist united front during World War II, the Viet Minh was the most efficient and powerful political grouping in the country. The French authorities and troops were in prison or dead, killed in the Japanese *coup de force* of March 1945.

The Viet Minh formed a government, the Democratic Republic of Viet-Nam (DRV), and a legislature, and held elections consolidating its power in Tonkin. The titular head of the state of Viet-Nam, pro-French Emperor Bao Dai, officially abdicated in August 1945 and recognized the DRV as the new government.

In southern Viet-Nam, called Cochinchina in French days, the Viet Minh were also strong and well organized, but so were a variety of other Vietnamese political factions including right-wing groups, religious sects, anarchists, and to Trotskyites. The Viet Minh were unable to establish a clear ascendancy in Cochinchina.

In September 1945 the British moved into Cochinchina to enforce the surrender of the Japanese armed forces and to free Allied prisoners. In order to restore "order" amid the chaotic Vietnamese political scene, the British handed over control of the country to France.

At that time the French had an Expeditionary Corps moving to the Pacific. Originally intended to participate in the war against Japan, the *Corps Expéditionnaire Français d'Extrême-Orient* served just as well to reestablish French authority in Indochina. Thus the French returned to Viet-Nam. But this was only in the south; in Tonkin the DRV was a constituted authority with an army, albeit ill-equipped and -trained. It was evident that, with only 64,000 troops in the Expeditionary Corps, the French Army could not simultaneously control Cochinchina and invade Tonkin.

The necessity for dealing with Vietnamese nationalism was recognized by the French commander in chief, General Jacques Philippe Leclerc. Leclerc reached an agreement with the DRV concerning French recognition of the independence and territorial integrity of Viet-Nam and its right to maintain an army to be assisted by France. The French Army returned peaceably to Tonkin while negotiations were in progress. But in mid-1946 the Viet Minh charged that France was not seriously committed to the independence it had promised for Indochina.

General Leclerc left Indochina in July 1946 and was replaced by Jean Valluy. During November a French sector commander at Haiphong, in Tonkin's Red River delta, provoked a serious confrontation between French and Viet Minh troops, after which a French Navy cruiser shelled a Vietnamese settlement in the city, killing more than 5,000 people.

War came about a month later. On the night of December 19, 1946, the Viet Minh made a concerted effort to overrun all French military positions in Tonkin. Great damage resulted from the battle of Hanoi, while at Nam Dinh the French garrison was besieged and nearly lost. The French deployed massive reinforcements to the north. Hanoi and Haiphong became bases from which the French moved out into the surrounding Red River delta. In the fall of 1947, General Valluy shifted the greater strength of the Expeditionary Corps to Tonkin for a major offensive called "Operation Lea." But it failed to catch the Viet Minh, who disappeared into the jungles and hills.

At first the French Army was supremely confident of the outcome in Indochina. Theirs was a modern European army with tanks, planes, ships, guns, and sophisticated communications and staffs. There were specialized units like paratroopers, who could make lightning strikes at an enemy by dropping out of the sky in a tactic known as "vertical envelopment." There was the magnificent Foreign Legion, whose combat ability was feared the world over. The French had total air superiority and complete control of the sea; their task forces and air strikes could range the length of the country. Nothing could stand against them.

In Operation Lea the French dropped paratroopers right on top of the village that housed the Viet Minh leadership. Ho Chi Minh and other DRV officials barely escaped in time. That was in August 1947; after that the French never again came so close to ending the Franco-Vietnamese war on their terms. The French Army was unbeatable in a pitched battle, but whenever it concentrated for an offensive, the Viet Minh avoided contact. The French mechanized forces could not follow the Viet-Nam People's Army into the bush and their infantry could not keep up with the pace of its battalions.

Thus the Indochina war became a source of increasing frustration for France. It was a stalemate, except that every day the list of the dead and injured grew, as did the drain on the French treasury. It became known as *"la guerre salle,"* the dirty war. After 1950 the National Assembly adopted regulations prohibiting draftees being sent to the war, which made Indochina even more the war of the professional army.

In 1953, Premier René Mayer offered the Indochina command to Henri Navarre, chief of staff to the commander of NATO ground forces in Central Europe. Lieutenant General Navarre did not want the post but was counseled by colleagues to accept and did so. He left Paris for Indochina on May 19. Navarre's instructions were to study the situation in Indochina and then report back to the government.

Navarre had impressed the government ministers as clear-sighted and intelligent, if sometimes a little obscure in his meanings. He was from the cavalry, traditionally the elite in the French Army, and had held a variety of staff and intelligence positions since before World War II. Navarre's combat experience was in the Riff campaign in Morocco in the 1920s, and then in World War II as chief of an armored unit that spearheaded the French Army drive into Germany in 1945. His command experience subsequently included the military division of Constantine, in Algeria, from 1948 to 1950 and then leadership of the French 5th Armored Division in Germany. Navarre was fifty-four years old when he was chosen for the Indochina command.

Navarre approached the strategic problem of Indochina as any good staff planner would have. Initially he refused to become bogged down in the day-to-day management of operations and instead spent time visiting the fronts, inspecting troops and facilities all over Indochina, conferring with subordinates and questioning Expeditionary Corps members on their combat experiences. Navarre had never been in Indochina until his arrival as commander in chief, so he brought a fresh perspective but no experience of the specific conditions.

During the inspection trips Navarre appeared to the troops as a cold and uninspiring leader. They began to call him the "air-conditioned general" because he seemed impossible to excite. Even a semi-official biography of Navarre printed in the Expeditionary Corps's bimonthly magazine saw the general as "master of his nerves" and as one man "with two faces." One of Navarre's old bosses, General Joseph-Pierre Koenig, whom he had served as secretary, gave him a white Persian cat that he liked very much. Navarre was quoted by Max Olivier as saying he liked cats "because they prefer to be alone and because they have an independent spirit."[1]

With his intelligence and refusal to become engrossed in the enthusiasms of some subordinates, Navarre could not fail to appreciate the military realities in Indochina: The Viet Minh were strongly established in Tonkin, where the Expeditionary Corps had assumed a defensive stance. Combined with the allied armies of the Associated States (Cambodia, Laos, and Viet-Nam), who were trained and armed by the French, the Expeditionary Corps possessed greater numbers than the Viet Minh, but this superiority dwindled to nothing because the troops were dispersed in small posts throughout Indochina. The Viet Minh, on the other hand, were building guerrilla strength even in the Red River delta. Above all, Vo Nguyen Giap, a former schoolteacher who now led the military arm of the Viet Minh, appeared to have the initiative—the Expeditionary Corps could only respond defensively and seemed unable to mount operations to successfully destroy their enemy.

General Navarre gathered many proposals from subordinates, ranging from one recommending the formation of partisan units in Viet Minh rear areas, to another proposal for the addition of bombers to the French Air Force. Navarre determined to ask for reinforcements from France for the Expeditionary Corps and to ask the Associated States to speed up their formation of native armies. He also decided to accumulate a general reserve so that the French could engage in offensive operations to match the Viet Minh's.

One proposal Navarre instantly accepted was a major increase in the rate of formation of Vietnamese Army units. This project was the idea of Vietnamese Army commander Nguyen Van Hinh, who began in December 1952 to advocate formation of light infantry battalions, smaller units that would have less firepower but that could be formed more quickly and in greater numbers as the Vietnamese Army expanded. These units would be able to hold cleared areas and free more powerful battalions for use in larger formations of the French Union forces. The Vietnamese called the light battalions *"Tieu Doan Kich Quan."* The program was approved in February 1953 and a month later the French asked the Americans to provide extra aid to Indochina to finance the Vietnamese Army expansion. On July 15, 1953, Bao Dai decreed general mobilization and extended the length of Vietnamese military service to two years.

Until 1953 the largest French units in Indochina were called *groupes mobiles*, which consisted of two or three thousand troops each, including some tank and artillery elements. But General Giap's army was operating in divisions of about ten thousand men. The People's Army had no tanks and until 1953 did not have many artillery guns either, but its divisions were still too large for an average *groupe mobile* to engage. Navarre wanted French divisions of a size equal to the Viet Minh's but possessing much greater firepower. He planned to form division command elements and put several *groupes mobiles* into each new division. These divisions would be maneuverable units, unlike the five territorial divisions into which the French had previously divided the Red River delta. Navarre planned to use the 1954–55 campaign season to consolidate the French position and form his battle force, anticipating a full-scale French offensive in the summer of 1955. He would make less powerful attacks sooner, indeed, immediately, so as to take a tactically active combat stance even while strategically on the defensive.

This concept of operations was presented at a meeting in Saigon on June 16, 1953, to which all the senior officers of the

Expeditionary Corps were summoned. Six combat divisions were planned, which would eventually have amounted to a French battle force of perhaps ninety thousand men. A major battle with the Viet Minh would be avoided until October 1954, when the Expeditionary Corps would be in a position to seek battle. The offensive would start with the elimination of the Viet Minh forces in central Viet-Nam as well as short, sharp blows from the Red River delta to keep the Viet Minh off-balance in the north.

The timetable for increasing the French Union forces called for formation of four combat divisions and eleven new mobile groups (including six Vietnamese) by April 1, 1954. By September, Navarre would add a paratroop division, a Vietnamese airborne group, and three more Vietnamese mobile groups. By June 1955 the plan would have added two Vietnamese divisions incorporating three additional Vietnamese mobile groups. Finally, the plan anticipated the formation of numerous Vietnamese light battalions: 54 through 1953, an equal number in 1954, plus 27 to be organized in the first half of 1955. Together the new forces would add about 161,000 men by 1955, bringing the total French and Associated States' manpower to about 640,000. Certain additions were also envisioned for the naval and air forces operating in the Far East.

General Navarre finished his presentation. He asked for questions. None of the eight other generals and admirals at the meeting had any major objections. For the Navy, Admiral Philippe-Marie Auboyneau agreed to create a French amphibious warfare group to facilitate surprise landings along the coast.

In the afternoon discussion turned to specific regions of Indochina and to specific planned operations. The Tonkin theater commander, Major General René Cogny, presented his own conception of French tactics for his command. Cogny insisted that the French should avoid battle in the Thai highlands, risking only partisan groups or highly mobile regulars there. At the same time in the delta, where Cogny believed that Viet Minh "rot" was increasing, he wanted to maintain a continuous offensive with sudden, sharp strikes against the Viet Minh bases on the approaches. Navarre responded favorably and asked Cogny to submit a list of proposed operations.

General Navarre himself emphasized only one specific operation. This was an offensive in central Viet-Nam (Annam) to wrest control of this country from the Viet Minh. Called "Operation Atlante," the offensive would use troops on the ground, amphibious landings, and forces in the Vietnamese Central Highlands to surround and destroy the Viet Minh regional command Interzone V. This regional command had established a vast base area despite its relatively few troops, estimated at 39,500 regulars and regional troops and 34,000 militia. Atlante could restore French control over this part of Viet-Nam and ensure the security of the positions around Hue and Da Nang.[2]

As Navarre said, "My principal aim is to break the force of habit. The Expeditionary Corps lacks aggressiveness and mobility. I am going to do my best to give it back those qualities."[3]

The concept of operations discussed at this meeting was incorporated into a memorandum on Indochina from Navarre to the French government. The fifty-five-page paper was completed on June 28.

General Navarre returned to Paris for consultations with the government on July 3, 1953. He stayed on for almost a month, presented the Navarre Plan several times before various groups, and had individual meetings with French officials. Three days after his arrival Navarre met with the General Staff for National Defense for a detailed discussion. The preamble to Navarre's memorandum stated that his plan was valid only if Chinese aid to the Viet Minh remained at the level of mid-1953. Navarre also noted that he could not offer the prospect of a total victory in Viet-

Nam. Rather, the best that could be accomplished was a *coup nul*, a military stalemate that would offer good conditions for a negotiated settlement.

General Navarre linked the military plan to an analysis of French aims in the Viet-Nam war. He offered three alternatives: maintenance of the Associated States within the French Union as defined in the 1949 Elysée Agreements; internationalization of the war with U.S., British, Australian, and other help; or a withdrawal from Indochina. General Navarre dismissed the withdrawal option with the observation that it would be very difficult to carry out without some accord with the Viet Minh. As for internationalization, that would be possible only if the Associated States were given independence without restrictions. On the other hand, keeping the Associated States within the French Union would require a military victory or at least sufficient success against the Viet Minh to create favorable conditions for negotiations.

Navarre summarized the possibilities for Viet Minh offensive action on the different Indochinese fronts in the 1953–54 campaign season and remarked that he was most troubled by the possibility of an offensive in Laos. On July 3 the French government had formally undertaken to help defend Laos in a treaty signed with King Sisavang Vong. Now Navarre asked the government for guidance on the extent of this obligation, speculating that it could impede fulfillment of his own new plan.

The response of the French joint chiefs of staff committee was articulated in a paper written two days after the meeting with Navarre. The paper was passed along to French Defense Minister René Pleven on July 17. It agreed with Navarre's need for reinforcements but expressed considerable doubt that the troops required could be supplied without adversely affecting the French military situation in NATO.

The French chiefs of staff also believed that the only aim to be considered, of the three presented, should be that of retaining the Associated States within the French Union. In other words, they opted for military victory in Indochina. Yet at the same time they bowed to military reality and did not advocate the defense of Laos except along a line north of the 18th parallel, which would have excluded most of upper Laos along with the royal capital at Luang Prabang. Instead, the French chiefs believed an attack on Laos by "foreign forces" should be dealt with by "a concerted action vis-à-vis China," specifically a diplomatic action by France, the United States, and Great Britain that would lead the Chinese government to dissuade the Viet Minh from renewing any Laotian offensive.[4]

All the French chiefs of staff were present when Navarre presented his plan to the new Cabinet of Joseph Laniel on July 24.

Once again the charts came out one after another and Navarre ran through his handwritten notes for the ministers. Most of the short discussion that followed was originated by the civilian ministers at the meeting. Navarre wanted the Cabinet to take a position on the defense of Laos, but the discussion was desultory. Some ministers worried about bad psychological effects the loss of Laos would have on the Associated States' war effort. Foreign Minister Georges Bidault insisted that in view of the recent treaty of friendship with Laos the country must be defended, but Prime Minister Laniel countered that nothing mattered more at the moment than protecting the vitality of the Expeditionary Corps.

Finance Minister Edgar Faure reported that the Treasury had calculated that the cost of the Vietnamese Army buildup envisioned by Navarre would amount to some 80 billion francs (about $230 million). The other measures Navarre wanted would add another 20 billion. France could not afford the cost.

"Not one *sou* for the Navarre Plan," declared Faure.

The minister of justice wondered how France could spend a hundred billion francs in Indochina without ensuring the defense of Laos in doing so.

Despite this discussion the Laniel government approved Navarre's buildup and general military strategy. It would keep the question of French reinforcements under consideration. There was no decision about the necessity of defending Laos; the Laniel Cabinet could not make up its mind. Navarre's staff aide, Captain Jean Pouget, later wrote that he could find "neither in my memory nor in documents" any trace of a choice on Laos.[5]

Although Faure could find no money in the French Treasury for Navarre's buildup, there was another possibility, discussed by the Cabinet on July 24. France would go to the United States for the money. Washington would pay for the Navarre Plan.

The first the Americans would hear of the Navarre Plan was in March 1953 from Premier René Mayer. At that time Mayer was saying that Indochina was the "misunderstood war" and asking for more compassion from the Americans, more understanding of the French procrastination in according real independence to Viet-Nam, Cambodia, and Laos.

Mayer came to Washington to discuss further increases in U.S. aid to Indochina. He explained the concept of forming Vietnamese light infantry battalions and training them using methods similar to those pioneered by the Americans in South Korea. However, the cost of the program would make it impossible to meet NATO force goals without additional assistance.

In the communiqué resulting from the Franco-American talks of March 1953, the governments "recognized that communist moves in the Far East obviously are parts of the same pattern . . . operations [in Indochina and Korea] cannot be successfully carried out without full recognition of their interdependence." The French were concerned that peace in Korea would reduce U.S.

interest in Indochina, but the March talks showed otherwise. The March communiqué declared that

> *any armistice which might be concluded in Korea by the United Nations would be entered into in the hope that it would be a step toward peace. It is the view of both governments, however, that should the Chinese Communist regime take advantage of such an armistice to pursue aggressive war elsewhere in the Far East, such an action would have the most serious consequences for the efforts to bring about peace in the world and would conflict directly with the understanding on which any armistice in Korea would rest.*[6]

The Americans promised that aid would not be reduced in Indochina if the Korean War ended. President Eisenhower also supported the request for $400 million in the fiscal year 1954 budget for Indochina aid.

As a result of the French request for supplementary military assistance, the United States dispatched a high-level military fact-finding mission to Indochina to examine the French war effort there. General John W. O'Daniel, commander of the United States Army in the Pacific area, was instructed to take two officers each from the Army, Navy, and Air Force and do a month-long study of conditions in Indochina.

The American officers arrived at Saigon on June 20, 1953. Between June 20 and July 10 the group toured Indochina and visited French bases. Navarre gave O'Daniel a copy of the memorandum he had prepared for the French government, and a detailed briefing of the Navarre Plan was made by the Expeditionary Corps's chief of staff, General Fernand Gambiez. The Americans returned to Pearl Harbor, where they spent four days writing up their findings.

The O'Daniel report was completed on July 14, 1953. It gave a highly favorable assessment of the French plans. It conceded that "though the new French High Command is prepared to take certain essential and highly desirable steps in the right direction, they will not, and perhaps cannot in view of political considerations, consider undertaking military campaigns designed to achieve total victory with the forces now available."[7]

O'Daniel's report was not the only important American military opinion. The Joint Chiefs of Staff had known since March of the program to form Vietnamese light battalions and commented on it in a paper to the Secretary of Defense during April. The Chiefs felt the French training plan could be improved, but they recommended that additional military aid be given provided that the money involved not come out of the Pentagon or monies already appropriated, and that the French make no reductions in Expeditionary Corps strength as they strengthened the Bao Dai army. By April 26 the cost of the light-battalion program alone had been estimated at $385.5 million.

While this additional assistance for France was being considered, however, the current Indochina request ran into trouble in Congress. Many senators and representatives were concerned over the continuing perception that France was pursuing a colonialist course in Indochina. At the same time, they were frustrated because all the U.S. assistance already given, and all the French military efforts in the war, still seemed to add up to no progress. Then the press reported that the French were asking for some $900 million for the 1954–55 fiscal year, more than double the request for fiscal 1954. In Congress a movement suddenly developed to *cut* funds to Indochina: funds for fiscal 1954 could be shaved by a quarter, to only $300 million. This congressional action would have had crippling effects for the French, who had actually reduced their military budget for 1953 in anticipation of U.S. aid.

Eisenhower stepped in to save the $400 million budget request. The task was not difficult. The 1952 election had produced the first Republican majority in Congress since 1946. Even so, the administration assumed a very tough rhetorical position. In his midyear report to Congress, Secretary of Defense Charles E. Wilson noted that "communist aggression in Indochina presents, except for Korea, the most immediate threat to the free world. For more than six years the communist forces, supplied with weapons and equipment from Communist China and Russia, have been waging open warfare."[8] Eisenhower remarked in his speech of August 4 to the Governors' Conference that "when the United States votes $400 million to help that [Indochina] war, we are not voting for a giveaway program. We are voting for the cheapest way we can prevent the occurrence of something that would be of the most terrible significance for the United States of America—our security, our power and ability to get certain things we need."[9]

French Foreign Minister Georges Bidault came to Washington in mid-July, meeting with the "Big Three" foreign ministers; there he impressed upon John Foster Dulles the necessity for extra military assistance to fulfill the Navarre Plan.

In the Far East another event occurred with profound implications for the Indochina war. On July 27 the three-year-long Korean War ended with the signature of an armistice at Panmunjom. That war, styled a "police action," was fought under the rubric of the United Nations, but it cost America 33,600 dead, another 10,300 who died of wounds or in captivity, 95,400 wounded soldiers, along with 4,400 other men who spent time in North Korean or Chinese prisoner-of-war camps. With the United States disengaging from direct combat in the Far East, there was considerable fear that the war in Indochina would intensify further. The French undoubtedly hoped that this would work in favor of their request for supplementary aid for the Navarre Plan.

One of the most important services performed by the O'Daniel mission was to transmit a copy of the Navarre memorandum to Washington, where it was analyzed by high-level military authorities. In one of his last actions as Chairman of the Joint Chiefs of Staff, General Omar Bradley sent a memo to Secretary of Defense Wilson commenting that the Navarre Plan represented "a marked improvement in French military thinking." Despite the cautionary note that "based on past performances" the Joint Chiefs had reservations in predicting actual results that could be expected from additional aid, Bradley recommended the supplementary funding for the French.[10]

Bradley retired to be replaced by Admiral Arthur Radford, formerly Commander in Chief, Pacific. Radford felt that the Navarre Plan was "almost a conscious point-by-point disposal of the previous objections of US military authorities."[11] The new Chairman of the Joint Chiefs of Staff also felt he could not let his predecessor's memorandum stand as written. On August 28, Radford addressed a new memorandum to Wilson arguing that the Bradley paper was too optimistic about the chances of French success. He pointed out that a progress report from the U.S. Military Assistance Advisory Group in Indochina reported that the French were as yet doing nothing to implement the agreements made with O'Daniel, seemed to have no plan for a major offensive in the fall of 1953, and were still only in the planning stages of the formation of combat divisions. Radford believed that supplementary aid should be contingent on French implementation actions. This became the Pentagon recommendation on the Navarre Plan.

Perhaps the most enthusiastic supporter of aid to the French for Indochina was John Foster Dulles, the fifty-third Secretary of State of the United States.

Dulles was the son of a Presbyterian minister from Watertown, New York. He attended Princeton University, graduated Phi Beta Kappa in 1908, and went on to a series of intellectual accomplishments at the Sorbonne, studying with philosopher Henri Bergson. He returned to the United States, where he studied law at George Washington University and graduated in 1911. Dulles combined his law work with an active political and literary career. He published a book called *War, Peace and Change* in 1939, which argued that war was tolerated as a means of settling disputes only because there existed no agreed way to effect changes in international relations peaceably.

He remained a staunch Republican all his life, associating himself with the Dewey wing of the party after New York Governor Thomas E. Dewey appointed him to a banking commission in 1943. In April 1950 he became a consultant to the State Department. His opinion then was: "If our conduct indicates a continuing disposition to fall back and allow doubtful areas to fall under Soviet Communist control, then many nations will feel confirmed in the impression, already drawn from the North Atlantic Treaty, that we do not expect to stand firm short of the North Atlantic area."[12]

In an article published in *Life* magazine entitled "A Policy of Boldness," he castigated U.S. foreign policy for an alleged lack of dynamism, for a reactive "treadmill" quality. Instead, Dulles favored active policies and implicitly supported "rolling back" the Iron Curtain as well as the use of covert operations to do so. The heart of the policy of boldness was contained in this passage:

There is one solution and only one: that is for the free world to develop the will and organize the means to retaliate instantly against open aggression by Red armies, so that, if it occurred anywhere, we could and would strike back where it hurts, by means of our choosing.[13]

Material from "A Policy of Boldness" was written into the foreign policy plank of the political program adopted by the Republican National Convention of 1952.

Dulles continued to work with the Eisenhower campaign and it was more or less assumed by many that he would become secretary of state. The feeling was so widespread that, Dwight Eisenhower later recalled, British diplomats approached him to say they felt it would be difficult to work with Dulles. Eisenhower says that he replied, "Now look, I know something about this man and he's a little abrupt and some people think he's intellectually arrogant and that sort of thing. It's not true. He's a very modest man and very reasonable and he wants to use logic and reason and good sense, and not force. And he will not be someone who's trying to wield the power of the United States as a diplomatic club."[14] Eisenhower did appoint John Foster Dulles and both assumed office in January 1953.

Dulles was a close personal friend of Vice-President Richard M. Nixon, another politician inclined to extreme rhetorical stances. Both men believed the United States to be in a life-or-death struggle with international communism. In his leadership of the State Department, Dulles made no effort to shield long-suffering Foreign Service officers beset by draconian "loyalty" investigations and "red-baiting" charges by Senator Joseph McCarthy and his allies. Dulles clearly believed in a Free World crusade against communism.

Not surprisingly, the Franco-Vietnamese war clearly fell within the parameters of Dulles's crusade against communism. Indochina was just another front in the Cold War. The Secretary of State made this clear in a speech he delivered to the American Legion in St. Louis on September 2, 1953. He declared that "a single Chinese communist aggressive front extends from Korea on the north to Indochina on the south." The Secretary insisted that U.S. interest in the Far East was not diminished by the end of the Korean War and warned, "There is a risk that, as in Korea, Red China might send its own army into Indochina. The Chinese communist regime should realize that such a second aggression could not occur without grave consequences which might not be confined to Indochina. I say this soberly in the interest of peace and in the hope of preventing another aggressor miscalculation."[15] Thus, Dulles seemed to attribute the Vietnamese revolution solely to Chinese incitement.

On September 1 the French presented an aide-mémoire in which they stated that the Navarre Plan was already being executed but that if supplementary U.S. aid was not forthcoming, "a complete reconsideration of the plan of operations in Indochina would be unavoidable."[16]

The Joint Chiefs' recommendation on the Navarre Plan came up for discussion at the National Security Council meeting of September 9. John Foster Dulles took the floor and explained that, in fact, French chances for winning were poor. But he argued that the Laniel government was the last French Cabinet that would have a chance to prosecute the Vietnamese war with a relatively free hand and without being forced into a negotiated settlement.

Dulles thought the supplementary aid was the best way to give the French at least some confidence of success.

The first man to speak after Dulles's exposition was Secretary of the Treasury George Humphrey. Humphrey said, "Well look, we've got a proposition here in which we've put an awful lot of money in the past. Mr. Dulles says this is the last hope of salvaging the investment. Therefore I think we should go ahead and make the further funds available."[17]

The French were told that same day of the favorable action. The Americans did make the aid dependent on political conditions—one was that the French should "complete" the independence of the Associated States. The United States also reserved the right to terminate the aid if the French military effort showed no progress.

By the end of September a new aid communiqué was ready and it was issued on the thirtieth. It said in part:

> The Governments of France and the United States have now agreed that, in support of plans of the French Government for the intensified prosecution of the war against the Viet Minh, the United States will make available to the French Government prior to December 31, 1954 additional financial resources not to exceed $385 million. This aid is in addition to funds already earmarked by the United States for aid to France and the Associated States.
>
> The French Government is determined to make every effort to break up and destroy the regular enemy forces in Indochina. Toward this end the government intends to carry through, in close cooperation with the Cambodian, Laotian, and Vietnamese Governments, the plans for increasing the Associated States forces while increasing temporarily French forces to levels considered necessary to ensure the success of existing military plans. The additional United States aid is intended to help make it possible to achieve these objectives with maximum speed and effectiveness.[18]

Dwight D. Eisenhower had entered office committed to balancing the budget, and reducing government spending and taxes as well. It was obvious that these aims could not be fulfilled if defense spending remained at high levels. Accordingly, the Joint

Chiefs of Staff under Admiral Radford developed a "New Look" military doctrine designed to give "a bigger bang for the buck."

First, as Radford explained to the National Security Council on October 30, economy was possible if the military was allowed to plan for the use of nuclear weapons whenever it was technologically feasible to use them. The Air Force and the Navy had the main roles in nuclear weapons delivery and received the lion's share in the proposed fiscal year 1955 budget. The Army budget would be cut by almost a third, to $8.8 billion. As a result Army strength, which had stood at twenty divisions and eighteen regimental combat teams when Eisenhower took office, would be reduced by three divisions and a number of independent units. The Army would end up with 1,164,000 men in 1955, about half a million less than its Korea peak strength.

The Air Force grew in the "New Look" 1955 budget, which anticipated a manpower increase of 20,000 and a budget increase of almost $1 billion. Navy aircraft carrier task forces and Air Force units would provide mobility and striking power for the U.S. armed forces, but for soldiers on the ground the United States would have to depend on local and indigenous forces allied with the United States. Thus supplementary aid to France for the Navarre Plan fell squarely within the tenets of the "New Look" strategy.

These points were formalized in a National Security Council document that was adopted at the October 30 meeting. The final version of this paper noted that the United States should continue to support French forces in Indochina and that "certain . . . countries, such as Indochina or Formosa, are of such strategic importance to the United States that an attack on them probably would compel the United States to react with military force either locally at the point of attack or generally against the military power of the aggressor." In addition a policy was set of delaying further withdrawals of U.S. troops from the Far East in order to avoid any perception of diminution of American interest in that area. The U.S. government foresaw possible situations in which it "should make clear to the USSR and Communist China, in general terms or with reference to specific areas as the situation requires, its intention to react with military force against any aggression."[19]

An important addition, which accommodated the Joint Chiefs of Staff, stated that

> in the event of hostilities, the United States will consider nuclear weapons to be as available for use as other munitions. Where the consent of an ally is required for the use of these weapons from US bases on the territory of such ally, the United States should promptly obtain the advance consent of such ally for such use. The United States should also seek, as and when feasible, the understanding and approval of this policy by free nations.[20]

The executive secretary to the National Security Council, James Lay, noted in the covering memo to the paper that prompt action should be taken to "conform existing arrangements regarding atomic weapons" to this stricture in the paper.

In the interest of alerting the Soviets to the active new U.S. policy, the Eisenhower administration decided to make a public exposition of the principles underlying the "New Look." This took the form of a speech by John Foster Dulles in New York to the Council on Foreign Relations on January 12, 1954. After saying he would speak about overall U.S. policies, Dulles declared the new aim was to make collective security more effective and less costly "by placing more reliance on deterrent power" and less on local defense against aggression. Instead, the United States would depend on "the further deterrent of massive retaliatory power."

Dulles thundered, "A potential aggressor must know that he cannot always prescribe battle conditions that suit him.... the way to deter aggression is for the free community to be willing and able to respond vigorously at places and with means of its own choosing." The United States would depend "primarily upon a great capacity to retaliate, instantly, by means and at places of our choosing." Dulles illustrated the concept, which came to be widely called "massive retaliation," with reference to Korea and Indochina and with the implication that the United States would act against the People's Republic of China in the event of any Chinese involvement in "local aggressions."[21]

As if to underline the Secretary of State's meaning, units of the Navy's Task Force 77, patrolling the waters of the Taiwan Strait, conducted extensive naval maneuvers during January 1954. Later that month Navy ships participated for the first time in maneuvers held by the Royal Thai Navy. Then, in mid-February, there was a joint British-French-American naval exercise held in the South China Sea.

By early 1954 when John Foster Dulles made his "massive retaliation" speech, the pieces were in place for Dien Bien Phu. The Navarre Plan had been approved and the U.S. Military Assistance Advisory Group was looking for results.

III

DIEN BIEN PHU

Navarre explicitly determined to limit his operations in 1953 and avoid a pitched battle with the Viet-Nam People's Army. However, as he had told the French Cabinet, he envisioned a Viet Minh move toward Laos as a real and threatening possibility. He prescribed a preventive action designed to prohibit movement of Viet Minh troops through the Thai mountains into upper Laos. The preventive action was the occupation of Dien Bien Phu.

After the Franco-Vietnamese war there would be official investigations in France concerning the selection of this Asian battlefield. The question, "Why Dien Bien Phu?" rang out repeatedly in later demands for new investigations, courts-martial, exonerations. It was much like the outcry in the United States in the years after Pearl Harbor or that following Franklin Roosevelt's Yalta agreements with Russia. The occupation of Dien Bien Phu was said to have been intended to close the door to Laos in the face of the Viet Minh. But in 1953 it was by no means self-evident that troops at Dien Bien Phu could do any such thing, or that the French position at Dien Bien Phu was not in fact intended for something else entirely: a deliberate effort to entice the Viet Minh into a battle on French terms.

Dien Bien Phu was one of the largest valley basins in mountainous northern Tonkin. The valley floor measured about nine miles long on its north-south axis and six on the east-west one. In the valley clustered perhaps eighty to a hundred small hamlets populated by about 25,000 inhabitants, mostly tribal Thai, who preferred the valleys, but also a sprinkling of tribal Meo, usually cliff dwellers, and occasional Chinese or lowland Vietnamese traders. Before World War II an airstrip was added and in 1945, Dien Bien Phu was the site of the first meeting between French colonial troops, retreating before a Japanese military offensive, and Free French officials who had returned to the Far East with the aim of reestablishing French control over Indochina. In 1946 the agreement between the Democratic Republic of Viet-Nam and the French allowed a garrison to be placed at Dien Bien Phu, and the French lengthened the old airstrip to accommodate larger transport aircraft.

It was this airstrip that gave Dien Bien Phu much of its strategic importance for the French, who used to classify airfields by the size of planes they could land. "*Morane*-able" fields were suitable for short-take-off-and-landing-type planes like liaison aircraft or helicopters; "Dakota-able" airfields were large enough to operate large transport aircraft like the C-47 Dakota. With Na San, focus of a major battle during the winter of 1952, and Lai Chau to the north, Dien Bien Phu shared the distinction of having the only "Dakota-able" airfields in the Thai mountain region. Because the French military positions in the Thai hills were wholly dependent upon air transport for provisions and reinforcements, the size of an airfield directly determined the size and quality of Expeditionary Corps forces that could be stationed at it. Only at "Dakota-able" airfields could the French base multibattalion maneuver forces with appropriate artillery and heavy-weapons support.

Some authorities stress the geographic position of the valley of Dien Bien Phu, and how it stood astride the main communications routes with Laos. General Navarre believes that French occupation of Dien Bien Phu prohibited a full-scale Viet Minh offensive into Laos. But the roads through the Thai mountains ended at Dien Bien Phu. Between there and Laos were only jungle tracks. Na San had also been on the road, and it is notable that French occupation of Na San did not prevent the Viet Minh from striking into Laos in April 1953. Actually, the direct road link from Tonkin to Laos was located too far south to be affected by French garrisons at either Na San or Dien Bien Phu.

The subject of the entrenched camp at Na San is worth raising because of its similarity to Dien Bien Phu. At Na San the Expeditionary Corps had placed battalions with artillery and relied on air supply. But once down on the ground the French battalions were nailed to it, confined to the entrenched camp they themselves had created. When Viet Minh General Vo Nguyen Giap invaded Laos, he drew the bulk of his forces away from Na San, but the French could still not maneuver. Only three times did they sortie out. For this they were forced to use elite paratroop and Foreign Legion battalions, with such lavish artillery and air support against such weak resistance that the Na San sorties were irreverently dubbed "banana operations" because after each one the French command handed out medals and citations as they would bananas.

Dien Bien Phu had been lost to the Viet Minh in December 1952 when a Vietnamese battalion there withdrew north to Lai Chau rather than attempt to hold the place against approaching Viet Minh troops. General Raoul Salan, before the end of his tour, had specifically foreseen the retaking of Dien Bien Phu as desirable for the 1953–54 season. Various staff officers commented on the possibility, and the proposal came to the ear of Navarre, who included it in his plan.

Implementation of the Navarre Plan began even before the commander in chief returned from his Paris trip. In July 1953 paratroops descended on Lang Son, a major Viet Minh supply transshipment center on the Chinese frontier, in an airborne raid that destroyed important depots. In September and October there were additional clearing operations and raids in and south of the Red River delta. Early in October a partisan raid was staged on Lao Cai, another Viet Minh supply center on the frontier.

Planning for the Dien Bien Phu operation continued apace. On November 2 the Tonkin theater command received orders that an airborne raid on Dien Bien Phu was to be carried out, preferably between November 15 and 20, but in any case before December 1. The plan called for a surprise airborne assault on the Viet Minh units in the valley by two French paratroop battalions, the largest force the transport aircraft then available to the French could handle at one time. The initial assault force would then be reinforced with five (later reduced to four) additional battalions and appropriate supporting arms, all together about 4,500 troops.

Arrival of the orders for the Dien Bien Phu assault had the effect of crystallizing opposition to the plan from within the staff of the Tonkin theater command. The Tonkin staff felt that Operation Castor, as the Dien Bien Phu attack was code-named, would divert badly needed combat units from the Red River delta to a peripheral area. Moreover, the staff argued, the Expeditionary Corps would be obliged to reinforce its assets at Dien Bien Phu once they were in place, diverting even more troops. Use of the valley as an offensive base, as at Na San, would come to an end once it was masked by even one Viet Minh regiment. The operations staff worried that Dien Bien Phu would become "like it or not" a *"grève de bataillons,"* literally a battalion meatgrinder.

An even more striking difficulty was raised by the commander of air transport planes in Indochina, Colonel Jean Nicot, in a report submitted on November 11, 1953. The French Air

Force colonel argued that sustaining a large combat force at Dien Bien Phu was beyond the capacity of French air transport. Dien Bien Phu, despite its "Dakota-able" airstrip, was not geographically well located for air operations. In the first place, the average flight duration would rise to over three hours, reducing the number of sorties that could be flown by each aircraft. Located at about 220 nautical miles from Hanoi, Dien Bien Phu was twice as far away as Na San had been, and there French air transport was stretched to its limit.

These arguments went forward to the Tonkin theater commander, Major General René Cogny. Nicknamed *"coco la sirène"* for his predilection for siren-blowing motorcycle escorts, Cogny was a self-professed "man of the delta." A lowly brigadier commanding a military division in Tonkin when General Navarre arrived in Indochina, Cogny was promoted and made commander of the whole theater.

Cogny could have spoken out against Dien Bien Phu at the June conference Navarre had held with his subordinates at Saigon. Instead he had said nothing. Cogny even spoke favorably of Dien Bien Phu in memoranda suggesting that it be made the "mooring point" for partisan bands that could range through the surrounding hills. Now, just a fortnight before the scheduled airborne assault on Dien Bien Phu, Cogny was faced with concerted opposition among his staff. Once again he did nothing. On November 12 he informed the French Air Force commander of the impending operation.

If it had rained on November 20, Dien Bien Phu might never have taken place. That morning the French were going to execute Operation Castor. Aboard a command aircraft were three generals empowered to call off the operation. But the weather reports held good and the flight was without incident.

At about ten in the morning the lead squadrons of a sixty-five-plane troop carrier formation reached the valley of Dien Bien Phu. The planes were carrying two of the best French airborne battalions in Indochina: Major Marcel Bigeard's 6th Colonial Paratroops and Major Jean Brechignac's 2nd Battalion, 1st Parachute Light Infantry.

The two French paratroop battalions together dropped 1,220 men. They encountered elements of the Viet-Nam People's Army 148th Regiment and attached units. The Viet Minh had buried stakes in the airfield to make it unusable for landings. A sharp fire fight developed on Major Bigeard's drop zone, and French casualties that day amounted to eleven dead and fifty-two wounded. However, the French successfully captured the headquarters of the 148th Regiment with all its papers intact.

The timetable called for the airborne drop of a third battalion plus supplies on the afternoon of the first day, and then the arrival of two more battalions the next day. The French also dropped airborne artillery and engineer elements, along with a bulldozer to help clear Dien Bien Phu's airfield.

The airfield was usable for small planes by November 22, and a week later Dien Bien Phu was open to all types of French aircraft. By that time reinforcement of the initial airborne spearhead had raised Dien Bien Phu to its full planned strength of 4,500 troops. On November 30 the Tonkin command issued its basic instructions for the Dien Bien Phu garrison: to guarantee, at a minimum, free use of the airfield, to hold this position to the last man (*sans esprit de recul*), and to retard buildup of Viet Minh forces by powerful attacks out of the Dien Bien Phu base.

General Henri Navarre made his first visit to the mountain valley on November 29, in order to determine the role of Dien Bien Phu in his overall strategy. Navarre stated his intentions in a personal and secret instruction on December 3. This directive noted the movement of large Viet Minh units toward the Thai mountains and specified points where the French Air Force should bomb the Viet-Nam People's Army's communications routes.

Most importantly, Navarre stated that he had decided "to accept the battle of the northwest" based on the "air-land base" of Dien Bien Phu. He envisioned a battle resulting in a decisive defeat for the Viet-Nam People's Army. Navarre, the general who was planning to augment the Expeditionary Corps's means and spirit before seeking out the Viet Minh, had now determined to fight a major battle instead.

Navarre's directive accepting battle at Dien Bien Phu was still en route to Hanoi when, more than eight thousand miles away at Bermuda, the leaders of the "Big Three" western alliance met for a summit conference at the British Caribbean resort. The Bermuda conference was the idea of British Prime Minister Sir Winston Churchill. Sir Winston had returned to office in Britain during 1951, hoping to follow his distinguished wartime leadership with another term as prime minister. He had now to cope with intense recession in the economy and a major counterinsurgency war in Malaya waged by the British Army and other Commonwealth forces.

Churchill, originator of the phrase "Iron Curtain" to describe Soviet control over Eastern Europe, cooperated in the Atlantic alliance. The British also accepted the ambitious goals for a military buildup fashioned at the Lisbon conference of the North Atlantic Treaty Organization in 1952. But harsh economic realities and the difficulties of war in Malaya forced the Churchill government by 1953 to seek a reduction of East-West tensions in order to focus resources on critical domestic needs. Following the March 1953 death of Soviet dictator Joseph Stalin, Churchill gave a speech in favor of "a meeting at the summit" with the new leaders of the Soviet Union.

The American response to Churchill's speech was to suggest instead a Western summit. In mid-July, Sir Winston suffered a major stroke, which left him partially paralyzed and much reduced in vigor. But following his recovery he went on to invite the American and French leaders to Bermuda, despite some opposition from the British Foreign Office.

Sir Winston's first thought was that the meeting could be billed as a reunion of wartime friends, an informal get-together without any agenda. But French Prime Minister Joseph Laniel had not been a wartime associate of either Churchill's or Eisenhower's, so the idea was abandoned. Of structure, Bermuda certainly had little. The meetings on the island ranged in subject from the European Defense Community to Anglo-French reactions to President Eisenhower's draft of a speech he would present at the United Nations the following week, offering "atoms for peace."

At dinner on December 5, Ike told Churchill and Anthony Eden, during a discussion of the risks of a renewal of war in Korea by China, that there was no logical distinction between conventional and atomic weapons. He also claimed the American people no longer distinguished between these types of weapons. Eisenhower's proposed speech threatened to use atomic weapons in Korea if the truce were violated. The British were surprised at the vehemence of the American position and they convinced Eisenhower to reject this atomic threat to China. But the diary of a close associate of the foreign secretary records that Eden was cast into "gloom" by Ike's intentions and said the prospects were too horrible to contemplate.

Meanwhile, the issue of the European Defense Community acted to sour relations between Britain and France. Churchill in 1953 accepted the attendant political risks in his country and pushed the EDC Treaty through ratification in Parliament. It was the French who had first proposed EDC and now they were laggard on formal ratification. A Churchill speech at Margate in

November bid France ratify EDC; it was so strained in tone that some Frenchmen recalled Sir Winston's role in 1940, when he deliberately ordered the destruction of a French fleet at Mers-el-Kebir.

Frenchmen could have no doubts about Churchill's feelings after they arrived at Bermuda on December 4. In their inimitable way the British perpetrated a series of calculated faux pas of protocol. As Laniel's plane arrived there was no band on hand to render *La Marseillaise.* Sir Winston also turned his back on Laniel in order to stroke the beard of a mascot goat that belonged to the Welsh Fusiliers regiment. When Eisenhower's plane arrived, Churchill quickly took the President aside, got in the first car of the motorcade, and drove away. Prime Minister Laniel was left to follow in a car with the subordinate officials.

The goat was present again at a formal banquet held on the second day of the conference. Agence France-Presse reported from Bermuda that the goat "has already been a little too prominent at this conference."

At the oceanside country club in Tucker's Town where the meetings were being held, Churchill was sitting with Laniel and Eisenhower but ordered drinks only for himself and the President. Only after the oversight was called to his attention by Ike, twice, was a drink brought for the French prime minister.

During the conference meetings Churchill, who was at this time using a battery-operated hearing aid, ostentatiously turned off the device when Laniel began to speak.

Laniel got the message. On the second day at Bermuda he retired to his hotel room with a "cold," not to emerge until the French delegation departed the island. The absence of Laniel left the French at a disadvantage in the discussions that followed. They had come prepared to lay their difficulties on the table for the Americans and British.

In late November the Soviet Union had agreed to a meeting of foreign ministers to be held in Berlin in January 1954. This meeting would both consider European problems and set up an international conference to be held on Far Eastern matters. Then an interview with Ho Chi Minh appeared in the Swedish newspaper *Expressen* in which Ho offered negotiations with France to end the Franco-Vietnamese war.

The Laniel government had just dispatched instructions to General Navarre to restrict his operations to the means with which he had been provided, when the Ho Chi Minh interview appeared. The government had also informed Navarre that he would receive only part of the reinforcements requested in July and that part of these must be considered to be an advance on replacement of future Expeditionary Corps losses. Although French Foreign Minister Georges Bidault said of the Ho Chi Minh offer that "foreign policy is not made in the back pages of newspapers," France was increasingly attracted to a peaceful settlement and needed to explain this to the United States.

At Bermuda on December 7, Bidault laid out the general considerations influencing French policy, much as Churchill and Foreign Secretary Anthony Eden did for the British position in Malaya. When the French mentioned the difficulty of finding reinforcements for Indochina, the Americans noted that the French battalion serving in Korea had been transferred to Indochina. John Foster Dulles fully approved of this troop movement, which he considered "an appropriate redeployment."

Foster Dulles also joked that he had asked a Frenchman from Indochina what was needed to win the war there and the answer had been "Syngman Rhee" (the president of South Korea).

Bidault broke in, "It's a deal."

Bermuda was dominated by the specter of the People's Republic of China. The possibility of an international conference on the Far East carried with it recognition for China, with perhaps such trappings as representation in the United Nations. To both of these possibilities the Americans were resolutely opposed. On the China problem, according to Secretary of State Dulles,

> *there were major differences between* [sic] *the three powers in their approach to this problem, especially as between the United Kingdom and the United States. It was the view of the United States that the best hope for intensifying the strain and difficulties between Communist China and Russia would be to keep the Chinese under maximum pressure rather than by relieving such pressure.*[1]

The U.S. view was that "politically and economically and to the extent possible without war, military pressure should also be maintained." The Americans were not interested in negotiations on Indochina.

After hearing from Bidault at Bermuda, both Britain and the United States should have understood that France desired to negotiate an end to the Indochina war. But only the British drew that conclusion. President Eisenhower noted only the French military report and later wrote of the French, "For the first time they were thinking of winning eventually."[2]

Six weeks after Bermuda, on January 25, 1954, a conference of the foreign ministers of Britain, France, Russia, and the United States opened at Berlin. It was the first such meeting of the World War II allies since late 1947.

In his opening statement to a plenary session in Berlin, Soviet Foreign Minister Vyacheslav Molotov advocated a conference on Far Eastern matters to be hosted by five powers, that is, the four nations meeting in Berlin plus China. But the very next day John Foster Dulles replied that "I would like to state plainly and unequivocally what the Soviet Foreign Minister already knows—the United States will not agree to join in a five-power conference with the Chinese Communist aggressors for the purpose of dealing generally with the peace of the world."[3]

At a meeting of the Western foreign ministers on January 28, however, Dulles seemed more responsive to Anthony Eden's assertions that the West could not afford to appear completely negative in the face of the Soviet proposals. All agreed that Molotov seemed to be dealing with more flexibility than previously shown by Soviet diplomats. At the plenary session that day the ice was broken by Georges Bidault. Though Bidault noted that it was difficult to believe in the peaceful intentions of the People's Republic of China "when the battlefield brings us proof every day of the opposite desire," he also declared:

> The French Government, in its concern to see peace restored everywhere as quickly as possible, has never hesitated to proclaim that it is ready, from this very day, to seize every opportunity to make peace in Indochina in full agreement with the Associated States. . . . Every form of conversation which would allow real progress to be made in the restoration of peace would be welcome.[4]

Progress began at Berlin when Molotov abandoned his insistence on a five-power conference. An acceptable alternative could be substituted.

In separate bilateral meetings Bidault rejected an offer by Molotov to help set up a meeting between French representatives and Ho Chi Minh. But for his part John Foster Dulles now agreed that Far Eastern questions could be discussed in conference with China, provided that it was not among the "convening powers" hosting the conference. On February 15, Anthony Eden proposed that a Far East conference make no distinctions between sponsor and invited nations.

Two days later Vyacheslav Molotov offered minor amend-ments to the British draft, ignoring the proposals previously made by the Soviets themselves. These were adopted in Berlin on Feb-ruary 18.

There would be a Far Eastern conference after all. It would convene in Geneva on April 26 and would first discuss a Korean political settlement. The conferees agreed that "the problem of restoring peace in Indochina will also be discussed at the con-ference," while, to satisfy the Americans, "it is understood that neither the invitation to, nor the holding of, the above-mentioned conference shall be deemed to imply diplomatic recognition in any case where it has not already been accorded."[5]

If it was necessary to hold a Far Eastern conference, the Eisen-hower administration felt that military success could only bestow a stronger negotiating position. In fact, while the Expeditionary Corps occupied Dien Bien Phu and the diplomats talked at Ber-muda and Geneva, in Washington a series of moves was in pro-gress to give even greater support to the French war effort.

Vice-President Richard Nixon and his wife, Pat, spent six "fascinating and frustrating" days in Indochina, from November 1 to 6, as part of an extensive Far Eastern trip. The Nixons were given the usual French VIP tour, shuttled among Saigon, Cam-bodia, and Hanoi. In Tonkin the Vice-President was taken on a visit to the front, in the southwestern Red River delta where the French were engaged in an offensive called "Operation Brochet" ("Pike").

Nixon met with General Henri Navarre, who told him that adding a fourth C-47 Dakota squadron was his most pressing need and wish. The Vice-President continued on his journey but passed Navarre's appeal along to Eisenhower. The Pentagon opposed giving the extra planes once it discovered, from a September 1953 survey, that the United States itself had only 1,312 C-47 aircraft available against a worldwide requirement for 1,432. Nevertheless, Ike agreed to supply them a couple of days after French paratroops dropped from the sky at Dien Bien Phu.

In addition the French promptly asked to borrow larger C-119s, "Flying Boxcars," a request also granted. On December 5 the U.S. 315th Air Division of the Far East Air Force began to ferry C-119s from U.S. bases in the Philippines to Cat Bi, a French air base near Haiphong in the Tonkin delta.

However, giving the French more planes did not automatically increase their aerial capacity, owing to the difficult French personnel situation. The United States had long been aware of these personnel problems and attempted to alleviate them in two ways. A covert method allowed the French to contract for the use of Americans who flew for Civil Air Transport, an ostensibly civilian airline formed in 1946 by retired General Claire Chennault, of Flying Tigers fame from World War II. CAT began to accept CIA missions, money, and investment until it became a CIA proprietary. When Chiang Kai-shek fled the mainland, CAT followed him to Taiwan and became the main component in the CIA station's clandestine capability there. By 1954 CAT was so large and well organized that it simultaneously carried out an airlift from Thailand to Taiwan, crew-training and maintenance for aircraft in a CIA covert operation in Guatemala, and operations in Indochina. CAT pilots first served in Viet-Nam in April 1953, when C-119s were lent to the French; they made the first American transport flight to a combat zone, to an entrenched camp in Laos, on May 8, 1953.

Civil Air Transport had called the Laotian airlift Squaw I. When fighting began at Dien Bien Phu, and the French asked the United States for expanded air transport capabilities, Washington loaned C-119s and provided for them to be flown by a combination of French and CAT crews. The CIA proved happy to oblige, and as the French crews would need to be trained, the CIA proprietary was in the air first. Civil Air Transport announced its agreement with the French—everything was made to seem as if this were a mere commercial transaction—to furnish twenty-four pilots on March 5. The proprietary would call its Dien Bien Phu airlift Squaw II.

The United States exercised command over Squaw II through the CIA station in Saigon, which put an officer named Cross in the north. The Air Force supervised operations, delegating that function to Colonel Maurice F. Casey, of the 483rd Troop Carrier Wing at Ashiya, Japan. Casey came down to Indochina three or four times a month to inspect and see what he could do. When CAT needed facilities Casey flew out a couple of planeloads of trusted Japanese workers from Ashiya. In at dawn, they were out before dark, leaving behind a spanking new building. Colonel Casey rode the right-hand seat with a number of the CAT pilots to check them out on the C-119. Most were soldiers of fortune but he remembers two crews of Indochinese. Some missions dropped napalm. Several flights were to Dien Bien Phu, where Casey looked at the hills overlooking the entrenched camp and advised the French to evacuate while there was still time. The entire operation was very closely held and participants were sworn to secrecy. Casey speculated that Dwight D. Eisenhower was the only person who really knew all the details.

In Washington the State Department denied a role in the matter. In Paris the French government at first denied the existence of any arrangement at all. Two weeks later the American pilots arrived in Viet-Nam in a group from Hong Kong led by Kirk Patrick. All of them were to fly the Dien Bien Phu run.

U.S. Air Force men also acted openly to carry out assigned duties. As the result of a special request by the French for assistance in conducting major overhauls of aircraft, a detachment from the U.S. 24th Air Depot Wing was moved from Clark Air Force Base in the Philippines to Nha Trang on the Vietnamese coast in January 1953. This unit remained on "temporary duty" at Nha Trang for eight months.

The first unit completed its mission and returned to the Philippines. At the same time, the Americans sent, in August 1953, another fifty-three Air Force officers and enlisted men to serve in specialist capacities, down to the squadron level, in the French Air Force. These men too were on "temporary duty."

At the very end of 1953, when the French encountered difficulty finding enough personnel to man the new air transport wing in Indochina, they turned to the United States once again. This time the request was made for 400 American mechanics to service French planes. Here was a serious matter that could be decided only by the President and the National Security Council in Washington.

In Washington the Eisenhower administration was engaged in a major policy review on Indochina, an interagency project sponsored by the National Security Council, the top defense decision-making body. The paper, entitled "United States Objectives and Courses of Action with respect to Southeast Asia," was completed on December 30, 1953.

It found that Southeast Asia was critical to American security, and that Southeast Asia, excepting Malaya, could be defended *only* by holding Indochina. In turn, "holding Indochina" was defined as doing everything possible for the success of the Navarre Plan. The United States should "employ every feasible means to influence the French government and people against any conclusion of the struggle on terms inconsistent with basic US objectives." This meant "that in the absence of a marked improvement in the military situation there is no basis for negotiation with any prospect for acceptable terms" and that "a nominally non-communist coalition regime would eventually turn the country over to Ho Chi Minh." In the event of intervention in Indochina by the People's Republic of China, or if China was "covertly participating so as to jeopardize holding the Tonkin delta area," the United States should give naval and air assistance to France in Indochina as well as provide the major forces to interdict Chinese communication lines "including those in China."[6]

The U.S. policy review concluded that a far greater danger was gradual deterioration of the French military position and of French and the Associated States' will to fight.

As the paper was circulated for comments, President Eisenhower was putting the final touches to his State of the Union address, which contained language asking for authority to continue assisting the French in Indochina. At a meeting with Cabinet members and congressional leaders on January 4, 1954, Ike agreed to specify "military assistance" when one leader asked if the authority granted would include the use of troops.

The very next day, speaking with a bipartisan congressional leadership meeting with reference to Korea, Eisenhower said that if the war flared up again the United States would "hit" China, including its Manchurian factories, "with everything we've got."[7] This statement was consistent with the strident tone embodied in the "massive retaliation" speech that Secretary Dulles was to deliver the following week, as well as with Dulles's repeated public warnings to China.

It was decided at the National Security Council that, in the case of Chinese intervention, the United States would provide for blockade of the China coast, covert operations in China to disrupt communications, use of Chiang Kai-shek's forces "as desirable and feasible" for operations in Southeast Asia, Korea, or China proper, and possibly air and naval action against suitable targets in China.

After the interagency study was approved the director of central intelligence was instructed to conduct certain contingency planning in conjunction with Secretary of State Dulles. President Eisenhower also directed Defense Secretary Charles Wilson to report on additional actions that could be undertaken to support the Navarre Plan. The obvious possibilities, of course, included giving the French additional aircraft (this time B-26 bombers) and also the 400 American military personnel they had requested.

The Joint Chiefs of Staff drew up a formal opinion for measures that could be taken in support of the Navarre Plan. The memo stressed the possibilities of approaching the French with a proposal for "a volunteer air group composed of personnel from various anti-communist nations or groups"[8] to serve with the French Union forces in Indochina. Another possibility would be temporary reduction of the French air commitment to NATO in order to augment their Indochina contingent. But the Joint Chiefs opposed additional U.S. military or civilian personnel except in certain highly specialized categories.

The French personnel request was then taken up by the National Security Council at its meeting on January 21. The Joint Chiefs' chairman, Admiral Radford, went to the White House prepared with a talking paper that offered yet a third solution for the aircraft maintenance problem: U.S. aircraft mechanics serving in Europe with NATO could temporarily replace an equivalent number of French mechanics who could be sent to Indochina.

The French finally agreed to make an effort to provide civilian mechanics, but they continued to insist on 400 U.S. Air Force men until at least June 15, 1954—to give them time to recruit suitable people for the task. Admiral Radford emphasized that there must be firm assurances that Americans would not be exposed to capture in Viet-Nam, a stipulation required by Secretary Wilson. The French categorically promised that there would be no problem.

On January 29, 1954, Secretary Wilson ordered preparations for 200 mechanics to be dispatched immediately to Indochina, with duty until June 15, 1954. On January 30 there was a meeting of the National Security Council Special Committee on Indochina that the President had organized. Deputy Secretary of Defense Roger Kyes wondered whether sending mechanics would lead to American ground troops in Indochina.

Walter Bedell Smith, Under Secretary of State, thought not. It was a question of maintenance, not combat units. "He felt, however, that the importance of winning in Indochina was so great that if worse came to worst he personally would favor intervention with US air and naval—not ground forces."

Admiral Radford agreed with Bedell Smith. Radford also departed from the stated Joint Chiefs' position to argue that a view based "on US action short of the contribution of US ground forces" was too "restrictive."

Gazing at his colleagues, Radford declared that "the US could not afford to let the Viet Minh take the Tonkin delta. If this was lost, Indochina would be lost and the rest of Southeast Asia would fall."[9]

Looking around the room Elmer B. Staats, Ike's budget director, had the sinking feeling that all of them were headed for trouble at Dien Bien Phu. Staats later recalled for the author how all the members of the Kyes committee were completely uncritical of what information the French had supplied to buttress their requests, which appeared woefully thin to him. Even Allen Dulles, director of the CIA, whose brief was to watch the French as much as the adversary, sounded no caution as the committee agreed to a report recommending approval of all French requests. The U.S. government had decided to send General John O'Daniel back to Saigon to do an updated report on French progress with the Navarre Plan. Allen Dulles obtained permission for his own specialist, Colonel Edward Lansdale, to be included in the group—even though the French had protested Lansdale's presence on the previous O'Daniel mission. Dulles inserted a note of caution with his hope that "our preoccupation with helping with the battle of Dien Bien Phu" would not be so great "that we were not going to bargain with the French as we supplied their most urgent needs."[10]

The first of over 200 men began to arrive by airlift from Clark on February 5, 1954. This raised the possibility of direct U.S. participation in Indochina as never before. One concerned citizen was Mississippi Democratic Senator John Stennis. On January 29, 1954, Stennis wrote the Secretary of Defense that "I have been impressed for some time that we have been moving steadily closer and closer to participation" and that the United States should "stop short of sending troops or airmen to this area."[11] Two days later, on personal rather than Senate Armed Services Committee stationery, Stennis addressed an identical message directly to Admiral Radford.

Dwight Eisenhower was responsive to such criticisms. Ike had a very acute sense for political trends and worked hard to preserve a middle ground, as he conceived it, upon which to stand. The President admitted to Republican congressional leaders on February 7 that he too shared the fear of seeing American troops in Indochina. But Ike thought it was worth it: "Don't think I like to send them there," Eisenhower said in front of Press Secretary James Hagerty, "but after all, we can go into Iran, Korea, Formosa, and Indochina with these technicians and not run a bit of risk. But we can't get anywhere in Asia by just sitting here in Washington doing nothing. My God, we must not lose Asia. We've got to look the thing in the face."[12]

Ike discovered that even Republican Senator Leverett Saltonstall, Chairman of the Armed Services Committee, was uncomfortable with the mechanics plan. After the political leadership meeting, the President called Secretary Wilson to discuss the kinds of assurances that could be made. Eisenhower was firm that, given the political climate, the U.S. airmen *must* be out of Indochina by the planned date of June 15.

Wilson was told to draft the necessary plans to get the American military personnel out, even if it meant spending money to hire civilians to replace them.

Such quiet assurances as the administration was willing to make did not satisfy Senator Stennis, who went public to criticize the dispatch of technicians after it was announced by the Pentagon on February 6. Stennis said, "First we send them planes, then we send them men"[13] and predicted the United States would end up with ground troops in Viet-Nam.

At his regular press conference on February 10, President Eisenhower was asked about Stennis's fears. Ike replied that "no one could be more bitterly opposed to ever getting the United States involved in a hot war in that region than I am; consequently, every move that I make is calculated, so far as humans can do it, to make certain that that does not happen."

Daniel Schorr, a correspondent for CBS Radio, followed up the President's reply with another question.

"Mr. President, should your remarks be construed as meaning that you are determined not to become involved, or, perhaps, more deeply involved, regardless of how that war may go?"

Eisenhower simply said, "Well I am not going to try to predict the drift of world events. . . . I say that I cannot conceive of a greater tragedy for America than to get heavily involved now in an all-out war in any of those regions, particularly with large units."[14]

As the President talked in Washington, the Air Force selected the best men from its bases at Tachikawa, Iwakuni, and Clark for temporary service in Vietnam. There was a spurt of volunteering as word circulated that airmen who participated would earn triple points toward ending their overseas tours (a couple of months later there would be massive danger to morale when the Air Force attempted to rescind this arrangement). Some volunteered just to get away from where they were. In the bitter cold of February in Korea, for example, navigator Neil Mesler was having coffee at the officers club at K-14, one of the Korean air bases near Seoul, when the squadron operations officer came by to ask who wanted to go to Indochina, which some had never heard of. The only question was whether it was warm there. When the answer proved affirmative several hands shot up.

The Americans moved to Vietnam by a top secret airlift code named "Operation Revere." It was conducted by Colonel Maurice F. Casey's 483rd Troop Carrier Wing stationed at Ashiya. Casey got very little advance notice for the operation. When the time came to brief the air crews security police came to surround the building. Only persons cleared for the operation were allowed to enter. The airmen inside were then warned to keep secret everything they heard. On later occasions when Indochina briefings became necessary air police similarly cordoned off the Ashiya operations building and similar security measures were imposed.

On February 4 three C-124 Globemaster transports flew from Tachikawa, another of the Japanese air bases, to Clark Air force Base in the Philippines. Later they were joined by a dozen C-119s and a fourth C-124. The C-119s on the run from Japan to the Philippines were flying to the limit of their range and had little margin for error. Fortunately there were no accidents. Over the next two days there were twenty-one flights to Indochina, nine by the huge Globemasters. The transports carried men and equipment first to Da Nang on the central Vietnamese coast, and then a smaller group to Do Son, near Haiphong.

Americans reached Do Son on February 5. This detachment was commanded by Major Kenneth F. Knox, a crackerjack maintenance specialist so good that in the Korean War, when the U.S. first acquired an intact MiG jet fighter, Knox was put in charge of keeping it flyable for an air technical intelligence exploitation team that included legendary test pilot Chuck Yaeger, who put the MiG through its paces to help identify its strengths and weaknesses. The airmen arrived a few days after Viet Minh raiders had hit an airfield and blown the noses off five French C-47s. One of the Viet Minh commandos had tried to escape along the beach side of the perimeter and had been shot down. His half naked body was among the first things the Americans saw as they arrived.

Worried as hell, the Americans had no guns or training in their use. Supply officer Russell De Somer, who had been in Japan with the maintenance group at Iwakuni before the Indochina adventure, begged for M-1 carbines from the Thirteenth Air Force, parent organization for the Japan-based units. He was turned down on the grounds that the Americans at Do Son were non-combatants. De Somer reasoned that the Viet Minh certainly would not make any distinction between French enemies and American "non-combatants," so he exploited the ambiguous identity and perch of his unit between U.S. organizations in Japan and the Philippines to make the same weapons request of the Philippines-based Fifth Air Force. This time the Americans at Do Son were given .45-caliber automatics, the carbines, and even a .50 caliber machinegun. De Somer then had to train the airmen to use them. One almost blew his head off. Major Knox's detachment also received a segment of the base perimeter to defend. Do Son was located south of Haiphong, on the coast of the picturesque Baie d'Along, and the Americans were posted along part of the beach, the same sector through which the Viet Minh had tried to escape after their earlier raid.

Knox's group were to do intermediate maintenance on French C-47 aircraft, the first of which arrived on February 9, just four days after the Americans themselves, to be completed, tested and handed back on the 12th. Knox discovered that his French opposite number was Lieutenant Colonel Gerrard Sermet, who he had met in early 1949 during the final months of the Berlin airlift. There were immediate headaches with security, which Sermet could not resolve, and morale. The men were bused to Haiphong for church or tours. Morale improved when a post exchange could be set up more than two weeks after arrival, and even more after two walk-in refrigerators arrived on February 25, permitting the Americans to make ice cream and assure a steady supply of frozen meat. Movie screenings began February 26 and ice cream would first be served two days later. Another morale booster was a hot shower—the Americans built the first hot shower at Do Son. Major Knox gained many points with the French when he granted permission to the Foreign Legion sergeant who headed one of the base security details for the French to bring their wives over and use the shower. One morning the Foreign Legionnaires brought their women to the shower, posted a guard, and were in and out within twenty minutes. The shower was left spotlessly clean.

The Americans were often confined to quarters. Security remained dicey. Fighting could be heard from the base. Sabotage was a constant worry. On February 20 gasoline supplies were discovered laced with water. After dark it was not safe to walk from the American compound at the south end of the Do Son complex to the French camp at the north. Knox lost his first master sergeant a couple of days after the sabotage incident, when the man made just such a nocturnal excursion seeking alcohol and female companionship. Found to be missing, a young communications man, Jack McDonald, was sent after him. After talking his way past the French guards, with difficulty, McDonald had to stay until morning and then brought back the sergeant, who had been roughed up a bit by the French. Disciplinary charges were brought against the man, who was quickly evacuated despite a ruling against sending out problem cases. Colonel Sermet, the French base commander, had words with Knox who then restricted his Americans even more tightly. Two days later, on February 24, over forty Viet Minh suspects were arrested in Do Son village near the French compound.

Not long afterwards the American deployment in the Tonkin Delta would be increased by a group working at the French air base of Cat Bi outside Haiphong. This unit included some Air Force C-119 crews of a provisional squadron drawn from the 483rd Wing, who were to ferry aircraft for maintenance and test them after servicing, along with training French and Civil Air Transport pilots to fly the planes. They also did some transport flights. Pilots of the unit, recalls Lieutenant Thomas Julian, joked that they were moving more barbed wire than anything else. The Air Force contingent was commanded by Major T. E. ("Ed") Yarbrough. An Army element of the 8081st Air Service Unit under Captain Donald Fraser was added to pack parachutes. The officers of this group, code named "Cat's Paw," were permitted to live at the Hotel de Paris in Haiphong, but the men were largely restricted to a barracks at Cat Bi base. The enlisted quarters were shabby but the men liked them, and they were receiving excellent per diem pay from the Air Force. When General Casey came for an inspection he was horrified and got the French to give up a better barracks for the Americans to use. The men were less enthusiastic about their new quarters. For Americans at both Do Son and Cat Bi, liberty in Haiphong meant access to nothing more than the hotel, two adjacent streets, and the cathedral.

This small area actually was a center for Americans in Tonkin. The Hotel de Paris, with its tropical architecture, cream color, green window shutters, and inner courtyard, was very typical of the surroundings. Tom Julian, one of the C-119 pilots, recalls that "Cat's Paw" was made up primarily of unmarried Americans whose location in the city permitted them at least some semblance of normality. The French post exchange, located just a couple of blocks away, enabled the Americans to get their sundries. Among others, Ed Yarbrough used the dining room of the hotel quite regularly. There he often noticed a man dressed in khaki clothes but no insignia who clearly seemed American. One evening Yarbrough went over to introduce himself and discovered the man was the local CIA representative. The CIA man knew who Yarbrough was and what the Air Force was doing and also had heard that "Cat's Paw" was having difficulty getting its supply requisitions up through channels to Colonel Casey in Japan. He asked Yarbrough up to his room in the hotel, where he pulled a footlocker out from under the bed to show a suitcase radio that gave him direct voice communication with Taiwan, Okinawa, and Japan. After that the CIA transmitted Yarbrough's requests, cutting delays by more than half.

Like Do Son, Cat Bi had its own security problems. In one such incident the provisional squadron received a visit from Major General Chester E. McCarty, who led the 315th Air Division, which included all the transport squadrons in Japan. McCarty inspected the unit and then grabbed a jeep and headed for Hanoi, where he wanted to get a look at Gia Lam air base. While he was traveling the Viet Minh pulled a major raid at Gia Lam and destroyed almost two dozen planes. One could easily have been McCarty's. After that whenever McCarty came to visit he would step off his airplane clad in combat fatigues with .45 automatics strapped to both hips and carrying a sub-machinegun. Colonel Maurice Casey made visits of his own, often enough that he became a good friend of General Rene Cogny. The French general soon had Casey staying with him when the American was in town, and sent groups of guards to escort the colonel. Casey found that Cogny had some sixty or seventy Vietnamese working at his own quarters, persons about whose loyalty that French did not seem especially concerned. Casey wondered why the Americans bothered with such secrecy since the Vietnamese obviously could learn anything they wanted about the U.S. activities.

Meanwhile at Da Nang base, where Lieutenant Colonel Walter A. Miller had moved in the lead detachment of the Americans sent to Indochina, life was also rather Spartan. The mechanics had to bring their own tools, for example. There was not toilet paper. Here the Americans spent the first couple of weeks just constructing a new barracks to house themselves. Still, once that work had been done the quarters were pretty comfortable. On one inspection visit General Otto P. ("Opie") Weyland, outgoing commander of the Far East Air Force, compared Da Nang with the bases up in Tonkin. "The difference between your place and theirs," Opie told the officers, "is chicken shit and chicken salad. You've got the chicken salad."[15]

The French worked different hours, and life suffered by comparison—the French had beer and wine, there were little shops selling alcohol and cheese right inside the hangars. The French would begin work about seven in the morning, then knock off for breakfast, then take a siesta after lunch. The Americans worked straight through. To airman Paul Cable it seemed a lot of effort to little effect, for the French Air Force did not fly very many missions out of Da Nang. When Cable saw inside the cockpit of one of the French B-26 bombers it was strewn with trash including wine bottles. It was the damnedest thing he ever saw. One of the senior maintenance officers at the beginning, "Sporty" Bannerman, was at Da Nang because it was a priority assignment, which his parent unit in Japan used to spirit him away from previous duty in Korea to play football. Bannerman, the star fullback of the Naval Academy team had run Navy to a 14-2 victory over Army in their 1950 game, before being booted out of the Academy for getting married. Following a short time at Da Nang Bannerman's unit could recall him to be a ringer on its league football team.

Relations with the French remained delicate, for despite their need of this help, the French seemed simultaneously arrogant and humiliated by the Americans beside them. And the Americans were bored. Airmen were not permitted into Da Nang town, while Frenchmen were going there all the time. The French base commander, Lieutenant Colonel Francoise Grogshillier, an experienced pilot with something like 190 combat missions, knew how hard it could be on the ground. Finally Grogshillier told his American counterpart that he would order French gate guards not to stop Americans and not to shoot at them, and if the U.S. detachment remained confined to the base it would be their own problem. That caused difficulties of a different sort, as will be seen later.

On the base there was at least one diversion—something the French Army called a *bordelle mobile de campagne*, a mobile field bordello. One could buy wine or beer and there were some pretty Vietnamese girls who wore necklaces with numbers on them. Airmen could choose a number and pay the madam, and afterwards be checked by a French Army medic to ensure they had contracted no sexually transmitted disease. A journalist who came through Da Nang later in the spring heard about the bordello and wrote it up for a story, but the chaplain of the 6424th Air Depot Wing, parent unit of the Indochina maintenance detachments, begged him not to run this part of his piece. After that the Air Force put the bordello off limits.

Meanwhile Far East Air Force arranged shipments of athletic equipment and books to the American technicians in Vietnam. At Da Nang the U.S. complex began to be called "Little America."

But not all was well at the picturesque Vietnamese port town. In the hills above Da Nang the Americans could hear the distant rumble of explosions. When asked the French merely shrugged. They said it was the sound of clearing mines on mountain roads.

IV

HELL IN A VERY SMALL PLACE

As the French pursued their requests to Washington for increased military aid, the Viet Minh were bringing about the very military crisis that Navarre thought he had avoided. They were already on the march into the Thai mountains when the French took Dien Bien Phu. General Vo Nguyen Giap had only to continue the operation already in progress to blockade the French within Dien Bien Phu. Giap could also choose to reinforce his move into the mountains and actually give battle at Dien Bien Phu. This basic strategic choice faced the Viet Minh in the fall of 1953.

Vo Nguyen Giap was just then entering his forty-third year. He had been characterized as a "snow-topped volcano" and was known for his iron will. In 1953 he engaged Henri Navarre in the mountains of Tonkin, despite the Frenchman's tanks and planes and in spite of the tremendous difficulties of mounting a battle hundreds of miles from supply bases. Now, at Dien Bien Phu, Giap did not shrink from the consequences of a showdown with the French.

By 1953 the Viet Minh divisions had become disciplined veterans in tightly integrated formations. Their communications and firepower had increased, to the extent that they copied a practice of the Soviet Army by forming, in the spring of 1952, a "Heavy Division" wholly composed of artillery, anti-aircraft, and engineer units.

The 351st Heavy Division took more than a year in the Chinese training camps polishing itself into a combat-ready heavy support unit. During this time the division was given and trained to use American-made 105mm howitzers (equal to any gun on the French side, save the heavy 155mm guns) captured from Chiang Kai-shek during the Chinese civil war. When it reentered Tonkin toward the fall of 1953, the 351st Heavy Division also contained an engineer regiment (the 151st).

One of the main problems the Viet Minh would confront as a result of a decision to fight at Dien Bien Phu was the logistical difficulty of moving and supplying the main battle force at a location several hundred miles from the major supply bases. To surmount the difficulty, the Viet Minh eventually were assisted by more than 75,000 local peasants, porters, and workers, plus engineer units and even occasional regular infantry in emergency situations.

On November 26, Giap issued an order of the day to the entire Viet-Nam People's Army, announcing the French occupation of Dien Bien Phu and proclaiming that the decisive battle of the war might be fought there. On December 6, General Giap issued a general mobilization order.

The 151st Engineers were ordered to open Provincial Road 41 to vehicular traffic as far as the approaches to Dien Bien Phu. The road needed to be widened between the Black River ford at Ta Khoa and the crossroads of Co Noi. There had been no regular vehicle traffic on the road since 1945, nor had it been maintained through the war. In many sections it was in poor condition; in some the jungle had reclaimed it completely. The Viet Minh also had to strengthen all the bridges and crossroads to bear a weight of at least twelve tons, the weight of a 105mm gun and its prime mover. The task was clearly massive. It ultimately involved the construction of sixty miles of new mountain roads.

Supplies for the Viet Minh arrived in China and were deposited in dumps at Nanning, Ching-hsi, or at Lang Son on the Vietnamese border. A fleet of a thousand *Molotova* trucks maintained by the Viet Minh transported the supplies to the bases in Tonkin. From there they could be moved by truck convoy or by human porters across the Red and Black rivers and to Dien Bien Phu. The total distance was over five hundred miles. The Viet Minh resorted to every expedient and they developed a very effective method of using specially modified bicycles to lift up to four hundred pounds of matériel. Trucks carried larger loads. According to the best available calculations, during the campaign the Viet Minh succeeded in moving at least seventy-eight hundred tons of supplies to Dien Bien Phu.[1] This compares very favorably with what the French were able to move in by air.

These supplies were moved despite the best efforts of the French Navy and Air Force to interdict the roads to Dien Bien Phu with bombing and strafing missions. Most were carried out by B-26 bombers of the French Air Force, which adopted a strategy of both heavy bombing of crucial "choke-points" and lesser bombing to establish roadblocks. During Dien Bien Phu, French bombers delivered six hundred tons of aerial munitions on twenty-three targets along the Viet Minh supply routes. Air Force B-26s flew 1,160 sorties solely against the supply routes, including 482 before battle was joined at Dien Bien Phu. At five points around Co Noi the French dropped 139 tons of bombs. The French also bombed six places within ten miles of the Viet Minh battle base of Tuan Giao. Here some 254 tons were delivered.

But the Viet Minh perfected methods of camouflage for troop units and supply convoys, which more often than not concealed them from French planes. The Viet Minh also strengthened their network of anti-aircraft gun positions throughout Tonkin, making it dangerous for planes in the airspace over the supply roads. By December 1953 the French Air Force had already made the decision to divert an increasing number of its aircraft from interdiction to flak-suppression missions to reduce this danger.

The Viet-Nam People's Army moved its troop units with the same determination with which it handled supplies. When General Giap issued his mobilization order of December 6, the first units of the 10,000-man 316th Division were already arriving at Dien Bien Phu. A regiment of the 304th Division came a few days later. According to their movement orders, intercepted by French intelligence, the 308th "Iron Division" would arrive at Dien Bien Phu on Christmas Eve and the 312th Division four days later. The first units of the 351st Heavy Division were expected December 26.

At first the French command could not believe Giap would move upon Dien Bien Phu. General Navarre hoped some of the Viet Minh were marching to Laos, not Dien Bien Phu. He also felt that Giap might be sending only elements of his divisions and not the entire army. René Cogny's Tonkin theater command took a less sanguine view and predicted the Viet Minh would have twenty-seven battalions in the valley by the New Year, as compared to twelve French battalions at Dien Bien Phu.

General Navarre issued his orders for the battle of Dien Bien Phu on December 3. A week later it was concluded that the entrenched camp could no longer be evacuated, but the high command optimistically added that victory would be certain. By the New Year, Navarre was no longer so confident. In a report that day to the Laniel government, he stated that the outcome at Dien Bien Phu was uncertain and suggested that additional reinforcements be sent for the air force in Indochina.

On January 20, French intelligence received extremely serious reports that Giap planned to begin his assault late on the afternoon of the twenty-fifth. For American readers, columnists

Joseph and Stewart Alsop wrote, "one thing, alas, is certain. A defeat at Dien Bien Phu or even a fairly mild French reverse will cause the same kind of reactions in Paris that Yorktown caused in London 171 years ago."[2]

The Viet Minh attack did not occur in January 1954. Some thought it had been halted by a desire to await the outcome of the Berlin conference. Others felt the Viet Minh realized they were trying to accomplish too much too quickly. Vo Nguyen Giap later wrote that the postponement had nothing to do with Berlin but related to a need to complete preparations. Giap says that critical problems were discovered only a few hours before the planned attack. He is silent about any role Chinese advisors may have had in this decision. Giap took advantage of the postponement to send some of his units at Dien Bien Phu, the 308th Division specifically, to raid Laos and further disperse the French reserves and to work on the Provincial Road 41 supply route.

This lull in January 1954 gave the French command one last chance to rethink Dien Bien Phu. Navarre's pessimistic report to the French government surprised Laniel's Cabinet, which had expected favorable news from Indochina. The government decided to send a special commission to Indochina to conduct a full study of the situation. Defense Minister René Pleven would head the mission and would be accompanied by the French joint chiefs under General Paul Ely. At a meeting of the Cabinet's Committee of National Defense on February 6, 1954, Pleven received full powers to make command decisions on the spot in Indochina, and he would have the senior military authorities there to back him up.

Pleven arrived at Saigon on February 9. In a working session at the Indochina command compound outside the Tan Son Nhut airport, Pleven told General Navarre that the government was not happy with the "hedgehog" strategy that had led to Dien Bien

Phu's occupation—this merely created "game preserves" for the Viet Minh.

General Navarre maintained that positions laid out as "air-land" bases had all the resources needed to withstand Viet Minh attacks. Navarre claimed the Viet Minh appeared to have abandoned the idea of attacking Dien Bien Phu because it was too strong for them.

General Pierre Fay, chief of staff of the Air Force, asked whether Dien Bien Phu's airfield would become flooded and unusable after a few weeks of the rainy season. Navarre did not know the answer to this critical question, yet the whole defense plan was based on aerial supply. He said he would check.

The next morning Pleven met with Army Chief of Staff General Clément Blanc along with Pierre de Chevigné, secretary of state for air in the French government. Blanc and De Chevigné were members of the Pleven mission who had come out sooner than the others to have more time to observe. Blanc had been to Dien Bien Phu. His reaction? "But this? It is Verdun."[3] De Chevigné stayed behind to spend forty-eight hours at the camp.

For a week afterward the Pleven mission made its fleeting tour of Indochina battlefields, including four days in Tonkin. On Thursday, February 19, two planes carried the mission from Hanoi to Dien Bien Phu. In order to avoid influencing the Pleven mission, General Navarre did not accompany it to the entrenched camp. Pleven and the others were given the standard VIP tour. It was a tour that had been given many times, even to Americans, and Dien Bien Phu had it down to a crisp routine. At Strongpoint Beatrice a Foreign Legion battalion was solidly built into place atop a hill on the edge of the valley. Here, Pleven was shown an example of French fortifications at Dien Bien Phu. In fact, the French were not dug in that deeply. Wood and other materials for fortification were not available in the valley and the Air Force had not been able to fly in more than token amounts. Paul Ely noticed the fragility of the dugouts on "Beatrice" and quietly took Minister Pleven aside to point this out.

A Foreign Legion lieutenant, commander of the company being inspected, suddenly spoke up without being asked.

"Mr. Minister, it would be a catastrophe if we didn't fight. We've got a unique opportunity to crush the Viets."[4]

Another portion of the tour was conducted by Colonel Charles Piroth, artillery commander of Dien Bien Phu. Piroth explained the artillery fire plan and later some of the French guns demonstrated their proficiency.

But there were disturbing portents at Dien Bien Phu. The commander of Strongpoint Gabrielle, Major Roland de Mecquenem, who had served with General Ely on the NATO Standing Group in Washington, came by looking concerned and asked to speak with Ely privately. The joint chiefs' chairman agreed to see De Mecquenem that evening, but the Pleven mission left Dien Bien Phu before nightfall. (Paul Ely would not see him again until the major returned from the Viet Minh prison camps, a lucky survivor.)

Also, Air Force General Pierre Fay took Pleven aside and advised him that the French should use the respite granted by Giap's abortive attack to evacuate Dien Bien Phu at whatever the cost might be. Fay insisted that otherwise the Expeditionary Corps was lost. He volunteered to take the responsibility and personally conduct the evacuation, using the Air Force in Indochina.

The defense minister was visibly shaken.

Paul Ely immediately intervened in the discussion. Ely emphasized how all ranks at Dien Ben Phu appeared to desire a Viet Minh attack and believed it would fail. Ely conceded the "tactical inconvenience of location"[5] relative to the French air bases in the Red River delta, but he insisted that Dien Bien Phu appeared to be a strong position that would require substantial forces to threaten it.

Upon his return to Hanoi, Pleven held a press conference. There, excited reporters told him of the agreement to hold another international conference on Far Eastern matters at Geneva.

Pleven was asked his opinion of the chances for a Viet Minh military victory and replied, "It is impossible for the Viet Minh to obtain victory."

Present at the press briefing was Brigitte Friang, a young journalist who was a veteran of combat parachute drops with the French Army. Friang was legendary in the Expeditionary Corps. As recently as December she had parachuted into Laos to witness a raid by paratroopers from Dien Bien Phu intent on making a junction with Franco-Laotian troops sent from the interior of Laos.

Upon hearing Pleven's assessment of Viet Minh chances, Friang insisted that she could not see how France could win either.

Pleven became angered. He tightly rasped, "Mademoiselle, I cannot respond to that. But I'll say that if I was in the position of Giap, I would be very uncertain about the news you have brought me this evening."[6]

The military report from the French chiefs of staff reached the conclusion that no decision could be reached in Indochina despite the forces at Navarre's disposal. Even heavy reinforcement of the Expeditionary Corps could not materially affect the outcome. Army Chief of Staff General Clément Blanc insisted that in view of the officer and NCO losses in Indochina, the war had to be settled during 1954. He favored withdrawal from the Tonkin "wasps' nest" to defend from the narrow neck of Indochina. Blanc believed this could be done without violating treaty undertakings with the Associated States and also thought Vietnamese leader Bao Dai could be gotten to agree with the plan. The other chiefs were not so specific in their recommendations, but there was general agreement that the development of a Vietnamese national army was the best option and that this should be the principal military and political aim in Indochina.

Defense Minister Pleven's own report to the Laniel government went along similar lines. The existing military situation made it impossible for the Viet Minh to inflict decisive defeats on the Expeditionary Corps, but the situation was precarious. Pleven felt French resources and morale were being dangerously worn down. The military balance was maintained only with increasingly costly operations, and the Navarre Plan could retard Viet Minh progress but not force Ho Chi Minh to make peace on terms favorable to France.

Pleven therefore recommended that every possibility be raised at Geneva for an acceptable solution. He opposed direct negotiations with the Viet Minh as a "betrayal" of the Bao Dai government. Rather, France and Bao Dai should negotiate a general military convention that would specify the stages and timing of an expansion of the Vietnamese Army that could replace the Expeditionary Corps. If Viet-Nam did not accept, Pleven argued, France should reconsider its military "obligations" in Indochina.

These reports were discussed before Laniel's Committee of National Defense at its meeting on Thursday, March 11, 1954. There General Ely presented the military situation and the conclusions of the Pleven mission. Ely is reputed to have said, "In my opinion, at Dien Bien Phu we are headed for disaster." But this phrase has by all accounts disappeared from the minutes of the meeting, which report that France had a substantial chance of success in the approaching battle in northwest Tonkin.

Pleven also raised the question of a hypothetical intervention by aircraft from the People's Republic of China. The French Far East air commander, General Henri Lauzin, had repeatedly warned that such action would destroy 60 percent of French air capability. Pleven could find no on-the-record assurances from the United States that it would respond to such intervention.

Georges Bidault admitted that no written commitments obtained. Only a verbal promise existed that the United States would reconsider the situation in the event of Chinese intervention.

Pleven noted an invitation to visit Washington that had been extended by Admiral Arthur Radford when the Americans learned of the Pleven mission. Pleven now proposed that Ely be immediately sent to Washington to take up this question with the Americans, as well as the more general problem of the increasing amounts of aid reaching the Viet Minh through China. The proposal was accepted, and Paul Ely was soon on his way to Idlewild.

In late February, General Giap suddenly ordered his 308th Division to return to Dien Bien Phu from its raid into Laos. The Viet-Nam People's Army was instructed to prepare for an assault upon Dien Bien Phu on "A-Day," eventually picked to be March 13. With the new attack date the Viet Minh changed their tactics against the entrenched camp. They began to build trench systems of their own, first to approach the French positions and then to surround them.

On March 10 French intelligence received information indicating the attack would begin late on the afternoon of the thirteenth. By that time all the Viet Minh artillery was in place and the concentration of assault forces opposite two of the French strongpoints had been almost completed.

In the entrenched camp there were varying opinions about whether Giap's attack would really come. The anticipation was excruciating.

The predicted hour was 5:00 P.M.

The time came and passed. At his bunker in the central complex of Dien Bien Phu, the commander of Airborne Battle Group 2, Lieutenant Colonel Pierre Langlais, decided to take the time for a shower. He had just stepped under the water outside his command post when Viet Minh cannon in the hills overlooking Strongpoint Beatrice began a massive bombardment of all Dien Bien Phu. Langlais ran for his bunker, but it was not as well protected as it could have been. Nor was the rest of Dien Bien Phu, due to the limited supply of construction materials for fortifications. Actually, only Dien Bien Phu commander Colonel Christian de Castries's headquarters and the camp hospital were housed in bunkers built to withstand 105mm artillery shells.

The result was that the French command took grievous losses in the Viet Minh's "A-Day" bombardment. The casualties included Colonel Jules Gaucher, commander of the Foreign Legion's 13th Half Brigade and the northern sector of Dien Bien Phu. In this sector were located Strongpoint Beatrice, which was clearly to be attacked, and Strongpoint Gabrielle. Gaucher's experience at Dien Bien Phu harked back to 1945, when he had been a junior officer among the troops in retreat after the Japanese coup. His death came when a shell exploded on his bunker at the very instant the staff met to decide on a replacement for the Foreign Legion battalion commander on Beatrice, who himself had just been killed by an artillery shell.

Colonel de Castries selected Lieutenant Colonel Langlais to take over the northern sector command. Langlais found that his telephone lines to the battalion commanders had been cut by the bombardment. So, news of his transfer, and the substitution of Major Hubert de Seguins-Pazzis as commander of the airborne battle group, had to go to subordinates by radio. Thus the Viet Minh, who had the practice of listening in to the French radio net, soon were informed of the success of their shelling.

The bombardment had crucial effects on the French position. One was to make it difficult and dangerous for the French artillerymen to work their own guns. The French guns were located in open pits—necessary to allow the guns to aim in any direction—and not fully dug in like the Viet Minh. French gun crews were thus far more liable to be wounded by nearby exploding shells that were not direct hits. Had the French crews worn flak jackets, many such losses could have been avoided, but there were no flak jackets in French hands and an emergency request had to be made for U.S. aid. The Americans were very cooperative in processing the request, U.S. veterans in Korea recall how they were suddenly told how, with that war over, they no longer had need of their flak jackets. They were asked to give the jackets back and told the equipment would be sent to Indochina. Nevertheless it was mid-April before any jackets arrived.

In any case the Viet Minh bombardment severely hampered the French, while the Viet Minh guns were not vulnerable. This was a total shock to artillery commander Colonel Piroth, who had given his word that with a half hour of warning his guns would silence any artillery the Viet Minh brought to Dien Bien Phu. But on the first day of the battle Piroth's guns fired a quarter of their ammunition supply without appreciably helping the defenders of Beatrice.

And Strongpoint Beatrice needed all the support it could get. The individual companies atop Hill 506, on which Beatrice had been constructed, were assaulted by two regiments of the Viet Minh 312th Division, which drove approach trenches to within sixty yards of the strongpoint. When the signal came for the attack, sappers destroyed the last French obstacles with explosive charges. One machine-gun post that had withstood the advance was captured after a Viet Minh section leader named Phan Dinh Giot blocked the embrasure with his body. Beatrice held off the first assault, but a second attack was begun before midnight. By the early morning of March 14 the Viet Minh completed their capture of Beatrice. The preplanned French counterattack had only been practiced on a map, was delayed in getting into motion, and was then halted when the Viet Minh offered a truce to exchange wounded. Beatrice was never recaptured.

Giap's bombardment effectively closed down the Dien Bien

Phu airfield, far more quickly than any monsoon rains would have done. In fact, almost the last man out was an American, Air Force Major Ed Yarbrough, who led the special air transport detachment then helping the French from Haiphong. A C-119 aircraft had lost an engine landing at Dien Bien Phu a couple of days earlier, and Yarbrough wanted to evaluate whether it could be repaired. His flight line chief at Cat Bi estimated that a crew of mechanics flown out with another engine could make the C-119 flightworthy in a day and a half. Yarbrough hitched a ride on one of the twice-weekly C-47 flights the French sent to Dien Bien Phu with frozen meat. It was March 13 around noon when they landed, and the major sat in a French dugout for a lunch of wine and bread when the Viet Minh opened fire on the airfield. The C-119 was completely destroyed. Colonel De Castries did not want the French air crew to leave, but he had no authority over Americans, and Yarbrough had orders not to be caught at Dien Bien Phu. A C-47 pilot through World War II with more than ten thousand hours in that machine—Yarbrough had flown 82nd Airborne Division paratroopers into Normandy in 1944—the American argued to De Castries he could fly out the French Dakota solo with no difficulty. He jumped into the Dakota and took off, highly unusual in a multiengine aircraft. Later that afternoon the Viet Minh opened their offensive against the entrenched camp. Yarbrough had to leave behind his interpreter, a young French paratrooper with excellent English-speaking skills named Bruno Balas, and often wondered what had happened to the man. Two decades later, by then an airline official retired from the Air Force, Yarbrough dined at the Pan American Clipper Club in Los Angeles to find his waiter was the very same Balas, who had survived Dien Bien Phu, fighting through the siege then marching out with the other French prisoners.

Meanwhile, the Air Force at that time considered the C-119 engines highly classified technology and was desperate to learn whether the engines on the plane at Dien Bien Phu had been completely destroyed. Major Yarbrough got orders to get back into the entrenched camp and checked. He flew a small liaison plane and took with him the Army parachute packer, Captain Don Fraser to confer with the French on their air drop needs. Lieutenant Tom Julian, who begged to come along on the mission but was turned down, remembers Yarbrough used a German-made aircraft, a Fieseler Storch of World War II vintage, a number of which were still active in the French air force in Indochina. Yarbrough snuck into Dien Bien Phu during a lull in the Viet Minh bombardments.

Hospital planes headed for Dien Bien Phu devised numerous techniques for diverting the Viet Minh anti-aircraft and gun crews, and with night landings managed to carry out some 324 wounded. But beginning on March 13, when the airfield came under intermittent artillery fire, some Viet Minh 75mm guns were even assigned the field as their primary target. Aircraft takeoffs and landings were more and more out of the question. A Dakota that landed on March 28 but was destroyed before it could take off became the last ambulance C-47 to get into the entrenched camp. Dien Bien Phu was essentially on its own. Its link with the Expeditionary Corps had broken.

On the evening of March 14 it was the turn of Strongpoint "Gabrielle." Here Major de Mecquenem's 5th Battalion of the 7th Algerian Rifles was fortified on a hill directly north of the main position at Dien Bien Phu. Gabrielle's tactical importance arose from the fact that it lay directly under the takeoff path of aircraft from Dien Bien Phu. If the Viet Minh could put antiaircraft guns on Gabrielle, the airfield would be irrevocably closed. Thus the Algerian battalion expected an attack and constructed the best-prepared defensive position at Dien Bien Phu. But these defenses were of little use against Viet Minh regiments willing to accept heavy losses.

Gabrielle was attacked repeatedly through the night. Major de Mecquenem, who stayed on voluntarily even though his tour in Indochina had ended, was wounded and captured. By the early morning only a handful of Algerian riflemen still held out in the last positions of Gabrielle. The Viet Minh suffered 2,000 killed, but the strongpoint was virtually theirs unless a counterattack was successful. The French counterattack got under way about 4:00 A.M., but it used an inexperienced unit, the 5th Vietnamese Parachute Battalion, which had just arrived at Dien Bien Phu. Together with a company from the 1st Foreign Legion Paratroops, the Vietnamese were moving toward Gabrielle when they were ambushed at a ford along the way. The troops froze, and the counterattack halted in its tracks.

By March 15, Giap had captured the entire northern subsector of Dien Bien Phu. Gabrielle and Beatrice allowed the Viet Minh to look directly into the central area of the entrenched camp, providing excellent artillery and anti-aircraft positions for the "Heavy Division."

By March 16 the French artillery had fired almost half its ammunition to no apparent effect. Colonel Piroth was despondent at this performance, and it is believed that the artillery commander lay down on his bed with a primed hand grenade and died in the explosion. Meanwhile, Colonel de Castries's chief of staff also had died, in a patrol action outside the entrenched camp. On March 17 tribal Thai serving the French Army and part of the battalion holding Strongpoint "Anne-Marie" deserted their position and went over to the Viet Minh. De Castries did not have the troops to replace them, so the two peaks of Anne-Marie were also lost. With Anne-Marie went the last two peaks within Dien Bien Phu valley that dominated the French airfield. Once Viet Minh anti-aircraft guns were emplaced there, even French air strikes in the valley would be affected.

On March 17 a report from the Viet Minh high command

summed up the operations: "The enemy has suffered a severe defeat . . . the essential part of his peripheral line of defenses has been destroyed, the greater part of the northern sub-sector and a part of the central sector annihilated, and the central airfield, the heart of the entrenched camp, directly threatened."[7]

There was only one good aspect of the French situation, which was the parachuting-in on March 16 of the 6th Colonial Paratroop Battalion as a reinforcement. This meant the presence of Major Marcel Bigeard, an officer of widely admired courage and initiative who was worth an extra battalion of reinforcements to French morale.

A stream of foreign visitors had passed through Dien Bien Phu during the winter of 1953–54. One was Graham Greene, who selected Dien Bien Phu as his topic when *The Sunday Times* asked him in 1963 to write an article on a decisive battle of his choice. Greene had been in Indochina gathering material for what later became the novel *The Quiet American*. He was at Dien Bien Phu for a day on January 5, 1954.

At the camp, Colonel de Castries invited Greene to lunch at the senior officers' mess. Greene recalled it as a scene "of evil augury." Colonel de Castries served excellent wine. He impressed the author as a man "who had the nervy histrionic features of an old-time actor."

Greene became involved in a conversation with Colonel Charles Piroth. The French artillery commander and another officer had begun talking about the evacuation of Na San. Suddenly, Colonel de Castries hit the table with his fist.

"Be silent," De Castries thundered. "I will not have Na San mentioned in this mess. Na San was a defensive post. This is an offensive one."

After lunch Greene asked his guide what De Castries had meant by an "offensive post." The officer scoffed at the notion and dismissed the power of the French tank squadron. What was needed for an offensive base, he said, was a thousand mules.[8]

There were also many Americans who visited the entrenched camp. Washington had no excuse for ignorance of conditions at Dien Bien Phu. The first visit by the head of the Military Assistance Advisory Group was on November 29, 1953, barely a week after the French reoccupied the valley. A December visitor was Lieutenant Colonel J. C. Foster, deputy chief of the Estimates Division at Far East Air Force intelligence. Colonel Foster spent three hours in the air surveying the environs of the entrenched camp in a plane loaned by the French.

Major General Thomas J. Trapnell was back for a second visit on January 14. He was followed on February 2 by General John W. O'Daniel, making a follow-up to his Indochina visit of the summer of 1953. O'Daniel's visit was a special one, requested at the highest levels of the U.S. government.

Trapnell did not think much of Dien Bien Phu, but O'Daniel's opinion was much more favorable. In a report of February 10 that was sent on to the White House, "Iron Mike" O'Daniel asserted his belief that the entrenched camp had adequate artillery, air, and armor support and that "a good job of fortification construction is being done." Moreover, O'Daniel declared, "I feel that it can withstand any kind of attack the Viet Minh are capable of launching."[9]

The report did warn that Dien Bien Phu was overlooked by hills of up to 1,000-foot height, at a distance of 3,000 to 5,000 yards, and that a Viet Minh force with two or three battalions of medium (105mm) artillery could make the area untenable. O'Daniel himself would have been tempted in the same situation to set up his strongpoints in the rim hills and not in the valley plain.

But O'Daniel's view was favorable enough to cause President Eisenhower to send an immediate cable to Foster Dulles, then in Europe. The President commented, "O'Daniel's most recent report is more favorable than that given to you through French sources."[10]

Another report was completed on March 9, 1954, and submitted to the deputy chief of staff for intelligence of the Far East Air Force. It predicted that medium caliber (37mm) antiaircraft guns sited along the limited aerial approaches to Dien Bien Phu could have "considerable success" against low-flying planes. The report also concluded, mistakenly, that the French exaggerated the threat and that the Viet Minh had no 37mm anti-aircraft guns. But when Giap's gun crews went into action on March 13, the medium anti-aircraft guns were very much in evidence. Several French planes were shot down in the very first days of the battle and others were destroyed on the ground at Dien Bien Phu.

Giap scheduled a series of raids on French air bases in the Red River delta before "A-Day." This action was of special concern to the Americans since USAF technicians had arrived in Viet-Nam and a total of 149 airmen were stationed in detachments around Haiphong, mostly at Do Son.

Early on the morning of March 3, Viet Minh commandos struck Gia Lam near Hanoi in a predawn raid that had been planned for more than eight months. The commandos penetrated without incident and were placing explosives and cans filled with gasoline under the engines of planes parked along the flight line when French guards saw them and opened fire. One commando was killed, but the others escaped and left twelve planes plus the Gia Lam repair shops damaged.

Four days later there was another predawn raid, this one at Cat Bi near Haiphong. Here were forty-four Americans of the Air Force "Cat's Paw" detachment, a small Army parachute packing unit, and some C-119 aircraft and their crews of the 816th Squadron under Major Edward Yarbrough. The commander, concerned at the morale of his enlisted men cooped up on Cat Bi base, had gotten some champagne. He and the officers were hosting a party for their enlisted mechanics at Haiphong's Hotel de Paris (the airmen, unlike their officers, were restricted to a dilapidated French barracks) when the attack took place and fortunately did not have to worry. At Cat Bi, behind double barriers of mines and barbed wire and protected by forty-eight bunkers, Lieutenant Colonel Brunet's airfield guards had a spectacular firefight with the Viet Minh, of whom five were killed or wounded. A unit leader and several more men were captured, and the French admitted to several wounded of their own. Four B-26 bombers and six small spotter planes were destroyed.

In the wake of the raids the French naturally hastened to repeat their assurances to the United States that American technicians in Viet-Nam would not be exposed to danger. Navarre was furious at the raids and blamed security at the air bases. In the hamlets and villages around Gia Lam some two hundred Vietnamese, laborers at the base, were arrested on suspicion of complicity. At Cat Bi the crack 6th Colonial Paratroops were put on airfield security duty for several days. The French also declared a state of emergency at Haiphong and established security zones around both Cat Bi and Do Son fields. Three additional rifle companies reinforced the guards at Do Son.

None of this kept the Viet Minh from striking again, which they did at Do Son. The signs built up for days. On March 6, when Cat Bi was attacked, seven Viet Minh were captured just outside the wire along the northeast perimeter. The road between Do Son and Cat Bi could not be used until after March 11. On the 7th the French had to bomb targets just a few miles outside the base. A Foreign Legion company reinforced Do Son. On March 12, on General Navarre's orders, Do Son went on stringent alert and Major Knox posted double guards on all his aircraft. All flyable planes left the base even though the weather was so bad some thought even ducks would not take wing. Three days later the base commander, Colonel Sermet, told Knox that 400 Viet

Minh had been spotted crossing a river in the area (2,000 enemy were estimated in the vicinity afterwards).

Do Son, on a peninsula south of Haiphong and fronting on the Baie d'Along, was just inland from the sea. Not only had the garrison been reinforced but Do Son was protected by three layers of barbed wire, with dogs running freely between the inner and middle barriers. The American mechanics here did intermediate maintenance on C-47 aircraft for the French. The effort to sustain the Dien Bien Phu airlift had been so intense the French were complaining the Americans were not checking out their planes rapidly enough. Knox tried to maintain the planes up to U.S. standards until explicitly ordered to meet lesser French ones instead. But all the service work came to a halt March 17, when a couple of Viet Minh commandos were captured in the evening on the hill east of the perimeter. A French heavy bomber hit the face of the hill with four 500 pound bombs within a half hour, but no one knew what to expect. The Viet Minh had carried plastic explosives, hand grenades and a machine gun. They had pictures of Joseph Stalin on their persons but did not know he was dead. The Americans were responsible for the security of a section of the base perimeter, along the beach where they had posted a machinegun nest. That afternoon Sergeant Jack McDonald, just returned from troubleshooting a problem at Da Nang, was assigned to be the noncom on the security detail because for the moment he had no bunk. When the alarm sounded in the night he could see nothing—the French typically turned off all lights at night—and detail chief Captain Winifred Ellis sent McDonald out to check. Again nothing seemed amiss and McDonald went back to his post in a large hospital tent. He fell asleep but suddenly awoke. All hell was breaking loose. McDonald got his knife and pistol and took cover beneath a tool bench. Ellis had a few riflemen along the beach. The rest of the Americans stayed in their quarters and took cover as best they could.

At Cat Bi, meanwhile, with nothing but the rumor that Do Son was under attack, Major Yarbrough told his C-119 crews to get ready for an emergency landing at nearby Do Son to rescue the American mechanics. Meanwhile Sergeant McDonaled tried to get on the radio to report on events at Do Son, but the logistics command network shut down in the evening, usually at 5 P.M., and he could not get through. He finally raised another radioman at faraway Clark Field on a ham radio, which only led to a later reprimand for going outside channels. The firing at Do Son died away between one and two in the morning. Major Yarbrough cancelled the alert for his pilots at Haiphong. The Americans at Do Son never could figure out how the Viet Minh had managed to get through the wire barriers. They soon began calling the Viet Minh "Ho Chi Minh's Red River Delta Boys."

On March 18 in Washington the French Mission requested permission to use the larger C-119 Packet aircraft on the Dien Bien Phu run. Thus, even as General Paul Ely flew through the night to the United States, the Americans were granting the request to use the Packets over the valley. It was another small step toward involvement—few French crews could fly the C-119s and most of the sorties would have to be flown under contract by Civil Air Transport, whose American pilots had just arrived in Tonkin.

The first C-119 flight to Dien Bien Phu occurred on March 19. It was not useful. Dien Bien Phu reported that the single six-ton pallet load of the plane could not be handled on the ground. The planes should be loaded with larger numbers of smaller consignments.

The Civil Air Transport pilots used C-119 aircraft the Air Force had loaned to the French. These were converted at Cat Bi, where Major Yarbrough's "Cat's Paw" mechanics repainted them in French insignia. For missions intended to drop supplies the mechanics also removed the C-119s' rear bay doors, which were replaced when flights were for troop transport or other purposes. The planes were flown by both CAT crews and French ones trained by "Cat's Paw" pilots. The U.S. Air Force pilots had strict orders to have nothing to do with the Dien Bien Phu airlift itself but that did not apply to enlisted men, some of whom went along as cargo kickers on the dangerous missions. Communications specialist Jack McDonald from Do Son would be among these men. Without Air Force—or CIA—knowledge, Ed Yarbrough sometimes flew co-pilot on the Packet flights. At least one Air Force pilot, Allen Pope, resigned from the service on the spot to join CAT and participate in the lift. He told colleague Lieutenant Tom Julian he could make more money with CAT (the pilots earned between $800 and $1,000 a month with an extra $10 per hour for combat missions). Wallace Buford, another Air Force pilot, had left the 50th Transport Squadron at Ashiya to join CAT's motley crew.

As for the actual fighting, the Americans were swiftly appraised of its progress. Secretary of State John Foster Dulles called his brother, the director of central intelligence, for a progress report at 6:05 P.M. on March 16. By this time Allen Dulles's information included the results of the previous day's combat at the entrenched camp. He told Foster that the French had lost some of their best troops and positions. The Viet Minh "fighters are fanatical," but had also suffered heavy losses. The Central Intelligence Agency was not yet giving up hope, although Allen Dulles would give the French no better than a fifty-fifty chance of success.

Allen Dulles reported to the full National Security Council on Dien Bien Phu at its meeting on March 18. The CIA now estimated that, in five days of combat, the Viet Minh had lost the equivalent of five battalions, the French two. French losses had been replaced by the drop of two paratroop battalions. The CIA did not change its estimate of the French chances for victory.

President Eisenhower subsequently observed, writing of this time in 1954, that "some of my advisors felt that the French had reached the point where they would rather abandon Indochina, or lose it as a result of a military defeat, than save it through international intervention."[11] Clearly the Americans had important questions to discuss with General Paul Ely.

Admiral Radford was told as much on the morning of March 19 when General Jean Valluy, just back from Paris himself, previewed Ely's imminent presentation: Military victory could not be achieved in 1954 or 1955, and the war could only be extended until 1956 by the participation of United States forces. Valluy also reported that at the upcoming international conference the French foreign minister intended to follow a negotiating strategy designed to prolong the negotiations and set the stage for American intervention.

It is not surprising that President Eisenhower was holding off-the-record meetings at the White House that day.

V

VULTURE CONCEIVED

Admiral Arthur William Radford, Chairman of the Joint Chiefs, epitomized the modern, forward-looking "brown shoe" Navy of aviators. World War II proved the worth of air-power and aircraft carriers, and the obsolescence of the traditional "black shoe" surface fleet. After the war naval officers from the aviation branches advanced rapidly, and Radford was well qualified even among the aviators. Born in Chicago in 1896, Radford graduated from Annapolis in 1916 and served aboard the battleship *South Carolina* in World War I. He went to flying school at Pensacola in 1920 and after that served in aviation units aboard ship, at the San Diego Naval Air Station, and in the Navy Department's Bureau of Aeronautics.

From 1941 until 1943, Radford directed aviation training for the Navy. As a rear admiral he was ordered to the Pacific to command a carrier task group of the famous Task Force 58. Off the Marshall and Gilbert islands, Radford won a Distinguished Service Medal for his direction of naval air operations. Following another stint in Washington he finished the war again leading carriers in the Pacific.

After 1945, Vice Admiral Radford commanded a fleet in the Atlantic and served as vice chief of Naval Operations. "Raddy"

Radford was a major figure in the Navy's so-called Revolt of the Admirals, which opposed the military doctrine of assigning the entire strategic air warfare role to the United States Air Force. Later, in 1949, Radford was promoted to full admiral and appointed Commander in Chief of the Pacific Fleet.

It was as CINCPAC that "Raddy" came to the attention of the future leaders of the Eisenhower administration. As CINCPAC the admiral was host to the President-elect on his trip to Korea. Ike had asked Charles Wilson to speak with "Raddy" and form an opinion as to whether he might be suitable for Joint Chiefs chairman. Wilson thought so. As for Eisenhower, of Radford the President recalls that "he was, as it turned out, that rare combination—a man of tough conviction who would refuse to remain set in his ways. Faced with new facts, he would time and again modify his views to fit them."

In his own memoirs Admiral Radford recalls that when Secretary of Defense-designate Wilson asked him whether he felt qualified to head the Chiefs, he replied that he did but that he favored the nomination of another naval officer, one who was not regarded favorably by Ike. It was Admiral Radford who took over the JCS in August 1953. Indeed one of his first official actions was to approve the Chiefs' formal comments on the Navarre Plan.

Radford was a masterful bureaucratic in-fighter. It was well he had accumulated good will in the Navy and had good relations with his successor as CINCPAC, Admiral Felix B. Stump, because on the Chiefs Radford attempted to play a balancing role rather than to emphasize Navy objectives. Often "Raddy" would side with the Army or Air Force when opinion on an issue among the Chiefs was evenly divided. Congressional members saw Radford as strongly committed to the President. Massachusetts Republican Senator Leverett Saltonstall believed that Radford was careful to maintain good relations with Congress and was personally friendly with a number of members.

Throughout his career Arthur Radford acquired a reputation as a man interested in the Far East. The reputation was justified, as even Paul Ely agrees. In 1950, Radford was already considering, although he professed to be puzzled about, measures to "maintain the peace" in Indochina. In October 1952 he visited Indochina, met French General Raoul Salan, and saw the entrenched camp at Na San, surrounded by the Viet Minh as it then was. A month later, the admiral sent a team of officers to Saigon to make arrangements for the contingency of U.S. naval deployment off Indochina.

In April 1953, when the Viet Minh were on the high road into Laos, "Raddy" was back in Indochina for another inspection. Salan found him greatly interested in the news that Chinese aid to the Viet Minh now included 105mm guns captured from Chiang Kai-shek. At that time Radford promised to support Salan's additional requests for military aid.

On February 16, 1954, Radford explained the extent of Chinese aid to the Viet Minh before the Senate Foreign Relations Committee. Supplies to the Viet Minh were tabulated at a thousand tons per month. Radford thought "their effort is almost maximum now" and that China would have great difficulty in increasing the flow, not only because of transportation difficulties but because of interdiction by the French Air Force. Asked what he thought of possible Chinese intervention with ground troops, he responded, "Well, Senator, it is a pretty good war the way it is and I discount the movement of large Chinese forces into this area because I believe the Chinese would have difficulty supplying such an operation."[1]

The official Joint Chiefs of Staff view of the impending Geneva negotiations was contained in a memorandum to the Secretary of Defense, which Admiral Radford, now Joint Chiefs chairman, signed on March 12, 1954. The paper argued that any solution involving partition of Viet-Nam would likely give the Tonkin delta to the Viet Minh, although the United States held this area to be the "keystone" of Southeast Asia. Consequently,

> *in the absence of a very substantial improvement in the French Union military situation . . . it is highly improbable that Communist agreement could be obtained to a negotiated settlement which would be consistent with basic United States objectives in Southeast Asia. Therefore, continuation of the fighting with the objective of seeking a military victory appears as the only alternative to acceptance of a compromise settlement.*[2]

The very next day the Viet Minh attacked Dien Bien Phu.

Public opinion was divided on the issue of Indochina. Press opinion largely supported the French. Opinion on Capitol Hill was more evenly divided, with many senators and congressmen sharing the fears of John Stennis that the dispatch of American technicians to Indochina could lead to the commitment of ground forces. The polltakers of the National Opinion Research Corporation in November 1953 found that 52 percent of Americans favored U.S. involvement, as in Korea, if communist armies attacked other countries. On Indochina specifically, polltakers had found 55 percent of Americans would favor use of the Air Force "if it looks like the Communists might take over all of Indochina." Only a third of those favoring air action would also support the use of ground forces. Some 35 percent of the sample opposed any use of force.

Official pronouncements assumed an aggressive stance. Under Secretary of State Walter Bedell Smith told a Senate committee on February 16 that he regretted the fact that in a democracy the American intention to send only military aid had to be made known: "I wish we did not have to tell them, for example, that we have no intention of putting ground soldiers into Indochina; I wish to God that we could leave that suspicion or that fear in their minds."[3]

Bedell Smith was careful to note congressional prerogatives in a situation like that: "We would not go into any all-out war anywhere or even approach it without coming to the Congress and placing the situation squarely before the Congress and asking for its decision."[4]

A week later, reporting to the same committee on the Berlin conference, Secretary Dulles declared, "I do not myself see any acceptable result there [Tonkin] short of a military defeat of the organized forces" of the Viet Minh, "forcing them into the position of having a guerrilla operation."[5]

However, at his press conference of March 10, President Eisenhower was asked by James J. Patterson of the New York *Daily News* what the United States would do if some of the Air Force technicians were killed or captured. The President replied, "I will say this: there is going to be no involvement of America in war unless it is a result of the constitutional process that is placed upon Congress to declare it. Now let us have that clear; and that is the answer."[6]

The public declarations of the administration were accompanied by secret military moves. On February 15 two carriers and a destroyer squadron then with the Seventh Fleet were ordered to the Philippines "to conduct training exercises as a cover for possible operations to assist the French in Indochina if such operations became necessary."[7]

Arriving at Subic Bay was the Navy's Carrier Division 3 with the ships *Wasp* and *Essex* and 143 aircraft between them. The division commander, Rear Admiral Robert E. Blick, suddenly got orders to load special high-frequency radio equipment on his ships to receive messages from French forward air controllers.

Vice Admiral William K. Phillips was sent to Subic Bay to command the fleet. There he organized a new unit called Task Force 70. On March 19 he was informed by the chief of naval operations that matters in Indochina were such that he should look for orders to sail, and be ready for air operations within three hours of command. The ships were brought to twelve hours' notice for sea. The next day, before General Paul Ely touched the ground in Washington, Phillips received orders to steam with his aircraft carriers to the entrance of the Gulf of Tonkin.

General Ely knew nothing of the American preparations when he arrived in the United States on March 20. While he was being taken from National Airport to the French Embassy residence, there was an off-the-record meeting at the White House among the President, Foster Dulles, Charles Wilson, Allen Dulles, and Douglas MacArthur II from State. Admiral Radford came in after the meeting began.

That night, on their way to the annual White House photographers' dinner at the Statler Hotel, President Eisenhower told Press Secretary Jim Hagerty that the Viet Minh offensive was very serious.

March 21 was a crisp, cold Washington Sunday. Paul Ely used the day to rest from his trip and talk with French Embassy people. At the White House there was another off-the-record meeting at 12:16 P.M. Eisenhower added Postmaster General Arthur Summerfield to the previous day's group. Summerfield specialized in giving political advice to the President. The Alsops' column reported that Ely would say the French could not win with the means at their disposal and must therefore seek a negotiated peace. *The New York Times* reported that Foster Dulles and the Joint Chiefs of Staff were considering proposals to send more planes, step up training of pilots and of the Vietnamese national army, and to specify the conditions under which the

United States would intervene directly. James Reston wrote that the policy problem was keeping the French in the war and that aid plans as well as intervention were under study.

The next morning Admiral Radford met General Ely and accompanied him to the White House. It was Radford's regular Monday morning appointment with the President, and he had called Eisenhower and asked if he could bring Ely along. Snow flurries dusted the city as the men traveled to the executive offices.

At 10:30 A.M., Radford and Ely met with the President for a half hour. Eisenhower kept the discussion on a general level and refused to be drawn into detailed questions of aid. Ike did tell Radford, in front of Ely, to do everything possible to fulfill French needs.

Radford subsequently wrote that he was sure Ely had gotten the wrong impression from the "pleasant interview" with President Eisenhower.

Ely later wrote that Eisenhower seemed to regard Dien Bien Phu with some anxiety and as a question of extreme importance.

At the end of the meeting the photographers came in for a picture-taking session and Ike was heard to tell Ely not to worry—the Free World had won World War II and would win again.

At ten that morning, before Eisenhower's meeting with General Ely, Secretary of State Dulles called Senator Alexander Wiley to set up a meeting with the Foreign Relations Committee member about a matter that had come up at the White House "this morning."

Later in the day Secretary Dulles called Helen Sioussat, a CBS employee in New York who was making arrangements for a speech Dulles was to give to the Overseas Press Club on March 29. Dulles had planned to speak of United States participation in the Caracas conference of Latin American nations, from which he had just returned. Now he told Sioussat that his speech would be important and it would probably be on Indochina.

Meanwhile, General Ely had gone with Admiral Radford to the Pentagon. Ely presented the Americans with a memorandum containing a long "wish list" of requests. In particular the French had trouble with G-12 parachutes (capable of handling 2,200 pounds) and their associated A-22 containers. The French were using a hundred a day just at Dien Bien Phu and would run out on March 26. The French also wanted 75 more planes including two dozen B-26s and 14 C-47 transports, 550 flak vests, 20 more landing craft, an increase in the monthly supply of 105mm artillery shells (from 70,000 to 100,000 in April and 150,000 after May 1954), and increased supplies of aviation fuel.

The CIA called on March 22 to say it had only three G-12 parachutes available in the whole organization, but Pentagon subordinates reported that eight hundred of the chutes had in fact been shipped by air on March 19 and were soon expected at Cat Bi. Several thousand more parachutes were scheduled to leave Norfolk by sea within a week, to arrive in Indochina about April 20. Another hundred parachutes were dispatched by air on March 23.

Many of Ely's other requests had also been anticipated. The landing craft were already in the pipeline, as were aviation fuel and metal landing mats called "Pierced Steel Plating." There was no problem with extra ammunition.

Ely's aircraft requests were more difficult. The Office of Military Assistance reported to Radford's aide Captain George W. Anderson that more B-26s were dependent on French training of aircrews. There was also the question of ground crews for the planes—French air commander General Lauzin said he expected two hundred additional American maintenance personnel to operate the new B-26 squadron the French wanted to set up. The Americans were already short of C-47 Dakotas and could not supply further aircraft without affecting U.S. capabilities. Only the small liaison planes requested by the French were already in the pipeline.

In the meetings with Ely, Admiral Radford was able to reach agreement on most points. The French were to be loaned additional C-119 Packets in lieu of C-47s, and B-26s would be loaned for the new squadron. The French agreed to extend the tours of 200 of their technicians and would send 450 more to Indochina by September. Fifteen B-26 aircrews in training would be flown to Indochina, and the USAF technicians would be released "within 8 days" of June 15.

The Americans rejected a request for twenty additional helicopters with eighty technicians to support them.

To the press Ely stated, "American aid for Indochina is constant and almost of a daily character. The continued discussions on this aid are more a matter of detail than anything else."[8]

Meanwhile, in Hanoi the French air commander for Tonkin also had a press conference on March 22. Brigadier General Jean Dechaux told reporters he'd be happy to have Allied planes help in the battle of Dien Bien Phu. He could find targets for ten times the number of planes currently in the Tonkin forces.

That evening General Ely was the guest of honor at a black tie dinner given by chargé Jean Daridan of the French Embassy.

John Foster Dulles had the delicate task of making the administration's public statement on the Ely visit. At a press conference on March 23, Dulles tried to minimize the importance of Dien Bien Phu. The battle was "a very gallant and brave struggle" but it was an "outpost" where "only a very small percentage of the French Union Forces are engaged."

The Secretary of State insisted "we see no reason to abandon the so-called Navarre Plan."

Victory could be anticipated in a year.

"There have been no . . . military reverses, and, as far as we can see, none are in prospect which would be of a character which would upset the broad timetable and strategy of the Navarre Plan."

When asked about the chances for a negotiated outcome at Geneva, Foster Dulles replied that if China would demonstrate its goodwill by halting all aid to the Viet Minh, that would greatly advance the possibility of a settlement. "That is a result which we would like to see."[9]

Immediately after his encounter with the press, Secretary Dulles was scheduled for lunch with General Ely, who had spent the morning meeting with the NATO Standing Group. Ely was accompanied by Jean Daridan of the French Embassy, and Admiral Radford. The meeting was crucial to General Ely's purpose in Washington.

The French general broached the subject of American action in the event of Chinese air intervention over Indochina. Ely also produced a written memorandum on the subject. Was the United States willing to combat China with its own air force?

In the short memorandum he sent immediately afterward to Eisenhower, which Eisenhower quotes in his memoirs, John Foster Dulles said that he would not, "of course," attempt to answer that question:

I did, however, think it appropriate to remind our French friends that if the United States sent its flag and its own military establishments land, sea or air into the Indochina war, then the prestige of the United States would be engaged and we would want to have a success. We could not afford thus to engage the prestige of the United States and suffer a defeat which would have worldwide repercussions.

I said that if the French wanted our open participation I thought that they ought also to consider that this might involve a greater degree of partnership than had prevailed up to the present time, notably in relation to independence for the Associated States and the training of indigenous forces.[10]

There also exists General Ely's version. He recalls that he began with a presentation on Dien Bien Phu and emphasized the conclusion that a military solution of the Indochinese conflict did not appear possible at a reasonable price under prevailing conditions. Ely implied a negotiated settlement at Geneva with his statement that France would be open to a "political solution" for the war.

Here, Ely recalls, Foster Dulles interjected that the administration, Congress, and American public opinion were quite irritated at the possibility of a cease-fire, which could only be obtained at the price of concessions to the People's Republic of China.

When Ely and Radford mentioned Chinese air intervention, the Secretary of State widened the discussion. Dulles was "visibly preoccupied" with the political conditions in which American intervention might be appropriate. But Dulles noted that he wanted to prevent China from making a miscalculation in intervention: the Free World would intervene if the situation deteriorated as a result of Chinese aid.

General Ely recalls he had the firm impression "that in the atmosphere created by the crisis of Dien Bien Phu the American administration was ready to study more seriously, which it had never done, the extreme limits where, in case of need, it could take its effort in Indochina."[11]

Admiral Radford's recollection is that Dulles answered that a request for intervention in the event of Chinese air strikes would be received and studied in light of the situation at the time.

Yet another account is contained in an executive study of the Indochina decision compiled by the State Department and the White House in August 1954. This statement, intended for public consumption, mentioned General Ely's fear that the French aircraft supplying Dien Bien Phu would be helpless before Chinese MiGs. "The Secretary of State said that he could not give, at once, a definitive answer to so serious a question." However, he pointed out that

> before the United States intervened as a belligerent, it would doubtless wish to take into account all relevant factors including the fact that such intervention could not be looked upon as an isolated act. Any such armed intervention would commit the prestige of the United States and would require it to follow through to a military success.[12]

At midafternoon General Ely met with the director of central intelligence for a *tour d'horizon* on matters of common concern, particularly psychological, clandestine, and guerrilla warfare. Probably the most important matter was a proposal that the United States should secretly take over funding of French partisans in Viet Minh rear areas.

Late in the afternoon General Ely proceeded to the sacrosanct E-Ring of the Pentagon where he was to attend a meeting of the Joint Chiefs of Staff in the Tank, their famous conference room. Before Admiral Radford and his colleagues General Ely repeated his presentation of the Indochina situation, including the need for a political settlement and French expectations that the United States would make concessions such as diplomatic recognition of China in order to secure a settlement. General Ely expected favorable results from the Navarre Plan in 1954–55 only on the assumption that Dien Bien Phu would not fall. At the same time

Ely affirmed that Dien Bien Phu had no better than a fifty-fifty chance of survival.

Radford agreed with Ely on the political and psychological importance of Dien Bien Phu. His conclusions were striking:

> As a result of the foregoing conferences I am gravely fearful that the measures being taken by the French will prove to be inadequate and initiated too late to prevent a progressive deterioration of the situation. The consequence can well lead to the loss of all of S.E. Asia to Communist domination. If this is to be avoided, I consider that the U.S. must be prepared to act promptly and in force possibly to a frantic and belated request by the French for U.S. intervention.[13]

Act promptly and in force? By his own account the admiral meant American air strikes conducted in Indochina. General Ely asked not only whether the United States would respond to intervention but also *how* it might respond. This led Radford into a discussion with Ely about specific arrangements for coordination of air forces over Indochina. Ely wanted precise staff agreements. Radford assured him that a great deal of joint planning had already been done for the contingency of American air operations over Indochina.

Admiral Radford pointed out that before the United States could commit such forces it had to have firm assurances on such questions as command and organizational lines, duration of support, and basing facilities. General Ely asked about constitutional arrangements governing the commitment of U.S. aircraft to combat. The French general pointed out that because he had been instructed to raise the issue of intervention, his government was clearly contemplating such a request if it was necessary to prevent defeat.

Radford told General Ely that the President had already agreed to take up any intervention request with Congress. *If* such a request was granted, the United States could have as many as 350 carrier aircraft in action within two days. The admiral observed that "prudence dictates that the matter should be explored on a higher level in order to be ready for such [an] emergency."[14]

General Ely hazarded the guess that his government would certainly request intervention if the Chinese entered the war, but he thought the Laniel Cabinet very concerned about provoking China. He would not venture to predict whether Laniel would go so far as to request intervention to save Dien Bien Phu.

The Frenchman's diplomatic caution was not matched by Admiral Radford. The very next day, "Raddy" sent his memo to Eisenhower, recommending American preparations to "act promptly and in force." Could the President seriously consider such drastic intervention?

On the morning of March 24, President Eisenhower read Dulles's memo. Ike was scheduled for a news conference that morning. At nine forty Jim Hagerty phoned Dulles about how the press should be handled. The Secretary of State told the President's press secretary that "Ely has been trying to get us to say we would put planes in [if MiGs appeared in Indochina], but we have not made any such agreement."[15] Dulles insisted the U.S. warning to China was contained in his St. Louis speech of September 1953. Hagerty told Dulles that Ike might announce Dulles's Overseas Press Club speech at his conference to give it more impact.

Eisenhower appeared before an audience of 212 in the Executive Office Building at 10:31 A.M.

After Eisenhower responded to a question about Geneva, Joseph C. Harsch of the *Christian Science Monitor* asked Ike for his "soldier's appreciation" of Dien Bien Phu.

The President reached back to his World War II experience as an Allied field commander to argue that the comparative odds, given a well-chosen position, should all favor the defender. Of course, Dien Bien Phu was in a valley astride a river, not so ideally chosen. Ike compared the position to that of the Allies at Anzio during the war.

"Some of you here were unquestionably at Anzio—that was after I left Italy, but I have gone back to that battleground—and there all the Allied forces were in an almost impossible position.

"They were lying on the plain, and the enemy had all of the observation positions to place all the artillery where they wanted to, and it is a terrible thing on morale."

The President would not prejudge the morale effects on Dien Bien Phu, but, "as I see it, there is no reason for good troops to despair of coming out of the thing all right."[16]

Ike joked about the French commander, De Castries, how he had been given the job "because apparently he is a very brilliant commander" and how if Eisenhower had been in command, De Castries would have been a general "the day before yesterday." (Just a couple of weeks later the French Army promoted De Castries to brigadier general despite his apparently broken morale; De Castries's subordinates had actually taken over tactical command of the defense at Dien Bien Phu.) Eisenhower claimed he had made this comment to General Ely, who remarked that the accolade would be entered in De Castries's personnel file.

Later that day Eisenhower met again with Dulles at the White House. When the talk turned to Indochina, Eisenhower said that he "agreed basically" that there should be no intervention unless the political preconditions were present for a successful outcome. However, the President did not "wholly preclude the possibility of a single strike, if it were almost certain this would produce decisive results."

The core of Dulles's account of this meeting with the President reveals how closely American policy on Indochina was tied to China itself:

> I mentioned that it might be preferable to slow up the Chinese Communists in Southeast Asia by harassing tactics from Formosa and along the seacoast, which would be more readily within our natural facilities than actually fighting in Indochina. The President indicated his concurrence with this general attitude.
>
> I said that . . . it would be useful for me in my speech Monday night to talk about Indochina and its importance to the free world, and to clarify and emphasize our attitude toward non-recognition of Communist China and its exclusion from the United Nations. I said there was developing somewhat of a landslide psychology in favor of "appeasement" of Communist China, and I felt something strong needed to be said publicly to check it. The President fully agreed, emphasizing the misconduct of the Chinese Communists, their seizure and retention of Americans as prisoners, etc.

For his planned speech to the Overseas Press Club Secretary Dulles had in mind "a paraphrase of the Monroe [Doctrine] address."[17] So, not only did the President refuse to exclude the possibility of an air strike, he agreed when the Secretary of State wished to extend to Asia an American doctrine of predominance within geographic areas.

General Ely had been scheduled to leave Washington on March 25. Before his departure Admiral Radford told him that an important meeting of the National Security Council was scheduled for that day, and Ely postponed his departure a day.

President Eisenhower customarily convened his National Security Council meetings at ten thirty on Thursday mornings. This Thursday, however, Ike had Admiral Radford in fifty minutes early and the council session itself was much larger than usual, including the full Joint Chiefs and service secretaries. As a last-minute addition, the President included his political advisor Jerry Persons.

Secretary Dulles announced that before the conference at Geneva, then a month away, the United States had to have answers to such "fundamental questions" as what it would do if France were tempted to "sacrifice the position of the free world in Indochina."

Dulles declared the United States either would have to write the place off or take the responsibility.

President Eisenhower listed four conditions he felt necessary for intervention: a request for assistance, perhaps from the Associated States; sanction for the action from the United Nations; other nations willing to join the United States in intervention; and congressional assent.

It would be some days before the President's conditions could be dealt with. The Planning Board was ordered to consider, prior to Geneva, "the extent to which and the circumstances and conditions under which the United States would be willing to commit its resources in support of the Associated States in the effort to prevent the loss of Indochina to the Communists, in concert with the French or in concert with others or, if necessary, unilaterally."[18]

Secretary Wilson raised the question of how the United States would respond if the Chinese sent in jet aircraft over Indochina. As recently as January there had been an incident in the air off Korea that had resulted in shooting and the loss of a Chinese aircraft. Wilson's concern was answered by Robert Cutler, who observed that an existing policy paper was quite clear on this point, providing for a range of military actions against mainland China. John Foster Dulles quickly agreed, but added he did not think the Chinese would send in MiG aircraft before the opening of the Geneva conference.

Eisenhower concluded that perhaps the time had come to explore with Congress what support could be anticipated "in the event that it seemed desirable to intervene in Indochina."[19]

That afternoon, Admiral Radford recounted in a 1965 oral history interview, General Ely was given the opinion that tactical air strikes on the surrounding positions could relieve Dien Bien Phu. For the first time Radford mentioned the use of B-29 bombers, which he thought feasible and which would greatly increase the fire power of any air strike. The big four-engine bombers could fly from Clark Air Force Base in the Philippines. Aircraft carriers could provide fighter cover if needed.

Once again Admiral Radford met with General Ely, on March 26. It was a tête-à-tête with a single interpreter. Radford said "with a certain insistence" that if France made a formal request, the United States would consider intervention with strategic air forces in favor of Dien Bien Phu.[20]

Radford judged Chinese aid to be considerable enough that heavy air bombardment could be executed without assuming the character of a provocation.

General Ely recalled, "This was a proposition whose importance could not escape me."[21]

Officially the two sides determined only to continue contacts on the military level. Ely would advise Navarre, and Radford would review all contingency arrangements for military cooperation.

That day at the White House there was a meeting of the Cabinet. The general subject of Indochina was included fairly far down on the agenda but at the last moment was rescheduled as the first item of business. The explanation was that in the United

States there had been a "general misunderstanding" about the Indochina war.

Secretary of State Dulles reviewed the situation for the Cabinet. He emphasized the political implications of the battle of Dien Bien Phu, the colonialism factor, and the discussions with Ely. Then he delivered an exhortation for U.S. action at Dien Bien Phu. Without it, as Dulles saw it, the "Reds" would "cut our defense line in half" in Southeast Asia.

Dulles predicted that the United States might have to take "fairly strong action" involving risks, but he insisted that "these risks will be less if we take them now rather than waiting several years."

When United Nations Ambassador Henry Cabot Lodge asked whether Viet-Nam couldn't be turned into "another Greece," Eisenhower the military man responded that the situations were different in that the Greeks were a "sturdy people" while the Vietnamese were "backward" and did not believe in the sincerity of French promises of independence. "France presents difficult questions everywhere you look."[22]

The Eisenhower administration was girding itself for action in Indochina. The numerous off-the-record meetings and comings and goings of officials confirmed that impression.

Did President Eisenhower have the legal authority to authorize such intervention? According to a long memorandum completed by Justice Department international lawyers at this time, there were less formal means than a declaration of war by which Congress could create or recognize a state of war, and there were no impediments to Congress and the President acting together. In his constitutional role as commander in chief, the brief asserted, the President had the authority to send armed forces outside the United States without resorting to a declaration of war. Under this "state of emergency" the President could exercise full powers for the duration.

The Justice Department memorandum also included a draft text for a congressional resolution authorizing both naval and air forces, "and should he find it necessary, land forces," to assist Viet-Nam, Laos, and Cambodia. It provided for any steps deemed necessary by the President to counter overt acts of aggression by any other country against the nations of Southeast Asia.

That day, before he met for dinner with John Foster Dulles, Admiral Radford informed U.S. commanders in the Far East that "circumstances" made it necessary to retain Task Force 70 in Indochinese waters for "at least" another six weeks.

VI

VULTURE TRANSFORMED

While politicians, diplomats, and military men cautiously discussed contingencies in Washington and Paris, the reality was at Dien Bien Phu and it was no mere contingency. The Viet Minh attacks of the first few days radically reduced the size of the entrenched camp and the drop zone in which supplies could be landed. The Viet Minh anti-aircraft guns acquired excellent positions on the former strongpoints of the French. But after their successes at Beatrice and Gabrielle, Giap's infantrymen changed their tactics. Instead of staging more mass assaults, the Viet-Nam People's Army began to dig its own trenches all around Dien Bien Phu; when the Viet Minh had finished protecting themselves with the trenches, they began to extend them toward the remaining French strongpoints.

On the French side it was painfully evident that once these approach trenches got close enough to the strongpoints, Giap's infantrymen would emerge again in their "human waves."

With the battle developing into a classical confrontation of siege warfare, Colonel de Castries informed Hanoi that he lacked specialists and combat engineering equipment for trench warfare. On March 23, Dien Bien Phu requested documents on trench warfare including four copies of the French Army's regulations on the defensive organization of terrain, a siege manual that had not been revised since 1916. In the valley the French troops were already encountering difficulties keeping the road open from Dien Bien Phu to its satellite position, Strongpoint "Isabelle."

While General Ely was in Washington, at Dien Bien Phu the French garrison fought several small battles on the road to Isabelle and mounted trench raids against the Viet Minh approaches to the main position. On March 27 the French made a sortie northward that reached halfway to former Strongpoint Gabrielle.

Concerned about the Viet Minh flak over the valley, the next morning the French conducted a major attack to the west of the entrenched camp. The attack cleared several Viet Minh flak positions. "Orchestrated" by Major Marcel Bigeard, the attack involved such large forces and consumed such a proportion of the stock of shells in the camp, however, that it was apparent the garrison could not often repeat operations of this size.

On March 27, President Eisenhower dictated to Foster Dulles a commendation of the fighters at Dien Bien Phu, which was sent as a letter to French President René Coty. Ike said:

In common with millions of my countrymen, I salute the gallantry and stamina of the commander and soldiers who are defending Dien Bien Phu. We have the most profound admiration for the brave and resourceful fight being waged there by troops from France, Viet-Nam, and other parts of the French Union. Those soldiers, true to their own great traditions, are defending the cause of human freedom and are demonstrating in the truest fashion qualities on which the survival of the free world depends. I would be grateful if you convey to the commander of the gallant garrison of Dien Bien Phu an expression of my admiration and best wishes.[1]

But it was not best wishes that the French needed at Dien Bien Phu. March 27 was the last day a French aircraft made a successful takeoff from the airfield at the entrenched camp. On the ground, every day the Viet Minh trenches came closer to the strongpoints.

On the night of March 30, General Giap began the second phase of his attack.

The new assault struck Strongpoints "Dominique" and "Eliane." On the eastern flank of Dien Bien Phu, these positions contained all the low hills remaining within the French defenses. Dominique and Eliane were the last obstacles to direct domination of the airfield by Giap, and they also protected the French Army's source of fresh water in the Nam Youm, the stream that flowed through Dien Bien Phu. Both strongpoints were composed of hilltop and interval positions; Dominique was defended by an Algerian rifle battalion and Eliane by a Moroccan one. Both also had small detachments of other units including paratroopers and artillerymen.

It rained at Dien Bien Phu throughout the day. In the evening the Viet Minh gunners of the 351st Division began another of their heavy bombardments. This destroyed four of the French 105mm guns and one of the 155mms. The Viet Minh infantry went in after dark. On Dominique and Eliane the French Union troops faced a veritable onslaught as two of Giap's divisions swept toward them. Not all the Algerians and Moroccans stood fast. In particular on Dominique two positions fell when Algerian rifle companies and Thai partisans disintegrated. At Dominique-3 the Viet-Nam People's Army's 312th Division was stopped by French artillery firing over open sights. On Eliane, Moroccans and Vietnamese paratroopers experienced some desertion but held fast. Still, the 316th Division seized the hill Eliane-1 and temporarily controlled critical Eliane-2.

If the Viet Minh could capture all these positions, they would have direct observation over the entire entrenched camp while the drop zone for French supplies would become hopelessly small. In a daring intervention Major Bigeard sent a company of his 6th Colonial Paratroops to reinforce Eliane-2 when he noticed that some of the Moroccans were still fighting in that position. The reinforcement broke the momentum of Giap's attacking troops and the French held the position.

Thus began what came to be called the "Battle of the Five Hills" for the five hill positions east of the airfield over which the fight raged. Combat raged for days in a sequence of Viet Minh attacks and strangulation efforts at night alternating with French counterattacks with artillery and air support by day. Twenty-one hundred losses were suffered by the French between March 28 and April 2—almost 30 percent of their casualties during the entire battle of Dien Bien Phu.

The tense military situation sharpened the need for urgency in diplomacy. Dien Bien Phu looked as if it might fall any day. In Washington, Admiral Radford mentioned one option to General Ely: an aerial bombardment, to be formally requested by the French government.

Ely carried the news back to Paris. The French themselves now had to decide whether to request air intervention.

Ely encountered the French ambassador to the United States, Henri Bonnet. He mentioned the intervention project to Bonnet and the two men considered the possibility of an air strike leading to open intervention by the People's Republic of China. Ely was gratified to discover that the ambassador agreed with him that the risk involved was small.

Next, Ely reported to Defense Minister René Pleven. Pleven immediately moved to schedule a meeting of the restricted Committee of National Defense.

The committee gathered on March 29 to hear the proposal brought by General Ely. Present at the meeting were Prime Minister Joseph Laniel, Pleven and other senior civil servants from the Ministry of Defense, Bidault and Maurice Schumann from the Quai d'Orsay, Marc Jacquet from the Ministry of Associated States, and the military chiefs of staff.

The major question considered was whether to request American air intervention. With it arose the related issues of whether such intervention would bring in China and whether the Expeditionary Corps could stand up to Chinese intervention and support the American air operations from its own air bases.

General Ely stated his opinion that an American air strike could be capable of breaking the Viet Minh siege ring around Dien Bien Phu while Chinese intervention would not necessarily follow. On the whole the risk was worth taking.

The French government did not immediately resolve these issues. Rather the Committee of National Defense determined to send an officer to Indochina to put the questions directly to General Navarre. The officer selected was Colonel Raymond Brohon of the French Air Force, chef de cabinet, or of personal staff, to General Ely.

Along the Potomac, activity continued as if the French government had already made the request for air intervention. The Americans had improved the concept of relying upon carrier air power by combining it with air strikes by U.S. Air Force B-29 bombers. This could multiply by many times the capability available from carrier aircraft alone.

In the meantime John Foster Dulles put the last changes on his Overseas Press Club speech. As was his wont, Eisenhower reviewed the text before permitting Foster to go ahead. Ike at several points inserted language *toughening* the text Dulles would deliver. In only one place did the President change a word to suggest the U.S. did not have a completely negative view of the upcoming Geneva conference. These pencilled changes by President Eisenhower put the lie to those theories which hold that the American project for action at Dien Bien Phu was the brainchild of Secretary Dulles and not the president himself. McGeorge Bundy, in a later study of the nuclear age, checked on this assertion only to be told by his own former White House secretary that the emendations were indeed Eisenhower's. *The New York Times* on the morning of March 29, 1954, reported the president had approved the speech Dulles was about to make.

Afterward, the speech was widely interpreted as an effort to prepare the American people for additional United States action on Indochina. Secretary Dulles warned:

> *The tragedy would not stop* [in Indochina]. *If the Communist forces won uncontested control over Indochina or any substantial part thereof, they would surely resume the same pattern of aggression against other free peoples in the area.*

Dulles cited President Eisenhower's stated view that Indochina was of "transcendent importance" to the United States. He then declared:

> *Recent statements have been designed to impress upon potential aggressors that aggression might lead to action at places and by means of free world choosing, so that aggression would cost more than it could gain.*

Dulles delivered the most explicit warning of American action that had yet been made on Indochina. Since it was desirable to clarify the U.S. position under all circumstances, Dulles said, *under the conditions of today, the imposition on Southeast Asia of the political system of Communist Russia and its Chinese Communist ally, by whatever means, would be a grave threat to the whole free community. The United States feels that that possibility should not be passively accepted, but should be met by united action. This might involve serious risks. But these risks are far less than those that will face us a few years from now, if we dare not be resolute today.*

In a powerful conclusion to this passage Dulles thundered, "Sometimes it is necessary to take risks to win peace just as it is necessary in war to take risks to win victory."[2]

That morning, Dulles had said on the telephone to Representative Walter Judd that the speech would ask for "united action" based on a recent congressional report in which Judd participated. After the speech he remarked to Senator William F. Knowland that he had had "to puncture the sentiment for appeasement before Geneva."[3]

On March 30, Dulles busily made arrangements to derive maximum advantage from the Overseas Press Club speech. Copies were sent to the embassies of Southeast Asian nations. When Jean Daridan, minister counselor of the French Embassy, called to ask how the Dulles speech should be interpreted, he was told that the United States was considering direct intervention that would stop short of actually replacing French troops on the ground.

Dulles had met with British Ambassador Sir Roger Makins two days before the speech and spoke with Makins on the phone that same morning. The British were given advance word of the "united action" formula and the intervention project. On instructions from London, Makins raised the point that agreement to joint action in principle did not commit Britain to joint military action. Dulles hastened to give the necessary assurances. Moreover, on the afternoon of March 30 the Secretary took Makins to the White House for a discussion with President Eisenhower, who in the meantime had been briefed on the capabilities of B-29 bombers by Air Force Chief of Staff General Nathan F. Twining. Dulles and Makins entered the White House by the rear entrance to avoid the press, and their meeting was held "off the record."

British official reaction to "united action" was not very favorable, but it was far less critical than British public commentaries. *The Times* of London commented on April Fools' Day: "It has not always been easy to let Mr. Dulles' speeches speak for themselves, however, because since he became Secretary of State he has often seemed to be reversing the normal tactics for a Foreign Minister and, instead of using his public statements to hint at policies, has made them stronger than the policies themselves." Two days later *The Times* added that Dulles's failure to consult with the allies *before* his Overseas Press Club speech "has been explained by the comment that moving fast creates a vacuum into which other interested countries cannot help being drawn."[4]

A crucial meeting occurred March 31 at the Pentagon; Radford called a secret conference of the Joint Chiefs, at which he asked them to determine what their recommendation would be if the French government requested the assistance of U.S. air and naval forces in combat. General Matthew B. Ridgway of the Army protested the secrecy with which the meeting had been called. In a memo written after the meeting Ridgway asserted that Radford appeared to have called the conference on no one's authority but his own.

All the Joint Chiefs—except for Radford—opposed intervention at that time, as Radford reported in a top-secret memorandum later that day to Defense Secretary Charles Wilson. But, "Raddy" continued, "the Chairman is of the opinion that such an offer should be made" anyway.[5]

President Eisenhower convened the National Security Council on April 1 in the Cabinet Room of the White House. The discussion focused on American policy toward Germany and the Philippines, but the real action that day occurred among a smaller group that stayed behind after the main body broke up.

The President directed that Congress be brought into the process of decision on intervention.

Ike went on to a lunch with businessmen Bob Howard and Walker Stone. Press Secretary Jim Hagerty saw Eisenhower "expound" informally about Indochina, which was "getting really bad." Evidently the President explicitly mentioned the possibility that the United States would have to send in the squadrons of two aircraft carriers to bomb the Viet Minh at Dien Bien Phu.

According to Eisenhower, "Of course, if we did, we'd have to deny it forever."[6]

At 2:54 P.M., John Foster Dulles called up with details about a planned meeting with congressmen. Dulles had been working with Thruston Morton to set up a congressional caucus. It had been decided to have perhaps two men from each party from each of the houses of Congress. Initially planned for the next day, the meeting was pushed back a day, to Saturday, April 3, so that it would be less conspicuous.

Foster had also talked to Attorney General Herbert Brownell about having "something to show" the congressmen in the form of a draft resolution giving authority to use force in Indochina. Dulles told President Eisenhower that he could show him a draft in the morning, but that, as a result, he might have to miss the scheduled Cabinet meeting.

The President said that nothing much was going to happen at Cabinet anyway. State could send Walter Bedell Smith in Dulles's place. Ike told Dulles to go ahead with the congressional meeting.

Six minutes later Dulles talked to Thruston Morton, in charge of organizing the mechanics of the briefing. Dulles reported the President's approval and the two discussed timing. Friday would be quicker but Saturday would be easier to keep quiet. Dulles hung up but called back again to say he had spoken with Admiral Radford, who emphasized rapidity of action, that "time is the question."

Radford had said, "If there is a disaster the President might be criticized for not doing something ahead of time."[7]

Thruston Morton succeeded in arranging a meeting for the State Department on Saturday, April 3.

But Thursday was April Fools' Day after all; that day, the proposal for aerial intervention began to unravel. It started with the British, whose response to Secretary Dulles's notion of "united action" was eagerly awaited in Washington.

Foreign Secretary Anthony Eden put the British view in a message to Ambassador Sir Roger Makins. Eden shrewdly suggested that he understood the United States was considering and had already *rejected* (rightly, in Eden's view) the intervention option. Britain no longer believed in the possibility of a French victory:

After earnest study of military and political factors, we feel it would be unrealistic not to face the possibility that the conditions for a favorable solution in Indochina may no longer exist. Failure to consider this possibility now is likely to increase the difficulty of reaching tripartite agreement should we be forced at Geneva to accept a policy of compromise.[8]

Makins passed these views along to John Foster Dulles and Walter Bedell Smith on April 1, and added that if it came to negotiation, Britain thought partition of Indochina to be the "least damaging solution."

This cautious reply from the British could have been expected. The Churchill government had been encouraging a more moderate approach to the post-Stalin Soviet leadership for over a year, and had also normalized relations with the People's Republic of China. Eden took a leading role in Berlin early in 1954 to set up the Geneva conference, which British foreign policy saw as a possible path toward improved East-West relations.

But in Washington, Dulles hotly argued for British reconsideration. According to Eden, Makins was told the aim would be "to compel China to desist from aid to the Viet Minh by the threat of military action."

Dulles insisted on a joint warning to China of air and naval action against the China coast. He said that "we possessed a military superiority in the area now which we might not have in a few years time. So if a warning was not heeded, we should now be in a position to put our threats into effect. Military action involved risks but the risks of letting Indochina go were greater."[9] Dulles bid the British diplomat to convey his message to the foreign secretary.

Dulles also reiterated his message the next morning when he received English journalist Henry Brandon for an interview.

Brandon asked whether the Secretary's March 29 speech was meant to herald United States entry into Indochina.

Dulles leaned forward, then he tipped his chair back.

He said, "I can tell you that American aircraft carriers are at this moment steaming into the Gulf of Tonkin ready to strike."

Had the United States actually decided to intervene?

"Not yet," replied Dulles, who evidently said that he personally favored the idea.[10]

The Churchill Cabinet was scheduled to meet in two days on the Indochina question. Dulles could expect his views to appear in the Fleet Street newspapers in time to influence the Churchill government, but he now knew that bringing the British into the intervention project would be difficult.

Another obstacle that developed simultaneously in Washington came from the Joint Chiefs of Staff. On April 1 its members were sent copies of Admiral Radford's memorandum to the Secretary of Defense that recommended offering intervention to France, despite the individual Chiefs' opposition to such an offer.

By the following morning there were formal papers on Radford's desk with the views of each of the Joint Chiefs on U.S. intervention in Indochina.

The most favorable view was that of Air Force Chief of Staff Nathan F. Twining, whose answer was "a qualified 'Yes.'" Twining was a general who believed in tactical bombardment. Graduating from West Point in 1919, he transferred to the Army Air Corps in 1924 and in World War II commanded air units in the South Pacific and Italy. In 1945, Nate Twining commanded the 20th Air Force in the Pacific, one of the major units conducting the B-29 bombing of Japan. Twining's opinion was recorded after the war: he was convinced Japan would have surrendered in a short time even if the atomic bomb had not been used. Now, in 1954, Twining favored intervention if the French would accept U.S. command of all naval and air forces and if the French would also make concessions on independence to the Associated States and U.S. training of the Vietnamese Army.

One of the papers to Radford did not really take a position. Chief of Naval Operations Admiral Robert B. Carney felt the Chiefs should "state the current capabilities" of U.S. forces and note that these could improve the French tactical position at Dien Bien Phu. Carney was not prepared to say that such an intervention would have a decisive effect. Possible consequences of U.S. involvement in the Indochina war should also be evaluated. Admiral Carney reaffirmed the opinion that the loss of Indochina should be averted if possible.

The viewpoint of the Marine Corps was stated by its commandant, General Lemuel C. Shepherd, Jr. Shepherd could not escape the view that action by American air forces "would be taken in the face of impending disaster and holds no significant promise of success." Any air offensive would have to be "improvised." At the same time the Viet Minh "are nowhere exposed at a vital point critical to their continued resupply and communications." Shepherd expressed regret at having to pen conclusions so contrary to his own natural inclinations, but the Marine Corps's stated conclusion remained that aerial intervention in Indochina would be "an unprofitable adventure."

Finally there was the memorandum from General Matthew B. Ridgway. The Army chief of staff's reply to air intervention was "an emphatic and immediate 'no.'" United States capability for effective intervention at Dien Bien Phu "is presently altogether disproportionate to the liability it would incur." Moreover, intervention "would greatly increase the risk of general war." Ridgway concluded, "If the United States, by its own act, were deliberately to provoke such possible reaction, it must first materially increase its readiness to accept the consequences."[11]

The chiefs of staff memoranda could not have been worse news for Admiral Radford. The Air Force and Navy, the services that would carry out any intervention, were not fully in support of this course of action. The Army and Marine Corps, which would have to do the fighting if air intervention failed, were completely opposed.

Admiral Radford was soon on his way to the White House for another meeting with the President. The gathering of 9:30 A.M. on Friday, April 2, was intended to refine the administration's position that would be briefed to the congressmen the next day. Dulles handed President Eisenhower the draft of a possible congressional resolution authorizing use of force in Indochina. The President read this over and said it reflected what he thought desirable.

Eisenhower insisted that the "tactical procedure" for the congressional meeting should be first to develop the thinking of the legislative leaders "without actually submitting in the first instance a resolution drafted by ourselves."

Secretary Dulles said that this was his intention.

Dulles then took issue with Admiral Radford, saying the two had some differences that ought to be clarified. Dulles said his view was that the authority derived from a possible resolution should be designed as a "deterrent," to give the United States leverage to develop strength in the area in association with other states. Dulles had already planned meetings with the ambassadors of several Southeast Asian states for the succeeding days. He then suggested that perhaps Radford saw congressional authority in a different way—something to be used in an immediate "strike" irrespective of any prior development of Allied unity.

Admiral Radford had little choice how to reply, having just been confronted with the Joint Chiefs' memoranda. He now said that he'd been thinking of a strike primarily in relation to Dien Bien Phu but "presently" he had nothing in mind. This was because, Radford said, the outcome at Dien Bien Phu would be determined "within hours."[12] In fact the French and Viet Minh were at that moment desperately fighting on the Five Hills east of the airfield at the entrenched camp.

At the White House that day Jim Hagerty recorded "our intelligence reports Chinese Reds moving into [Indochinese] territory—not in great numbers yet but in special advisor and technical departments."

The meeting at the State Department between congressional leaders and representatives took place in one of the fifth-floor conference rooms near John Foster Dulles's office. The United States Constitution gives all war-making powers to Congress even though the Chief Executive, the President, is considered commander in chief of the armed forces. Any act of force in Indochina undertaken by President Eisenhower would have invited impeachment if made without some kind of congressional action. Ike himself had told the press in mid-March that there would be no American intervention without consultation. The State Department meeting of April 3 was intended as such a consultation.

There was an impressive array of congressional leadership at the gathering that morning, five senators and three representatives including the senior party leaders of both parties in both houses of Congress. For the Republicans, Senator William F. Knowland, Senate majority leader, and Speaker Joseph Martin headed the group. Both men were identified with the China Lobby and had long interest in Far Eastern affairs. The Democratic leaders were Senate minority leader Lyndon B. Johnson and House leaders John W. McCormack and J. Percy Priest. McCormack kept notes at the meeting. For the executive branch there were Secretary Dulles and Admiral Radford. Substituting for Defense Secretary Charles Wilson were his deputy Roger Kyes and Navy Secretary Robert B. Anderson.

Dulles began by saying that the President had asked him to call the meeting. The government needed a congressional resolution enabling it to carry out air and naval action in Indochina. Dulles alluded to the "deterrent" role of such a resolution—its mere passage might make the use of it unnecessary. He emphasized that at this crucial juncture the President wanted Congress to feel the same way he did on the issue.

Admiral Radford then took over for a briefing on the military situation and contingencies. Radford used a map of the Pacific to illustrate the importance of Indochina. He described Dien Bien Phu under siege, but said that because of slow communications he was not even sure that the entrenched camp, at that very moment, was still holding out.

Secretary Dulles reinforced Radford's talk. Indochina was the key to Southeast Asia; if "the Communists" got it "and nothing was done about it," it would be only a question of time before all Southeast Asia, including Indonesia, would go. America could ultimately be forced back to Hawaii, as before World War II. Dulles thought the President should have congressional backing to use air and sea power if he felt it necessary "in the interest of national security."

Radford revealed the plan for intervention from the aircraft carriers and B-29 bombers the Americans had available.

Then discussion began.

Senator Knowland, who liked to end his meetings with the Kuomintang toast "Back to the Mainland!" announced he favored giving Eisenhower the authority to use force.

Radford was asked if an air strike would be an act of war and he replied in the affirmative.

What would happen if the air strike didn't work? There would be follow-up attacks.

Would troops be used?

Both the Secretary and Admiral Radford pointed out that the administration did not now contemplate the commitment of land forces. The congressmen replied that once the flag was committed, the use of land forces would inevitably follow.

The congressional group, particularly Georgia Democratic Senator Richard B. Russell, active on the Armed Services Committee, showed very little confidence in the French. Nor could they have been relieved when Radford said that three weeks earlier he had been sure air power would have defeated the Viet Minh, but that now it might already be "too late."

Kentucky Senator Earle C. Clements asked Radford if the intervention plan had the support of the other Joint Chiefs.

"No," Radford responded.

How many agreed?

"None."

"How do you account for that?" puzzled Clements.

Admiral Radford said, "I have spent more time in the Far East than any of them and I understand the situation better."

The other key question was put by Lyndon Johnson. Senator Johnson had helped to show, during the Truman-MacArthur controversy, how America was unable to fight a general war against China and how General MacArthur had exceeded his writ in advocating such a strategy. Now Johnson noted that Republican Senator Knowland himself had publicly complained of a war (Korea) in which the United States carried 90 percent of the burden. Who would carry the burden in Indochina? What nations would be America's allies?

Secretary Dulles admitted that no allies had yet been enlisted.

Clearly more legwork was necessary before Congress would be satisfied.

Because of the cautious attitude concerning immediate unilateral action, Dulles never showed the draft resolution he had in his pocket. The joint resolution accused "the Chinese Communist regime and its agents in Indochina" of "armed attack against Viet-Nam." Authority given under the resolution would last until June 30, 1955. If passed, the resolution would have given President Eisenhower the power "to employ the Naval and Air Forces of the United States to assist the forces which are resisting aggression in Southeast Asia, to prevent the extension and expansion of that aggression, and to protect and defend the safety and security of the United States."

The conclusion of the meeting, according to Dulles's record, was that "if satisfactory commitments can be obtained [from allies], the consensus was that a Congressional resolution could be passed giving the President power to commit armed forces in the area."[13]

While other senators directly expressed their reservations, the minority leader himself actually took a position much akin to that of the president. Another way of interpreting LBJ's comments at the April 3 briefing is to see them as Johnson simply asking how well the administration had planned to line up *bipartisan* support for the initiative. This point is reinforced by the fact that immediately *after* the session with Dulles, Senator Johnson went right on to take soundings among his Democratic colleagues about their positions on Vietnam intervention.

Lyndon Johnson made no speeches of advocacy, but his newsletters to Texas constituents consistently *supported* intervention in Indochina. It has never been disclosed previously, but Johnson's newsletters, which often reflected his thinking and were written by aide George Reedy, other assistants, occasionally LBJ himself, always with a careful eye to leadership, repeatedly made the case for U.S. action in Indochina. The April 3 meeting, for example, is explicitly recalled in Senator Johnson's April 15 newsletter, which advised that in Indochina "we are at the crossroads" and talked of the need to make "hard decisions—the kind that will tax all our determination and willpower." Johnson asserted that the fall of Indochina "would be disastrous to all our plans in Asia," warning of the loss of rich tungsten, tin, and rubber sources, and raising the specter of "the loss of all Southeast Asia and probably all of Asia. Ultimately, we might be driven out of the Pacific itself!" The punctuation was Johnson's.

The Senator's information may have been dated—he wrote voters earnestly about Vietnam's rubber and tin (nonexistent)—but he backed Ike's domino theory, publicly worried about fighting elsewhere if Indochina were given up, and lauded the French at Dien Bien Phu. One speech Lyndon Johnson did make, in late April, *after* the notorious meeting with Dulles and Radford, offered a resolution for federal funds to keep open a tin smelter in Texas, one of the few left in the United States at that time. Beyond the pork barrel politics was LBJ's argumentation in support of his initiative: the senator argued that keeping the smelter open another year was critical due to the situation in Indochina. With a group of Bolivian businessmen trying to buy the smelter, Johnson worried that the loss of Indochina could cut the free world off from sixty-five percent of its tin supplies, and make it vulnerable to price fixing by South American cartels. The only correspondence in the record during this period between Seantor Johnson and President Eisenhower concerns the tin smelter. Whether his information on tin in Indochina was correct or not, this material shows that Lyndon Johnson had his own reasons to perceive a national security problem in Indochina.

Johnson's newsletters also mentioned the matter of allies for intervention. In the April 15 issue that recollected the bipartisan meeting with Dulles and Radford, LBJ's comment was: "Shall we continue without clear assurances that others will join us? Or shall we withdraw altogether and fall back upon the concept of Fortress America?" The choice among these stark alternatives was clear. The Senate minority leader's rhetoric cast the isolationist view in a pejorative way. Johnson's words were not those of an opponent of intervention.

In his April 24 newsletter Senator Johnson referred to a briefing Foster Dulles had given senior congressmen after his first trip to Europe and just prior to his departure for the NATO meetings and Geneva. Johnson declared that a Viet Minh victory in Indochina "would be a heavy blow to freedom" that would leave communism "in a commanding position *to take over the entire continent of Asia*" (Johnson's italics). Lyndon declared that any decision on U.S. involvement would have to have the full support of the American people, but again his rhetoric seemed designed to convince Texans, at least, that intervention was the sensible course.

Lyndon Johnson also made these arguments repeatedly, both during Dien Bien Phu and during the negotiations at Geneva, warning of the need to intervene if they failed. In the April 24 newsletter Lyndon Johnson's language ran *"Indochina is a rich prize"* (his italics again) and maintained, "It is impossible to exaggerate the seriousness of the situation." The senator's office put out the identical text as a press release a few days later. Johnson took that line in spite of the fact that few of his constituents (at least measuring by the views expressed in letters to LBJ) favored the Indochina intervention Johnson was advocating here: sixty-three of the seventy Texas constituents expressing opinions opposed any Indochina intervention. Not until May 1, with Dien Bien Phu on its last legs, did an LBJ newsletter state that he shared the prayers of Americans who hoped the crisis "will not end in another war to be fought by our young men." Even after the fall of the entrenched camp, Johnson's May 15 newsletter, terming the loss of Dien Bien Phu a major setback, quoted LBJ's floor speech in the Senate on the occasion: "we are ready to meet the President and the Administration *more* than half way. As responsible men, *we are ready at any time to cooperate in the preservation of our country*" (Johnson's italics).[14] Like some other American leaders, Lyndon Johnson seems to have changed his position on an Indochina intervention, and his first view was not the one historians usually attribute to him.

Meanwhile, at 1:44 P.M. of April 3, shortly after his session with congressional leaders, John Foster Dulles called the President at Camp David and told him "on the whole it went pretty well." The Secretary of State reported that some serious problems did come up. Congress would be "quite prepared to go along on some vigorous action" if the United States was not acting alone. Congress also wanted to see peoples of the area actively involved.

Dulles suggested that President Eisenhower might want to write a letter to Prime Minister Churchill asking for British support of "united action." Eisenhower agreed to let the State Department work up a cable on a personal basis to Churchill and bring it back to him for changes.

Eisenhower and Dulles also agreed on a consultation conference to be held in Washington with Britain, Thailand, the Philippines, and the ANZUS powers—Australia and New Zealand—on "united action."

Meanwhile, at the State Department after the congressional leaders' meeting, the press office put out a one-sentence statement saying that congressmen had been given a periodic briefing on Indochina.

That morning the *Times* reported Viet Minh capture of two positions in the Five Hills at Dien Bien Phu. Senator Knowland declared that the news from Indochina convinced him that the situation was extremely serious. "Whether Indochina remains outside the Iron Curtain or falls within may well be determined in the next few months," declared the California Republican, who had served in the Senate since 1945.

The State Department's press release on the congressional leaders' meeting happened to note the presence of Admiral Radford. Reporters immediately began to pester press assistant Henry Suydam about the significance of this. Suydam repeatedly refused to enlarge on the one-sentence statement. The reporters took this to mean that Radford's presence had been significant.

Despite the optimism of the State Department record on the congressional leaders' meeting, from April 3 the proposal for Indochina intervention underwent significant change. From a straightforward effort to arrange favorable conditions for an air strike, the project slowly evolved into a longer-term effort to create a Southeast Asian alliance structure. This did not mean that the idea of aerial intervention was discarded, only that the United

States began to follow a two-track approach, enlisting support for intervention to be followed by an alliance. John Foster Dulles was a great supporter of alliances and he worked very hard for this one. The demand for allies to assist in intervention even made it easier for Dulles to advocate a Southeast Asian treaty organization along the lines of NATO. But, curiously enough, these changes were developing before the French government even made its request for intervention to save Dien Bien Phu.

None of this had yet happened when Colonel Raymond Brohon left Paris on his emergency mission to Indochina. Colonel Brohon's task was to equip the Laniel government with Navarre's view of a possible intervention so that the Committee of National Defense could make a decision on a request to the Americans. Cosmopolitan and cultured, Colonel Brohon knew Washington after serving there on the French Military Mission. Known to General Navarre from his participation in the Pleven mission, Brohon was ideally placed to give the Indochina commander in chief a complete view of the complex issues surrounding intervention.

Brohon arrived in Saigon only to discover that General Navarre had left Expeditionary Corps headquarters for Hanoi, where he could observe events at Dien Bien Phu more closely.

On April 1 in Indochina (thirteen hours ahead of Washington), Colonel Brohon met Maurice Dejean, the French High Commissioner for the Indochinese states, who was en route to Hanoi himself. The two flew north in the High Commissioner's personal plane.

Only a quarter hour after Dejean's plane landed at Gia Lam, the High Commissioner hosted a dinner at Maison de France with Generals Navarre, Pierre Bodet, and Cogny. It was raining hard in Hanoi. After dinner there was a secret discussion among the officers as Colonel Brohon presented the Radford plan and the concerns of the Committee of National Defense.

Brohon explained the concept of using numbers of American heavy-bombardment aircraft along with carrier air support. The Laniel government was interested in General Navarre's opinion. According to some accounts Colonel Brohon also raised the possibility of using atomic weapons in the strike. With several such atomic weapons the aircraft could destroy both the Viet Minh supply base at Tuan Giao and the close-in siege positions where the Viet Minh had placed their artillery and anti-aircraft guns.

According to these same accounts Brohon also pointed out the dangers involved: However small the blast radius of the tactical nuclear weapons, thermal radiation from the detonations could reach the French garrison on the valley floor. Moreover the targets would have to be unmistakably marked on the ground, and the yellow-colored markers available in Indochina would be hard to see from the height of the B-29 bombers.

General Navarre said little, instead promising a decision in the morning. After the meeting the three generals repaired to the radio room at Tonkin headquarters, where they learned from the latest messages that the Viet-Nam People's Army had just captured Huguette-7, another position at Dien Bien Phu.

The next morning at nine sharp the same group met at Maison de France. General Navarre's opinion was negative.

Dejean left with Brohon for Saigon at midafternoon. Brohon continued on to Paris, where he arrived on April 4. He went immediately to General Ely's home, where he began to detail Navarre's doubts about intervention. But even as the two men spoke Ely received a cable from Navarre. The cable read, "The intervention of which Colonel Brohon has informed me can have a decisive effect, above all if it is made before the Viet Minh [general] assault."[15]

In Saigon, where Expeditionary Corps staff officers expected to have to deal with American military men on the operation, a code name was selected for the intervention project. The code name was Vautour ("Vulture") and it had already been used once for one of the bombing points along the Viet Minh line of supply to Dien Bien Phu.

In Paris the Navarre cable created an immediate crisis situation. As soon as Colonel Brohon had finished briefing Ely, both officers went to Defense Minister René Pleven to inform him of Navarre's first impressions and his new change of heart. Pleven was not optimistic about Indochina—two days ago the minister had said to American journalist Marquis Childs that to win in Indochina on the order of three additional paratroop divisions and a thousand more planes would be needed. "Naturally," said Pleven in answer to Childs's question, such a force could only be provided by the United States.

Today, Pleven was also in a sour mood. That afternoon he had been trapped for ten minutes in a crowd of hostile demonstrators from the Association of Indochina Veterans while participating in the Ceremony of the Flame, held annually at the Arc de Triomphe. Now General Ely had come to say that Navarre wanted the air strike.

Pleven did not hesitate. He immediately telephoned Prime Minister Laniel at the official residence, the Matignon. Laniel called a meeting of the Committee of National Defense for that same evening; General Navarre's cable mentioned urgency and, though it failed to predict an exact date for the next major Viet Minh offensive at Dien Bien Phu, it did give a range of six to ten days' time. Operation Vautour would take a certain amount of time to organize and execute. The hour was already late.

Grim faces lined the conference table at the Matignon that night. The prime minister believed nothing should be denied that offered any possibility of a favorable outcome at Dien Bien Phu, this in spite of the attendant dangers of a Chinese response. No member of the Committee of National Defense appears to have objected to this government position: not Pleven, who had counseled negotiation after his February inspection visit, nor Georges Bidault, whose concessions at the Berlin conference helped make possible the scheduled Geneva talks. The effect an act of force in Indochina would have on the prospects of attaining a negotiated settlement at Geneva can readily be imagined, but the Committee of National Defense had no difficulty deciding to make a formal request to the United States to carry out the Vautour air bombardment.

The telephone rang in the American Embassy at eleven P.M. Maurice Schumann of the Quai d'Orsay asked Ambassador C. Douglas Dillon to come to Laniel's residence immediately.

At the Matignon, Ambassador Dillon was received by Foreign Minister Georges Bidault in Laniel's office. Laniel himself joined them a few moments later. Dillon reported they said that "immediate armed intervention of US carrier aircraft at Dien Bien Phu is now necessary to save the situation."

The fate of Dien Bien Phu would "probably be sealed" if the entrenched camp did not receive assistance by the middle or end of the week.

Bidault catalogued the extent of Chinese involvement established by French intelligence. Most serious perhaps was the claim that forty Viet Minh anti-aircraft guns were actually radar-guided weapons manned by Chinese troops. The French claimed these guns were shooting up through cloud cover to hit the planes supporting Dien Bien Phu. The French also claimed the Chinese specialists had installed and were maintaining the telephone lines between Viet Minh command posts. Although the French claimed the presence of two thousand Chinese advisors, they would only confirm fourteen Chinese present in Giap's headquarters.

Bidault informed Douglas Dillon that the French Air Force realized that Vautour could lead to a Chinese air attack on the Tonkin air bases. The request for air intervention was being made despite this danger.

The French foreign minister finished his presentation with some very strong language. "For good or evil the fate of Southeast Asia now rest[s] on Dien Bien Phu. . . . Geneva w[ill] be won or lost depending on [the] outcome."

This was the first time that Douglas Dillon heard about intervention or Vautour. Dillon knew the United States was contemplating additional actions in Indochina, but he had had no idea of the specifics. Dillon's startled reaction is reflected in the slightly incredulous tone of his cable, which reported the intervention request to Washington: "Ely brought back report from Washington that Radford gave him his personal (repeat personal) assurance that if situation at Dien Bien Phu required US naval air support he would do his best to obtain such help from US Government."[16]

Since 1946, France had resisted every suggestion that its Indochina war might be "internationalized." That night, April 4, 1954, propelled by desperation before the specter of defeat, the French made a volte-face. No one had told them that the vulture they wished so fervently to fly had already been relegated to a subsidiary role in a transformed policy of "united action."

VII

"THE TIME FOR FORMULATING COALITIONS HAS PASSED"

Most of the day on April 4 it was just a quiet Sunday at the White House. Though it was cold, Jim Hagerty went out to play golf. The President and Mamie Eisenhower did not even arrive back from Camp David until 8:20 P.M. Awaiting Ike were Foster Dulles, "Beetle" Smith, Admiral Radford, Roger Kyes, and Douglas MacArthur II, who met to discuss the results of the canvass of congressional leaders conducted the day before. The group went upstairs to the President's study.

While it was abundantly clear that Congress wished to attach preconditions to any Indochina intervention, it was also true that what Congress wanted was not much different from the policy goals stated in National Security Council documents approved by President Eisenhower himself.

The President agreed to recommend United States participation in the Indochina war if the congressional preconditions were met. The conditions stipulated that the United States operate as part of a coalition of interested nations including nations of Southeast Asia; that France accord full independence to the Associated States; and that the French agree to accept U.S. training for the Vietnamese national army.

Writing in 1963 about his decision, President Eisenhower agreed "there was nothing in these preconditions or in this Congressional viewpoint with which I could disagree; my judgment entirely coincided with theirs."[1] In interviews given in 1964 and 1967, however, the former president emphasized his initial total opposition to intervention and maintained that he only later decided that Vautour was feasible.

In both interviews Eisenhower pointed out the disadvantages of the French garrison at Dien Bien Phu. The former president remarked that he made these objections clear to French representatives—"You boys are taking an awful chance, I don't think anything of this scheme," or "I can't think of anything crazier . . . [to] establish . . . an immobile force . . . in a fortress and then ask the enemy to come to invest it," or "as a soldier, I was horror-stricken." These musings were intended for history. The record shows that the United States government went ahead to underwrite the Navarre Plan without warning Navarre against any specific operations. Far from opposing intervention then, President Eisenhower favored the action provided certain conditions were met.

Eisenhower also gave the oral historians an interesting comment on the military efficacy of bombing: "After these people are deployed all around Dien Bien Phu and secreted in the jungle, how are you, with a few air strikes, to defeat them?"[2] The 1954 record shows both that at the time there was a more positive view of the effects of air bombardment and that an intervention like Vautour was thought to have psychological benefits for the French, in addition to its military value.

Some writers tend to excuse Eisenhower and argue that the President opposed intervention and did so by posing preconditions for it that he knew could not be met. Unfortunately this argument is belied by the extent to which President Eisenhower worked together with Dulles and Radford to achieve the "united action" precondition.

For example, Eisenhower's letter to Winston Churchill urged the Prime Minister to press for British support on "united action." The letter was one of the major subjects at the White House Sunday night meeting. Not only did Eisenhower change the wording of the State Department draft, he also suggested passages from Churchill's memoirs of the prewar years, *The Gathering Storm*, that could be worked into the text.

"Geneva is less than four weeks away," noted the letter to Churchill. The President saw a dangerous possibility that the Eastern bloc powers could drive a wedge between some of the Western Big Three. Eisenhower expected both of them were following the news from Dien Bien Phu with "the deepest interest and anxiety."

> *But regardless of the outcome of this particular battle, I fear that the French cannot alone see the thing through, this despite the very substantial assistance in money and materiel that we are giving them. It is no solution simply to urge the French to intensify their efforts. . . . This has led us to the hard conclusion that the situation in Southeast Asia requires us urgently to take serious and far-reaching decisions.*

As for Geneva, the President noted "there is no negotiated solution of the Indochina problem which in its essence would not be either a face-saving device to cover a French surrender or . . . a Communist retirement." Eisenhower believed "somehow we must contrive to bring about the second alternative."

To put "teeth" into his concept, President Eisenhower advocated some kind of ad hoc grouping or coalition of nations, which must be strong and "must be willing to join the fight if necessary." Ike then reminded Churchill of the years before World War II: "If I may refer again to history; we failed to halt Hirohito, Mussolini and Hitler by not acting in unity and in time. That marked the beginning of many years of stark tragedy and desperate peril. May it not be that our nations have learned something from that lesson?"[3]

After the White House meeting that night, aide Douglas MacArthur II returned to the State Department. He did not reach his Foggy Bottom desk until 10:15 P.M. Sitting on the desk was a cable from Paris. It transmitted the French request for air intervention in Indochina. MacArthur suddenly realized his night was just beginning. He reached for the telephone.

General Vo Nguyen Giap arrived on March 31 at his forward headquarters overlooking the valley. He had come up from the People's Army main headquarters at Thuan Chau. The command post at Dien Bien Phu was set along a small stream and camouflaged in a thick wooded area east of the entrenched camp. Late in March, Viet Minh sappers completed construction of an underground complex dug into the hillside—over three hundred meters of tunnel with all the necessary offices and communications equipment for the operational command. These caves would be home to Giap for the next six weeks at least.

Giap was met by the Viet-Nam People's Army chief of staff, General Hoang Van Thai, and they quickly moved to the map room to review plans for the attack on the entrenched camp.

The Viet Minh had been carrying out the second-phase attacks with unbelievable success. On the western face of Dien Bien Phu the People's Army already occupied the low hills of Strongpoint Anne-Marie, which had been abandoned by the Thai mountaineers. They had closely invested several positions, including Huguette-7, which managed to survive a strong Viet Minh attack the night before Giap's arrival. East of the airfield, in the Five

Hills, the Viet Minh had captured three of the hills in the first attacks. On position Eliane-2 the French retained a dominant bunker complex although the Viet Minh had driven them out of the defense works on the lower spur of the hill. Losses had been heavy. During the day French paratroops massed for a counter-attack against the commanding heights Eliane-1 (468 meters) and Dominique-2 (505 meters). The attack once again was coordinated by the redoubtable Major Bigeard and was briefly successful in regaining both positions, but at such heavy cost that the French, who received no airborne replacements that day from Hanoi, evacuated the positions. Many of General Giap's *bo dois* had also become casualties; indeed, the regiments of the People's Army 312th and 316th divisions, which fought on Eliane, Dominique, and Huguette, had been decimated.

General Giap's decision was given immediately. The People's Army should renew the attack that night. The 316th Division should use a different regiment against Eliane-2. Giap also ordered the 312th Division, east of the airfield, to divert French attention from Eliane by attacks on the eastern sector of the entrenched camp.

That night new attacks were launched on both the eastern and western faces of Dien Bien Phu. In the west at Huguette-7 the badly outnumbered remnants of a company of the 5th Vietnamese Parachute Battalion held on to their position by means of a clever stratagem. They abandoned all but one part of the strongpoint, concentrated there, and hit the confused Viet Minh in the remainder of the position with well-directed artillery fire. A dawn counterattack by the paratroops reoccupied the strongpoint from the remaining Viet Minh.

On Eliane-2 in the east the battle was a virtual repeat of that of the night before. The Viet Minh 316th Division charged up the hill, almost carried the entire position, was halted by the shock action of French tanks, then withdrew to hold the lower part of Eliane.

On April Fools' Day the Viet Minh again attacked Huguette-7 with Le Trong Tan's 312th Division, which finally broke through after several nights of assaults. The Huguette-7 position fell during the early morning hours of April 2.

To the east of the entrenched camp, on Eliane the Viet Minh offensive effort seemed to have petered out for a time. Now the French organized another counterattack under Major Bigeard, who had become Dien Bien Phu's deputy commanding all offensive actions. With artillery and seventy-one combat air sorties to support him, Bigeard launched his own former battalion, the 6th Colonial Paratroops, together with the 1st Foreign Legion Paratroops, in a frontal attack over the peak of Eliane-2 to eject the Viet Minh on the lower slopes. Again Major Bigeard's paratroopers were successful. In the Five Hills battles alone it is estimated that the Viet-Nam People's Army lost from 2,000 to 3,000 men. The number of wounded is unknown, but in that war it was estimated at roughly twice the number of dead. Some accounts put the total of Giap's medical personnel as low as two surgeons and five advanced medical students. The implications for the number of Viet Minh casualties in the Five Hills battles are staggering.

To Tuan Giao, Giap sent for replacements from the camp of some 25,000 recruits established there. He also reached out to available regular units to pull them into the siege: two battalions of the 304th Division, which had been engaging pro-French partisans in the highlands, were ordered to drop this mission and return to the siege lines. Another regiment of this division, one of the few remaining regular units in the vicinity of the Tonkin delta, was ordered to Dien Bien Phu on April 2. General Giap still felt the morale of his troops to be shaky, so a week later the People's Army began to increase the number of political cadres it assigned to combat units. It is also said that China agreed to send an extra 720 tons of ammunition to Dien Bien Phu, plus a regiment of sixty-seven 37mm anti-aircraft guns of the Chinese Army. French intelligence claimed these troops crossed the Tonkin border on April 10.

That same day at Dien Bien Phu, Lieutenant Colonel Bigeard, recently promoted, mounted another attack in the Five Hills. This time the French dug an approach trench themselves, to within thirty meters of the Viet Minh position on Eliane-1. In a lightning assault the 6th Colonial Paratroops were on top of the People's Army soldiers. The Viet Minh troops resisted for a time, then panicked and fled. The next day the hapless regiment commander of this unit of the 308th Division was executed for negligence. But after the Eliane-1 debacle the People's Army regained its former poise. The Viet Minh would not again waver.

In the entrenched camp the French had their own problems. On April 2, when it appeared the garrison had pulled through the Five Hills battles, the French government awarded a special unit citation to the troops. Two weeks later Christian de Castries was promoted to brigadier general and most of the other senior officers, like Bigeard, ascended one rank. But decorations and promotions could not make up for lack of fighting men. The aerial lifeline to Dien Bien Phu was erratic at best. The Viet Minh antiaircraft was downing French combat and transport aircraft with numbing regularity. When the weather was bad, no transports would come at all. The really depressing days for the French in this monsoon season were those when it was beautifully sunny at the entrenched camp but no planes came because it was raining in the Tonkin delta.

Another problem was reinforcement of Dien Bien Phu with new combat units, especially paratroop battalions. Late arrival of reinforcements caused the collapse of more than one French counterattack. At the same time, the French command was reluctant to send more paratroop units because its reserve had gotten dangerously low. General Navarre was carrying out his "Atlante" operation as planned and two or three of the scarce parachute units were in Annam or Laos. This left only three on reserve in Tonkin, reduced to two after the 2nd Battalion, 1st Parachute Light Infantry was committed to the entrenched camp early in April. That meant barely twelve hundred men were available to reinforce Dien Bien Phu.

Every day Lieutenant Colonel Langlais lost more men in his efforts to hold the Eliane and Huguette positions. The two sides were fighting classic trench warfare by now, using raids, small commando actions, and sudden, sharp infantry attacks.

Plans to save Dien Bien Phu by a ground operation were drafted at this point by Lieutenant General John W. ("Iron Mike") O'Daniel, who had earned his sobriquet in World War I for fighting on over twelve hours with a bullet in his face. His plan might have come from the same war, or at least World War II. Told by Radford that General Navarre would pay the closest attention to U.S. ideas on military options, O'Daniel cobbled together a plan for an overland relief column to move by road from Hanoi to Dien Bien Phu. Not completed until April 24, the option would be briefed to French high commissioner Maurice Dejean but not Navarre. It would have required use of every French armored unit in the Tonkin delta plus a division worth of mobile groups to be brought up from Central Vietnam. With sufficient air support O'Daniel thought the plan could work, but he spared no thought for how the French, already strained by the flight requirements for the entrenched camp, were to come up with the planes for this attack. Iron Mike also did not consider how his force would be able to negotiate roads not used by the French in a decade, or how it could itself avoid ambush, especially traversing the Viet Minh's own supply routes. Clearly the O'Daniel plan was absurd; the most charitable thing that can be said about it is perhaps that the idea was more suited for European-style operations. The plan, about which Navarre inevitably heard, did not endear Iron Mike to him.

The only real possibility for an overland attempt—and that a very slim one—was to mount a relief expedition from Laos. The French had considered this and begun planning as early as December 1953, about the same time as Navarre decided to accept battle at Dien Bien Phu. The idea for this operation, code named "Condor," was for a column to make its way from the Laotian royal capital of Luang Prabang, about 120 miles from Dien Bien Phu, to a point close to the mountain valley, where the French would secure a drop zone for a landing by an airborne battle group of three battalions and the combined force would enable the Dien Bien Phu garrison to break out to the southeast. Execution became the responsibility of the capable regional commander for northern Laos, Colonel Boucher de Crevecoeur.

An old Indochina hand with two pre-World War II tours in the colony, plus wartime experience with the British Far East commando group Force 136, Crevecoeur had parachuted into Indochina before the end of that war to set up guerrilla bands to fight Japanese. Later he had helped in the French reoccupation of Laos. Rising in the ranks and known as a fighter, what the French called a *baroudeur*, as well as a military intellectual (de Crevecoeur would eventually become one of the French theorists of revolutionary warfare), the colonel had already held the northern Laos command for six years. He well knew the difficulty of any overland trek toward Dien Bien Phu, where treacherous mountains covered by jungle made the ground distance much greater than the air mileage. French mountain posts that might have helped the relief mission had also been swept away by the Viet Minh in the large scale raid their 316th Division made toward Luang Prabang in February 1954. Because of these difficulties Colonel de Crevecoeur got his forces in motion even before Giap launched the assault on the entrenched camp.

The forces available to the French were limited. Crevecoeur had a single mobile group, the French equivalent of a U.S. regimental combat team, called the *Groupe Mobile Nord*. The unit comprised four battalions, its backbone the 2nd Battalion of the 2nd Foreign Legion Infantry and the 1st Laotian Paratroop Battalion, the remainder a couple of Laotian light infantry battalions. The Foreign Legionnaires had special incentive for this operation since the first battalion of their regiment was trapped inside Dien Bien Phu itself while a number of other Legion units were also in garrison there. Colonel Then, who led the mobile group, divided it into two columns and took with him the 4th and 5th Laotian Light Infantry. French Lieutenant Colonel Yves Godard led the other column with the legionnaires and Laotian paratroopers. The French and Lao troops hacked their way north and northeast using river valleys that cut through the mountains. They eventually reached Muong Khoua, site of a French post overrun in a bloody battle the previous year, but could proceed no further.

In Paris the French chief of staff, General Ely, saw American reporter Cyrus L. Sulzberger toward mid-April and told him that it would be exceedingly difficult to save Dien Bien Phu overland from Luang Prabang because of the complicated process of assembling the forces and the near impossibility of moving them through the mountains. These remarks were echoed by General Navarre, who sent Tonkin theater commander René Cogny a secret letter on April 15 that instructed him to consider alternatives to Condor if he judged the operation too hazardous. At Hanoi the next day senior officers gathered to assay the possibilities. An attack to sever the Viet Minh supply lines in the vicinity of the Red River, the option closest to O'Daniel's rescue plan, was rejected because its short term impact at Dien Bien Phu would be minimal. The option of an airborne landing northeast of the entrenched camp had to be rejected because the battalions that might carry it out were instead being fed into Dien Bien Phu as reinforcements. The same factor made impossible the air drop called for in the original Condor plan.

General Cogny and Colonel Crevecoeur ended up concocting a fresh overland operation they called "Albatross." The *Groupe Mobile Nord* was now merely to hold the positions it had reached on the Nam Ou river as a forward base while the close approach would be attempted by commandos and partisan bands. Even this reduced effort required supplies at a rate of 45 tons a day, a significant fraction of the level needed by Dien Bien Phu itself, and a major draw on French aerial transport capabilities, in fact one more reason the French needed their American support so much.

The partisan groups belonged to French intelligence, which ran a counter-guerrilla command called the *Groupement Mixte d'Intervention* (GMI). This Indochina-wide command had mobilized about 15,000 indigenous fighters to combat the Viet Minh, and roughly 3,000 of them were Lao. Major Roger Trinquier ran the GMI and came up to a forward command post at Khang Khai in the Plain of Jars to supervise Operation Albatross. Trinquier set in motion a number of partisan groups, given the names of fruit such as "Grapefruit" (*Pamplemousse*) and "Banana" (*Banane*). One group was led by Lieutenant Vang Pao, who would gain fame in the later CIA secret war in Laos. Vang Pao would act as the rear guard for the partisan formations. The partisans radiated around a maneuver force made up of French commando units, one of which came to Nam Bac to protect the headquarters of Colonel Molla, in overall charge of Albatross. From there Molla threw a force of commando units into the hills southwest of Dien Bien Phu, including 33 Commando from Cogny's command, under Captain Bréhier, and 610 Commando from Central Vietnam, under the field command of Captain Henri Lousteau.

At the final briefing held at Nam Bac, Lousteau was told that Dien Bien Phu could not hold out longer than May 10. But by the time all the French pieces were in place it was April 29, in reality long since too late. All the forces in northern Laos together amounted to perhaps 5,000 troops, Giap had 50,000. The portents were hardly good. Lousteau's 610 Commando managed to ambush one Viet Minh unit but otherwise stayed out of contact. The commandos maintained radio silence for they knew the Viet Minh could easily intercept their messages. By May 4 they were in position in an arc to the south of Dien Bien Phu, ready to protect a parachute landing. The next day they learned that no paratroop units were left. Rain fell ceaselessly. Lousteau ordered patrols of four or five soldiers to fan out from his positions. Whatever was about to happen he was ready for it.

When the Paris embassy cable arrived on April 5 the President was probably in bed. Secretary Dulles had been called to the State Department by MacArthur and he talked to Eisenhower by phone after midnight. The two agreed to speak in the morning. Dulles called again at 8:22 A.M.

The Secretary of State was holding Dillon's report of the conversation at the Matignon. Dulles read portions of the cable over the phone, then he remarked that "in principle we have already answered this in the negative."[4]

Ike seemed upset there was any official French request at all—the President maintained that Admiral Radford thought he had been speaking to General Ely in confidence.

Dulles was sure Radford hadn't made any commitment on behalf of the United States. Dulles himself had been present when Ely was given the clear impression that political resolution was required prior to any military action.

The President suggested that Dulles speak to Radford, tell him that what was in the cable was impossible, and ask him whether he had any alternatives in mind.

Nine minutes later Dulles was talking to Radford. Dulles told him that the President "feels we have to say we cannot commit an act of war except under the kind of program" that incorporated "united action." The admiral was reconciled to this response, but he did suggest one alternative—the Chief of Naval Operations had said "he has seen messages that there are pilots in France [for B-29s], and we could get planes there in a week for these pilots."[5] Radford was not giving up on immediate action in Indochina.

Nor, for that matter, was John Foster Dulles, who was scheduled to appear before the House Foreign Affairs Committee that very day. Ambassador Dillon's cable, besides its intervention request, contained information obtained by the French about Chinese participation with the Viet Minh. Now Dulles asked Radford whether this intelligence could be mentioned on the Hill either openly or in disguised form. Radford felt it could not do any harm, and that day Dulles made widely reported charges that China had taken its aid to Indochina to new high levels. But inside government the specific French claims were checked by the Central Intelligence Agency, which reported back the next day that there was no "special intelligence" from Saigon that confirmed this activity. Even worse, the French command in Indochina saw press reports of Dulles's claims about Chinese involvement and issued a public statement denying that it had been the source for any of the allegations.

At the White House Monday morning President Eisenhower saw five Republican congressional leaders for breakfast, where they were briefed by Harold Stassen on the foreign aid program and told that Dien Bien Phu would have fallen already if the United States had not provided extra assistance under the Navarre Plan. Stassen also told the Republican leaders that the 1954 foreign aid request would soon be ready, would be smaller than that for the previous fiscal year, but would include over a billion dollars for the Indochina war, more than a third of the planned total.

Ike himself said to the GOP leaders, perhaps a little ruefully, "if the French are stiff [enough] to come through this, I'll forgive them for a lot of things they cause[d] me to worry about over the last four years."[6]

The President went on to meet with the full Joint Chiefs in his office at 10:30 A.M. An hour before, a cable with the official U.S. reply to the Laniel government request had left the State Department. In the message Secretary Dulles explained that the United States was doing everything possible to create a congressional, constitutional, and public opinion basis for "united action," but that "as I personally explained to Ely in presence of Radford, it is not . . . possible for [the] US to commit belligerent acts in Indochina without full political understanding with France and other countries. In addition, Congressional action would be required. After conference at highest level, I must confirm this position."[7]

Although for the moment President Eisenhower was working along with Radford to develop "united action," the admiral's problem with the President was to maintain his enthusiasm.

Matt Ridgway had his first chance to put the Army's case, opposing intervention, directly to Eisenhower at the Joint Chiefs' meeting with the President. As the general later recalled, "I was greatly concerned to hear individuals of great influence, both in and out of government, raising the cry that now was the time and here, in Indochina, was the place to 'test the New Look,' for us to intervene." Ridgway objected to the "old delusive idea" that intervention could be "on the cheap," with naval and air forces alone. He was convinced the Army would have to follow on the ground any act of force from the sky.[8] Radford could not help realizing that the man sitting in the President's chair once had been sitting where Matt Ridgway was when the first big postwar crises erupted in Europe. If Ike began to align with the Army viewpoint, any chance for action in Indochina was ended.

For the moment the President stayed on board.

Meeting in the afternoon, the National Security Council Special Committee on Indochina made four recommendations, incorporating "united action" but clearly postulating circumstances under which unilateral action might be necessary. The first point on the special committee's program was to accept nothing short of military victory in Viet-Nam. Secondly, the United States should endeavor to obtain French support for this objective but failing it, should oppose *any* settlement at Geneva. In the event a settlement still resulted from the conference, the United States should take immediate steps "aimed toward continuation of the war in Indochina, to include active US participation without French support should that be necessary." The last recommendation was for "united action"—that every effort be made to obtain a concert with other interested nations.

Also discussed was a study of military force requirements for Indochina intervention ordered by President Eisenhower on March 25. The study identified six measures to be taken for intervention, ranging from congressional approval to military mobilization planning to publicized military moves designed to make readily available the necessary naval and air forces. An annex detailed the force requirements: three Air Force wings with 8,600 men and a Navy carrier group with 35,000 sailors and airmen. These forces would be needed for action in concert with France (Operation Vautour) or for "united action." In the case of unilateral intervention the study added ground forces amounting to one airborne and six infantry divisions, a total of 275,000 soldiers. Significantly, the study built around the assumption that atomic bombs would be "available for use as required by the tactical situation and as approved by the President."[9]

The military options paper went forward from the special committee to the National Security Council, where it was the first item of business on the afternoon of April 6. The full Joint Chiefs, not only Arthur Radford, were present for the meeting. Ike was in a very serious mood. Richard Nixon recorded in his diary that "it was quite apparent that the President had backed down considerably from the strong position he had taken on Indochina the latter part of [last] week."[10]

Decisions were taken at the meeting to focus American efforts prior to the opening of the Geneva conference (now only three weeks away) on formation of a regional grouping for the defense of Southeast Asia, and on gaining British support for U.S. objectives in order to strengthen U.S. policies in the Far East.

Admiral Radford and Deputy Secretary of Defense Roger Kyes were scheduled for a follow-up meeting with congressional leaders the next day. President Eisenhower ordered them to try "urgently" to obtain congressional support for both lengthening the service and increasing the number of Air Force technicians detailed to Viet-Nam. Radford found this desirable, but as far as he was concerned, discussion of a Southeast Asian regional grouping was a "tangential issue."

Charles Wilson raised a French request made on April 6 for ten or twenty B-29 bombers, said to be based on Navarre's feeling that even a small intervention by air power might save the day. Though Indochinese air bases were possibly too small for these big planes, the French believed that the United States could allow use of facilities at Clark Air Force Base and also supply the necessary bombs and ammunition. General Navarre also apparently directly approached an American detachment commander in Tonkin, Major Ed Yarbrough, about getting at least some B-29s for the French to play with.

On April 7 Secretary Dulles did offer the French fifteen B-29 bombers provided they supplied the air crews. But the French had no pilots to spare and their crews would have needed at least four months training before they were able to fly those bombers on a mission. Admiral Radford was right to insist that the French could never get B-29s flying in time to make a difference, and he won support from General Twining. Nevertheless B-29s with French roundel markings were spotted at Clark Air Base in the Philippines, ready for another mission that was not to be.

In Washington the National Security Council Operations Co-ordination Board secretly considered forming a new "private" air corporation to fly three squadrons of F-86 jet fighters for the French, and Dwight Eisenhower himself suggested that pilots hired for this new company be trained to fly B-29s, in case the question of loaning them arose again.

The White House press corps was puzzled by the holding of a National Security Council meeting on Tuesday, two days ahead of President Eisenhower's normal weekly routine. Press Secretary Jim Hagerty announced that this week it "seemed more convenient." The presence of the full Joint Chiefs was not explained.

The congressional follow-up occurred on April 7. The legislators had not become more enthusiastic about the idea of intervention in the ninety-six hours since their exposure to it. George Reedy, a political advisor on the staff of Senator Lyndon B. Johnson, has recorded the reactions of some Democrats whom Johnson sounded out: While Senator Walter F. George was concerned that the United States would lose face if it did not act in force, Oklahoma Senator Robert S. Kerr, a big, ham-fisted oilman, ended the debate when he pounded the table and "allowed that he was more concerned with losing another part of his anatomy if we did go in."[11] Even politicians of the President's own party were only lukewarm. Radford and Kyes were, therefore, not able to get the commitments the President had asked for.

Meanwhile there was another setback in the effort to achieve an international "united action." On April 7, President Eisenhower received Sir Winston Churchill's reply to his urgent personal letter. The British statesman refused to be drawn in by Ike's allusions to the years before World War II. All matters would be discussed with Secretary Dulles in London. There was no discussion of Dien Bien Phu, no support for "united action," nothing.

It should have come as no surprise to John Foster Dulles that the British did not view "united action" with favor; he had been told as much by Sir Roger Makins on April 1. This impression had received further confirmation when Winthrop Aldrich, U.S. Ambassador to the Court of St. James's, reported from London on a long talk with Foreign Secretary Anthony Eden on April 6. Eden was quoted as saying that the seriousness of the military situation in Indochina had been exaggerated.

Eden had said, the "French cannot lose the war between now and the coming of the rainy season however badly they may conduct it."

The French understandably recoiled from the rebuff Washington made to their desperate appeal for military intervention. As soon as the appeal was put in motion, General Paul Ely had sent his aide Colonel Brohon on another trip to Washington. On April 8 there was a painful scene as Brohon met with Admiral Arthur Radford.

Brohon began with a French concession—the Expeditionary Corps agreed to accept twenty-five to fifty American officers to assist training the Vietnamese Army. Then the colonel got to his main point. General Ely was disappointed and embarrassed by the American response to the French request for aid. His impression had been that the request would be followed by a prompt affirmative reply. Proposals for long-range political action would be too late to save Dien Bien Phu. The Laniel government was beginning to think it had made a blunder in making the request.

But as Radford reported, "Ely now has reservations and grave doubts that the combination of French and native forces and *only* US material assistance will any longer be adequate to carry out the Navarre Plan."[12]

This report went to John Foster Dulles just before he departed for an important diplomatic trip to Europe. The visit, Dulles explained to the Cabinet on April 9, was an effort to strengthen Allied unity in advance of Geneva. Foster "expressed hope of exerting effective US leadership in a situation made extremely delicate by political considerations in France and England."[13] Dulles outlined the Indochina situation in answer to questions from Herbert Brownell. Then President Eisenhower noted how the outlook for Dien Bien Phu had been improved by recent French counterattacks (on the Five Hills) and stressed the need for effective assistance to France.

It is clear from this record that intervention was not rejected despite Washington's brusque reply to the Laniel government. At a news conference in the Executive Office Building on April 7, Eisenhower articulated publicly the "domino principle" for the first time. The argument that Indochina, and Tonkin especially, was a strategic key point had been made in national security decision documents before, but it had never been made by a President on a public occasion.

Just under two hundred journalists turned out for the conference. Eisenhower appeared for twenty-five minutes and he came without any opening statement. The conference began with a discussion of the power of the hydrogen bomb and with allegations about the loyalty of Edward R. Murrow, the noted broadcast reporter. It was the height of that period's political witch-hunts and, in fact, Senator Joseph McCarthy was at that moment preparing to hold the televised hearings on the loyalty of the United States Army that shattered the power of his image and broke his political career.

The Indochina question was asked by Robert Richards of the Copley Press: "Mr. President, would you mind commenting on the strategic importance of Indochina to the free world?"

Eisenhower began, "You have, of course, both the specific and the general when you talk about such things."

Then he referred to the specific value of the locality, including the tin, tungsten, and rubber from Southeast Asia; he also mentioned the many human beings that might "pass under a dictatorship inimical to the free world." Then Ike came to what he called broader considerations.

"You have a row of dominoes set up, you knock over the first one, and what will happen to the last one is the certainty that it will go over very quickly. So you could have a beginning of a disintegration that would have the most profound influences."

Eisenhower declared that loss of the other countries of Southeast Asia would only "multiply the disadvantages," that Asia could not afford to "lose" more than the 450 million people in China, that the fall of Southeast Asia would "turn" the United States defensive perimeter along the rim of the Pacific, and that it would move to threaten Australia and New Zealand while excluding Japan as a vital trading partner.

The President concluded, "The possible consequences of the loss are just incalculable to the free world."

But to the very next question Eisenhower conceded that there had been no responses to his formula for "united action," which was not true, since the British had already indicated their displeasure.

A very telling comment, since the National Security Council documents had been insisting for years on independence for the Associated States, was the way President Eisenhower pulled his punch on a question about independence. He said, "I can't say that the Associated States want independence in the sense that the United States is independent. I do not know what they want."

Ike would not comment on taking the Indochina issue before the United Nations, but here the President made an oblique reference to "united action" when he said, "I do believe this: this is the kind of thing that must not be handled by one nation trying to act alone."[14]

Not sharing Ike's concern for "united action," the American press exhibited unqualified approval for intervention. Articles reporting rumors of military action under consideration by the administration made no effort to be critical. Editorial support in varying degrees was given by many major newspapers. Jim Hagerty, who thought Ike's press conference of April 7 had not come off too well, was undoubtedly surprised at *The New York Times's* editorial treatment of the "falling domino" theory: The falling dominoes had already been seen at work in Europe under Hitler and Stalin. "In almost every case these insatiable dictators relied on the fall of one country to open the way to the conquest of the next. In Asia the prospect is even more menacing."[15] Prominent columnist Walter Lippmann warned that the fall of Dien Bien Phu would complicate the Geneva talks. The object of American diplomacy should be "to see to it that in the military stalemate the West has a strong negotiating position which eliminates the need and the danger of a political surrender."[16] Lippmann thought his aim could be accomplished only with military force sufficient to ensure that the Viet Minh could not take over any ports on Viet-Nam's coast.

Other, more cautious, views were expressed in the press. One of the most perceptive was that of Richard Rovere in a piece that appeared in *The New Yorker* magazine on April 8. Here Rovere wrote of John Foster Dulles:

> . . . *although he has recently given the impression in his speeches, press conferences and congressional testimony, that American intervention, if it comes, will be a response*

to further Chinese intervention, it is patent that in his
mind it is not the action or inaction of the Chinese Com-
munists that really matters but the success of Communist
armies of any national or ethnic composition.

Rovere felt that Indochina had become the most pressing of all
the problems in Washington, "exceeding in urgency even what
to do with our rapidly multiplying megatons." Moreover, Rovere
observed, "No doubt exists as to what sort of mandate Mr. Dulles
thinks he ought to be given. He plainly believes that we should
not flinch at doing anything that is needed to prevent a Communist victory."[17]

But the road to victory, such as it was, now lay through
London and Paris. "United action" had become a precondition to
intervention. Dulles was convinced he could reach agreement in
personal talks with British and French leaders. It was not quite
what Drew Pearson had heard—that Dulles's aim was to "whip"
the British and French into line.

Under Secretary of State Walter Bedell Smith told Admiral Radford on April 8 to go ahead with briefing General Sir John Whi-
teley, British representative on the NATO Standing Group.

Radford outlined the seriousness of the Indochina situation.
Although the Joint Chiefs believed there was no purely military
reason why a French defeat at Dien Bien Phu might affect the
overall position of the Expeditionary Corps, the "psychological
aspects" could "cause reactions in Indochina and in France which
could lead to a collapse."[18] Radford reminded the British of previous interallied meetings that had been held to forge a common
approach to Southeast Asia and insisted that Dien Bien Phu must
be held.

Admiral Radford told the British general that the United
States recognized that Britain was already fighting in Malaya. Its

contribution need be only moral support and token participation, even just a few ships withdrawn from the British contingent off Korea. Radford conceded that the American military were not unanimous in their views concerning the consequences for the French of a defeat in the Tonkin mountains. He also stated his personal opinion that an ultimatum to the People's Republic of China in advance of military action would be a mistake. The British general agreed that the matter was urgent and that he would get off an immediate report to the Churchill government.

While frenzied activity to gain support for direct intervention and "united action" continued, many Americans were working quietly around the clock in support of the French military effort. Dien Bien Phu was the reason for preliminary military moves in the United States, Japan, and Germany; actual military support detachments in Indochina; active operations in Japan and the Philippines; Task Force 70 in position off the Vietnamese coast. These quiet but entirely serious measures put the United States in a position to move much more forcefully if it determined to do so.

Once the French could no longer land planes on the airfield, they recognized the need to get more paratroop units to Indochina; Paul Ely mentioned this to Admiral Radford during his Washington visit. In early April, Foster Dulles worked throughout one night expressly to set up an air transport arrangement to move these troops to Indochina. Dulles and Radford were understandably annoyed when they discovered later not only that the French had not completed training the two proposed battalions, but also that the French Defense Ministry wished to delay implementation until late April in order to reduce the burden on their military budget. Thereafter, Radford had to be concerned with maintaining secrecy over this airlift of paratroopers, since the Viet Minh would gain an obvious advantage from knowledge of the imminent arrival of reinforcements for Dien Bien Phu.

Alerted to assume the mission on April 3, 1954, United States Air Forces in Europe at first planned to use C-119 planes of its 322nd Air Division for the planned lift. Several days later, however, India, in its effort to encourage settlement of the Indochina war, refused overflight rights for the American airlift, which precluded use of the medium-range C-119 transports.

The Air Force switched to long-legged C-124 Globemasters of the Military Air Transport Command. The 62nd Troop Carrier Wing was directed to deploy thirteen of its C-124s forward to Rhein-Main Air Force Base in Germany in a highly classified air movement. It was intended that the planes pick up the French airborne troops when they were ready to move. They would avoid Indian airspace by flying over the ocean and refueling on Ceylon (now Sri Lanka). There, at Negombo, north of Colombo, a little-used British air base provided facilities to the planes. French soldiers, and the small numbers of sailors and airmen who went on this airlift, traveled in mufti, not wearing uniforms or carrying weapons.

But none of these forces materialized at Dien Bien Phu. An American official who saw the 7th Colonial Paratroops, the first unit to arrive at Da Nang, reported to President Eisenhower that it appeared understrength—he cited no more than 350—and this entailed delays while the battalion was fleshed out with Vietnamese recruits.

The airlift was a highly classified operation, but no one could miss the appearance of the huge Globemaster planes at a major French airport loading French passengers. American reporters in Paris detected the military movement immediately. When newsmen began asking questions at the Pentagon, spokesman Fred Seaton called Jim Hagerty for instructions.

Seaton told Hagerty that "more than has ever been admitted," U.S. planes had been carrying French military personnel. A Pentagon press statement had been drafted with the approval of Ike's political advisor Sherman Adams. The simple seven-sentence statement said U.S. planes were carrying "certain French Union personnel" and landing them outside the combat zone in Indochina. The measure was held to be entirely normal within "the existing military assistance program."

Secretary Wilson released this statement at the Defense Department, with the result that the secret airlift was immediately reported and followed in the press. As early as April 22 military writer Hanson Baldwin of *The New York Times* concluded that the paratroop reinforcements would be too little and too late for Dien Bien Phu.

The special American airlift from Clark Air Force Base to Indochina was so extensive it swamped the 6426th Air Depot Wing, which happened to lack any ground transfer section. Brigadier General Albert Hewitt had to send in ad hoc detachments from Far East Air Logistics Force units in Japan. By the end of April there were 634 additional personnel at Clark, including 86 civilians, just to lend a hand on the Indochina airlift. A month later there were twice as many. The activity continued to be very hush hush—one airman at the Korean field known as K-2, near Taeju, was told never to mention the lift. Necessity for additional C-119 and C-47 aircraft due to Indochina proved so acute the man was denied leave in Japan for want of planes to carry people on furlough. Transferred instead to Panmunjom, the airman discovered Army troops beginning to grouse they were being denied leave as well. He tried to explain how Indochina was affecting Korea but was constrained by the secrecy. Airlift work was constant. In March came an emergency lift of parachutes, in April one of smoke bombs. Flak jackets were also delivered by air, but transshipment problems in Tonkin prevented early arrival at Dien Bien Phu. Scheduled air service to Cat Bi and Da Nang began February 8, at three times a week, and expanded to four flights in March. There were a total of 1,800 flights. Before its end on August 1 the U.S. airlift had carried 10,354 passengers and 7,600 tons of freight.

On April 20 the airlift finally moved 514 French troops to Vietnam. Most were the 7th Colonial Parachute Battalion, the lead unit the French had prepared for the move. Five "Globemasters" under Major Michael F. Robinson flew first from Germany to Orly field outside Paris, where they picked up 456 French soldiers and airmen. The planes went on to Wheelus Field in Libya, and were joined by another C-124 that had flown to Al Ouina, Tunisia, to pick up another 84 French troops. One C-124 spare aircraft went directly from Rhein-Main to Wheelus.

From Libya the American aircraft continued their seven-thousand mile direct flight to Da Nang, Vietnam. Refueling stops occurred in Egypt, Saudi Arabia, Pakistan, Ceylon, and Thailand. Once over the Bay of Bengal air-se rescue for the airlift became the responsibility of the 2nd Air Rescue Group from Clark Field. The "Globemasters" reached Da Nang on April 24. All the C-124s had carried double crews, for twenty-four men each, so that the planes could save time and maintain secrecy for the mission, code named "Blue Star."

At Marseilles on May 5 began a second wave of the Blue Star lift which delivered 408 men of the 3rd Foreign Legion Paratroops and 44 French Air Force personnel to Da Nang. This time the C-124s were at Da Nang just as Dien Bien Phu fell, when the Viet Minh permitted evacuation of a number of badly wounded French soldiers. The men were flown to Da Nang where they were put aboard the same Blue Star aircraft. Meanwhile at Da Nang, airman Paul Cable was amazed to encounter a friend, a C-124 crew chief named Jewell, whom he had not seen in years. Another of the Globemaster crew chiefs would become a leader of dissent against the Vietnam war more than a decade later. In the meantime, none of the French paratroopers showed up at Dien Bien Phu. A U.S. official who saw the 7th Colonial at Da Nang reported to Eisenhower that it appeared understrength—he cited no more than 350—and this entailed delays while the unit was fleshed out with Vietnamese recruits.

There were American combat aircraft in the skies above Indochina, just as other American planes penetrated the airspace of neighboring mainland China. Most of the planes were from Task Force 70. This Navy carrier group sailed form Subic Bay on March 22nd. The fleet steamed to a patrol area in the South China Sea that lay within several hours of launch points that could be used for its aircraft to intervene in the fighting in Tonkin. The task force had the ostensible mission of conducting "fair weather training." The American naval forces were on station near the Gulf of Tonkin before General Paul Ely departed Washington bearing his explosive proposal for intervention.

A couple of days before the task force sailed, President Eisenhower had received a Radford briefing on the Navy's South China Sea capabilities. The carrier *Essex* embarked Air Tactical Group (ATG) 2 under Commander Lucian C. Powell, whose four squadrons and associated detachments totaled 72 aircraft. The heterogeneous group included three types of Navy jets: the F2H-3 "Banshee," the F9F-2 "Panther," and the F9F-6 "Cougar." These 44 jets were complemented by 28 prop-driven AD-4 "Skyraider" attack planes.

Carrier Air Group (CAG) 17 under Commander Leroy D. Swanson was aboard flagship carrier *Wasp*. This unit comprised 14 of the new F9F-6s and 32 older Banshee jets. Swanson also had another 23 Skyraider attack planes. A full strike with these aircraft could carry more than thirty tons of bombs. That was a significant amount where the load of a typical French air mission amounted to just a few thousand pounds.

The task force was in the capable hands of Vice Admiral

William K. Phillips, temporarily sent from his post on the U.S. West Coast with a small staff to take over ships sent from the Far East Command to CINCPAC. "Sol" Phillips was already familiar with existing arrangements for air support in French Indochina—he had served as chief of staff to both Radford and Stump at CINCPACFLT, the command for the Pacific Fleet, where he had been replaced by Herbert Hopwood. Phillips had been with Radford when the 1952 staff agreements on airpower were negotiated with the French. Sol was also an experienced combat leader. In the Atlantic in World War II he had led an antisubmarine escort group during the worst days of the battle for the North Atlantic. Later, in the Pacific, Phillips had commanded the close escort for one of the groups in the famous Task Force 58. He had skippered the antiaircraft cruiser *Oakland*, participated in the Battle of the Philippine Sea, and protected the carriers during the initial airstrikes on Iwo Jima. The CINCPAC at the time of Dien Bien Phu, Admiral Felix B. Stump, thought Phillips a splendid fleet commander.

Admiral Phillips's task force was divided into several units. The main striking power resided in Task Group 70.2 with the two aircraft carriers of Carrier Division 3, under Rear Admiral Brobert E. Blick on the carrier *Wasp*. It amounted to an all star team. Carrier Division 3 had seen constant service off Korea and become highly skilled in air support work. Admiral Blick had won the Navy Cross at Leyte Gulf for saving the crippled escort carrier *Santee*. In addition to the carriers there were underway replenishment ships in Task Group 92.2 (Captain George H. Browne) plus an independent unit with the submarine *Bluegill*. The carrier force had an escort of eight destroyers.

Before departing Subic Bay the task force loaded special high frequency radio equipment suitable for talking to French air controllers in Indochina. Task Group 70.2 then began to cruise about sixty miles off Cap Ron on the Vietnamese coast. *Wasp* reported, "underway at high speed for distant operating area off eastern coast of Indochina.[19]

Various incidents occurred during the fleet deployment. On March 24 a Cougar from the *Essex* crashed into the deck barrier on landing and another came down with one of her leading wheels not extended. A third Cougar the next day had a tail hook failure on landing. The latter accident took place in spite of the fact that a couple of weeks previously *Essex* had had all her F9Fs grounded for corrective action on tail hooks. In all Commander Powell's pilots flew 778 sorties during March and 739 more in April. The group bettered even this performance during May with 1,367 flights, average flight times during those months stood at about 1,500 hours. Flagship *Wasp* suffered a breakdown in one of her catapults just before this cruise began, and her record of 861 sorties in March dropped to just 255 during April, but this ship would be at the center of operational activity, with more than double the number of flight hours on "service" as opposed to training missions.

Despite problems with both aircraft and weather (in April the *Essex* was forced to cancel almost a third of her planned jet aircraft missions due to low wind conditions, which precluded generating enough air flow over the bow to get the jets into the air), the American aircraft carriers maintained a steady stream of flight activity. In fact their efforts compare favorably with French air operations. The French air force and navy together mounted 1,494 strike sorties over Dien Bien Phu during April. Task Force 70 fell short of that, but if the *Wasp* had not had the catapult or aircraft problems she did, and had performed at March levels, there would have been more U.S. sorties than French ones. If the Americans had maintained March levels of aerial operational activity and had not been forced to cancel missions, they could have approached the level of overall French performance, which for all of northern Indochina in April 1954 came in at 1,937 combat sorties.

On March 25th and again two days later the radars aboard the *Wasp* recorded air contacts that were tracked on a course and speed and appeared to be echoes from a single aircraft. When fighter planes were sent to investigate, however, they reported only haze, no visible targets, birds or clouds. Radar operators aboard ship had nevertheless plotted the intercepts and seen their air patrols merge with the blips, which did not blur or break up when magnified. The spurious radar contacts in the South China Sea repeated an incident the carrier *Langley* had had in these waters with Task Force 58 toward the end of World War II. The experience would be repeated again, quite notoriously, in 1964, in the Gulf of Tonkin incident that helped draw the United States into active combat in its Vietnam war. Failure to take into account the earlier experiences at the time of the Gulf of tonkin contributed to Washington's confusion in 1964.

On March 25 CINCPAC recommended to the Chief of Naval Operations that Phillips be ordered to secure reconnaissance photographs of airfields in southern China. Admiral Carney approved the recommendation and instructed CINCPAC accordingly on March 29. The task force commander asked for authority to sail deeper into the Gulf of Tonkin to bring his ships into range of the reconnaissance targets. Admiral Phillips's request was granted. Task Group 70.2 began to steam in an area only about 125 miles south of Haiphong. On March 30 Phillips received orders to extend his deployment in Indochinese waters for another two weeks.

In this heated atmosphere the Navy's top commanders clearly behaved as if they believed important events were in the offing. At the end of March Admiral Carney sent a dispatch to CINCPAC informing Stump of the Washington talks with General Ely. The next day Carney cancelled a long-planned visit to Pearl Harbor.

On April 3 he told CINCPAC to go ahead with operations deeper in the Gulf of Tonkin provided Task Group 70.2 took precautions to avoid discovery. Carney waited until April 7 to inform Admiral Stump that no decision had yet been made on an Indochina intervention and that none was currently anticipated.

Meanwhile, once the Pacific Command received approval for missions over China Task Force 70 became even more active. On April 4 the aircraft carrier *Boxer*, steaming directly from Pearl Harbor, entered the South China Sea to reinforce the carrier group in the Gulf of Tonkin. That night Admiral Phillips took off from the *Essex* on a scouting flight over Dien Bien Phu to see conditions there for himself. Three days later the task group received a new requirement for photographic coverage of Dien Bien Phu and the Viet Minh supply lines. The pictures were to be in by April 12. There was also an early April photo recon mission over the Chinese airfields and supply center at Nanning. On April 7 the French Air Force reported sighting seven contrails and six jet aircraft at altitude over the northern edge of the Red River delta, and the next day the Viet Minh claim to have sighted jet aircraft over Dien Bien Phu. On the 9th the *Essex* lost two of her planes at sea, one a jet the other a Skyraider, both from engine failures.

On April 2 General Ely was informed by Radford that the Americans had arranged for a visit to Navarre by the chief of staff of the Pacific Fleet, Rear Admiral Herbert G. Hopwood. Hopwood's assigned mission in Indochina was to review the existing staff agreement on control of U.S. carriers in the event of intervention.

Herbert Gladstone Hopwood was chief of staff and aide to Admiral Felix Stump, the man with operational control over U.S. warships in Indochina waters. A Pennsylvanian, Hopwood numbered among the Annapolis class of 1920, officers commissioned a year early to fill the Navy's ranks just after World War I demobilization. He served with the Yangtze Patrol and also distinguished himself as a staff aide. The war years 1940–44 he spent working for the Join Chiefs of Staff, then returned to sea as captain of the light cruiser *Cleveland* during eleven months of the bitterest fighting in the Pacific, including the kamikaze battles and fire support for the American return to Corregidor. During the Korean War Hopwood commanded a cruiser division, and then all cruisers and destroyers in the Pacific Fleet. He had been chief of staff to Stump, Pacific commander, since September 1953. There is every reason to believe Hopwood enjoyed the confidence of CINCPAC.

Admiral Stump was told the particulars of the Radford-Ely discussions by the chief of Naval Operations. Thus Hopwood likely knew of them as well, in particular since at that time CINC-PAC had to arrange individually for transfers of exotic weaponry such as tactical nuclear bombs (of which more later). But in Saigon he merely reviewed the 1952 arrangements with General Navarre. Neither officer found any problem. Navarre, who the previous day had made a difficult decision to ask Brohon to go ahead and request American bombing, could see Hopwood was talking of a related topic. Navarre raised the matter of Operation Vulture.

Hopwood told Navarre nothing. The admiral was concerned with communications, target information, timely intelligence, not political questions. He would pass the general's questions to his superiors.

Rebuffed in his inquiry on Vulture, General Navarre remarked that in recent days several flights of jet aircraft had been detected over Tonkin. Navarre presumed the planes were American. He did not object to the flights, but he wanted advance information about them.

In the Gulf of Tonkin on April 10 the French Navy sighted Task Force 70. It was a morale boost for those in Hanoi who heard about it. But the day before, in Washington, Secretary of Defense Wilson called the White House about ordering Admiral

Phillips back to Subic Bay. Although the telephone note-taker wrote for the record that the President did not sound too sure of himself, Eisenhower told Secretary Wilson, "I guess we might as well let them come back."[20]

VIII

MR. DULLES GOES TO EUROPE

O n April 10, John Foster Dulles went to Europe in order to achieve Western support for the American "united action" policy before Geneva. Dulles had received a certain amount of encouragement in separate meetings he held with the ambassadors of smaller countries—Thailand, the Philippines, Australia, and New Zealand. The Thais went along immediately. Australia and New Zealand were waiting to see what London would do.

As Dulles left the capital Under Secretary of State Walter Bedell Smith was at the CBS broadcasting studios appearing on *The American Week* television program. Bedell Smith warned of the dangers he saw; rhetorically he asked, "Can we allow, dare we permit, expansion of Chinese Communist control further into Asia?" Answering his question in the negative, Smith posited that the stake in Indochina was "the human freedom of the masses of people for all that enormous area of the world." As Drew Pearson put it to his diary, "there is no question but that the administration is trying to whip up more and more public sentiment for Indochina."[1]

The China question as seen in London looked much different than in Washington. In preparation for Dulles's visit, Foreign Secretary Anthony Eden penned a preparatory paper in which he concluded, "I cannot see what threat would be sufficiently potent to make China swallow so humiliating a rebuff as abandonment of the Viet Minh." Eden rejected the U.S. assumption that the threat of retaliation would coerce China into such an action, since he believed in a distinction between warning against some new action and halting Chinese activity already in progress. Eden felt a threat would have no effect, and any ad hoc coalition would then be faced with a choice between an ignominious retreat or war with China.

Eden also rejected the specific military program entailed in a threat to China. He recalled the Korean conflict and noted that the British chiefs of staff believed at that time that neither blockade of mainland China nor bombing of Chinese internal and external communications would have been effective. Eden could see no reason why the situation should be different in connection with Indochina. He believed that Washington had not weighed the consequences of its policy and that "it does not seem that the Americans have formed any clear conception of the military operations which they propose should be conducted against China if threats fail to produce the desired result."[2]

Eden was not alone among the British in his views of American policy. The British Cabinet had discussed Indochina in the first week of April and was in broad agreement that any Western involvement should be avoided.

Dulles wasted no time after his arrival in London on April 11. Following dinner at the U.S. Embassy he held the first talk with Eden. Dulles gave a long exposition of U.S. government reasoning, beginning with the domino theory and a warning to the British concerning their interests in Malaya should Indochina fall. Dulles asserted that the French could no longer deal with the situation, that the battle at Dien Bien Phu had reached a crisis stage.

"Three weeks ago," said Foster Dulles, "the US Joint Chiefs of Staff suggested intervention by air and naval forces." Now the American diplomat alluded to U.S. aircraft carriers already in place off the Viet-Nam coast.

"Mr. Dulles," recalled Anthony Eden later, "did not consider that the United States should act alone on this matter."

The British Foreign Secretary, noting American concern for Malaya, explained at some length that the military situation there was improved.

Dulles then made a gesture toward British concerns—he said the United States was no longer talking of a joint warning to China but of a coalition that might develop into a Southeast Asia defense alliance.

Eden was more receptive toward the longer-range objective of an alliance, but he noted that careful thought must be given toward which nations should be included, citing India as an example. As for intervention, Eden believed it doubtful the Indochina situation could be improved by purely military means. The West should at least see what the other side had to say at Geneva.

It was clear no further progress could be made that night. Dulles, according to Eden, steered the talk toward related topics. Eden recalled that "he wondered whether France was not, by a process of historical evolution, inevitably ceasing to be a great power. I declined to be drawn into direct comment on these observations and said that we, with our experience in Malaya, could understand the difficulties with which the French were confronted."[3]

Formal discussions occupied the next two days but added little to the Dulles-Eden exchange of April 11. The British agreed to preliminary discussions about a regional security arrangement. Dulles reiterated that he was convinced Indochina was the place for intervention. He declared his confidence that Congress would allow the President to use air, naval, and possibly even land forces. Dulles also drew an analogy between Indochina in 1954 and Manchuria in 1931, when the Western powers failed to unite to halt Japanese expansion in Asia, and the German reoccupation of the Rhineland in 1936, a step on the road to World War II.

Britain was not convinced. There was more talk about the ad hoc coalition or regional pact—the British again proposed participation by India, while the Americans countered with a suggestion that the Chiang Kai-shek regime on Taiwan should become a member. Eden also explained that the British chiefs of staff did not believe intervention in Viet-Nam could be confined to air and sea power. Moreover, British public opinion would be firmly opposed to a commitment to become involved in the Indochina war before Geneva.

The communiqué from these discussions indicated only vague agreement between the British and Americans. The British were "ready to take part" with other nations in an "examination of the possibility" of establishing a collective defense. Nothing was said about the timing of such an "examination," but the Americans acceded to language that did specify that "it is our hope that the Geneva Conference will lead to the restoration of peace in Indochina."[4]

It became immediately clear that, aside from Churchill's and Eden's cautious attitudes, the British government's hands were not free in the matter of joining any coalition for action in Asia. Eden informed Parliament of the project on April 14. When opposition leader Clement Attlee made a statement mildly approving the proposal, he was subjected to an unprecedented attack by Aneurin Bevan, another prominent opposition member. Bevan resigned from the Labor Party's policy committee (the "shadow cabinet") the next day, but many felt he would not have made so complete a break without broad public support.

But, amazingly, the Secretary of State maintained he had garnered British support for his concept of a coalition. He told reporters before leaving London that his idea of a successful settlement was "the removal by the Chinese Communists of their apparent desire to extend the political system of Communism to Southeast Asia."

Did that mean a complete withdrawal of communists from Indochina? "That is what I would regard as a satisfactory solution." Was there any possible compromise? Said Dulles, "I had not thought of any."[5]

China. The threat from China. The theme was woven into American diplomacy throughout the Dien Bien Phu crisis. Just what was the extent of the People's Republic of China's involvement in the Indochinese war?

There is a clear record of U.S. intelligence perceptions of Chinese intentions with respect to Vietnam in the National Intelligence Estimates (NIEs) produced by the Central Intelligence Agency.

The record of NIE predictions goes back to December 1950, when NIE 5 maintained that "direct intervention by Chinese communist troops may occur at any time." The CIA's view changed as time passed and there was no PRC intervention outside Korea. In August 1951 NIE 35 concluded that the future development of the Korea situation would probably influence a Chinese decision to get into Vietnam. The national estimate put at 10,000 the number of PLA specialists serving with the Viet Minh but predicted that the French Expeditionary Corps would be able to withstand Viet Minh forces even if supported by as many as 30,000 Chinese specialists. The CIA also predicted that the Chinese could not support many more than 100,000 troops in any invasion of French Indochina. The NIE noted that the PLA was improving road and rail links to the Vietnam border and thus gradually increasing its ability to sustain forces in Tonkin. The Chinese were also refurbishing some of the forty-four airstrips in the border region left over from World War II, when Kunming had been one terminus of the "Hump" air route into China.

An equally detailed appreciation was given in NIE 35-1, issued by the CIA in March 1952. This national estimate concluded flatly that that Chinese would not intervene and foresaw only four circumstances that might lead the PRC to enter the Indochina war. These circumstances were: to counter a Western or Nationalist Chinese blow; as a diversionary attack in the event of a general war in the Far East; if a serious threat to China was not judged met by its present policy; or, if Peking concluded that "the West intended to attack Communist China regardless of the latter's policies in Southeast Asia." Even if the Chinese did intervene logistic difficulties would limit them to "a series of limited offensives." The estimate of the force the PLA could sustain in Vietnam was raised to 150,000. The CIA also concluded that China would be unlikely to use jet aircraft in Vietnam while the Korean war continued but that "employing only piston-type aircraft, [the Chinese] would probably, with surprise, have the capability to neutralize the French Air Force in Tonkin."

It should be noted that even while the estimators were reaching the conclusion that the PRC might intervene to counter a Western or Nationalist blow, they were not told of some CIA covert operations encouraging just such blows in a secret war between Taiwan and mainland China. CIA operatives forged an alliance with Kuo Min Tang armed troops who had fled to northern Burma under General Li Mi. The KMT troops actually took over an area of the country and established regular supply routes from Taiwan. With CIA support in weapons and Civil Air Transport (CAT) supply flights, which landed to refuel in both Saigon and Bangkok, Burma was used as a base for regiment-sized forays into Yunnan in April 1951 and August 1952. Several CIA advisors on the operations were killed in China. In the fall of 1952, however, the KMT Chinese attacked the Burmese government, which went to the United Nations in March 1953 with its case that Chiang Kai-shek directed Li Mi from Taiwan. The KMT agreed to a demobilization and the CIA-proprietary airline CAT flew 1,925 persons from Thailand to Taiwan in an aerial evacuation in the fall.

General Li Mi of the KMT executed a deceptive demobilization, however. Evidently many of the persons flown to Taiwan were not Chinese but impressed locals, while few weapons were surrendered. The first party of fifty Chinese brought out no weapons at all but only a huge nine-foot by fifteen-foot portrait of Chiang. In March 1954 the Burmese began a full military offensive against the Chinese and succeeded in driving many into Thailand. During April and May, when other Civil Air Transport pilots were pushing their C-119 "Packets" over the Viet Minh flak at Dien Bien Phu, CAT planes moved 4,600 more Chinese to Taiwan. On May 30, 1954 General Li Mi announce the dissolution of his "Yunnan Province Anti-Communist Salvation Army."

The Nationalist "salvation army" was not the only CIA covert operation against China. On Taiwan, Civil Air Transport provided mechanics for Chiang's planes that flew missions over the mainland, as well as for CAT planes doing the same thing. Some of the flights were used to infiltrate agents and teams as well. By March 1954, the CIA had accumulated on Okinawa a supply of 4,300 500-lb. capacity parachutes for actions in the Far East. In December 1952, CIA officers John T. Downey and Richard G. Fecteau were actually captured in China in their "Dakota." The Nationalists claim an average of fifteen clandestine flights through PRC air space in a month. The CIA role was enough so that its Taiwan station increased rapidly to number of 1,000 by the mid-1950s, one of the largest overseas CIA concentrations. Meanwhile, in his New Year's message for 1954 Chiang Kai-shek promised a "near future" return to the mainland while on Easter Chiang declared a "holy war" against Peking.

Evidently Peking did not allow these covert operations to affect its policy against open intervention in Indochina. The CIA estimators again recognized this in NIE-91, approved by Allen Dulles on June 4, 1953. The consensus in the estimate was that the PRC would continue and perhaps raise the level of its aid to the Viet Minh but would not invade Indochina in the period before mid-1954, whether or not hostilities were stopped in Korea (they were). On this point the Joint Intelligence Group dissented and stated as a footnote that the evidence was insufficient to draw any conclusion at all. The estimate still projected that only about 150,000 PLA troops could be maintained in Vietnam but credited these troops, together with the Viet Minh, with a capability to capture the Tonkin delta before assistance could arrive for the French.

American intelligence still believed that with surprise a Chinese air intervention might make small scale but damaging attacks on French installations in Tonkin and perhaps could neutralize the French air force. Sufficient piston and jet aircraft were available for this independent of the situation in Korea. But because of the lack of improved airfields in south China and supplies stockpiled for an offensive, the NIE did not think China had a capability for sustained air action in Indochina. The Chinese air force could not move to the south without preliminary basestocking and other preparations that could be detected and would take several months.[9]

After mid-1953 the Americans were especially alert for any indications of a Chinese move south. In July 1953 American photo reconnaissance planes were sent to obtain pictures, or "covers," of the three Chinese airfields on Hainan island. Only the one at Haikou was found to be serviceable. In the fall, French intelligence claimed that a Viet Minh pilot training school had been started at Nanning and that the Suichi airfield was being prepared for jets. CINCPAC sent an aircraft to obtain a "cover" of Suichi and found no evidence for the French claims. CINCPAC noted that in fact Chinese jet strength at Canton was lower than previously. In reporting this development to Admiral Radford during October, Edwin Layton commented that the Joint Intelligence Group felt the French were exploiting an alleged Chinese jet threat in order to obtain jets for the French air force in the Far East. The Chinese were estimated to be able to put only 120 aircraft over Tonkin, not including jets because the three known jet airfields in South China, those in the Canton complex, were too far from Tonkin to fit the radius of action of the Chinese MiG-15s.

Another informative incident occurred in March 1954, when the U.S. ambassador to Vietnam, Donald Heath, misunderstood a remark by an American air attaché. Heath was told that the Chinese airfield at Nanning was so good that perhaps jets might be stationed there without preparations. Heath immediately cabled Washington that the Chinese communists had put a squadron of jet fighters at Nanning. In Washington, the USAF Directorate of Intelligence replied that it had no information to confirm either jet aircraft at Nanning or construction of a jet-capable airfield on Hainan. The Air Force's information was pretty recent too—the fields of the Canton complex were photographed in January 1954.

Actually aerial reconnaissance was a widely used intelligence method. Between July 1953, when the Korean war ended, and January 1954, the People's Republic charged its airspace had been violated 135 times. United Nations forces in Korea admitted thirteen of these incidents but charged Peking with twenty-six violations of its own, half a dozen of them in the last month. Another violation occurred on January 22 when a reconnaissance B-45 accompanied by U.S. jet fighters encountered a formation of Chinese jets. A Chinese MiG-15 was shot down despite Peking's aircraft outnumbering the Americans, just as in the war Chinese and

Russian air losses had run at eleven to one against the Americans.

But another air incident was the last thing President Eisenhower needed. Informed of the event the President said he didn't want to hear about it, that the United States would act as if nothing had happened unless the Chinese brought it up. The stance endured for days until the Pentagon itself inadvertently spilled the news.

Along the Indochina border the People's Liberation Army typically maintained five armies, 150,000 combat troops. The manpower figures of the Liberation Army were impressive. But Chinese equipment and technology were inferior. The problems were most acute in the Chinese Air Force. That service arm had had to undergo the transition from piston to jet engines virtually under the gun, with enormous losses of pilots and planes in Korea.

Because of Korea most of the Chinese facilities capable of handling jet aircraft were located in central and northern China. In the southwest near Viet-Nam there were few jet-capable fields; virtually the only ones were Tien Ho, Nan Hai, and the field code-named "White Cloud." All were near the port of Canton, where the Chinese based seventy jet fighters. All Chinese IL-28 jet bombers were based near Peking. With these airfields the Chinese were too far away to intervene effectively over the Tonkin delta. Jet bombers could have deployed forward to the Canton complex for Indochina operations, but then the Chinese planes would have been operating without fighter cover, a very risky proposition considering the American jet fighters on aircraft carriers in the South China Sea.

The broad outlines of Chinese aid to the Viet Minh were apparent in varying degrees to the Western intelligence services. For their part the French often interpreted information in such a way as to emphasize the danger of Chinese intervention in Viet-Nam. Before the People's Liberation Army even reached the Tonkin border, in March 1949, the French had been responsible for reports that Chinese communist troops were fighting with the Viet Minh in a few areas and had seized for a time part of the coastal village of Mong Cai.

The French were also quick to call attention to fluctuations in People's Liberation Army strength near the Indochina border. They estimated an increase from 50,000 to 120,000 during 1950–51. General de Lattre further raised that estimate to 150,000 in talks in Washington during September. Before the end of the year René Pleven declared that Liberation Army strength had increased from 170,000 to 290,000 men in six months. Claims like these were extreme, as were some of the claims about Chinese aid to the Viet Minh, like one made in 1952 that alleged 20,000 to 30,000 Chinese in Viet-Nam.

The basic framework for assistance was established by the Chinese in 1950. Peking agreed to *sell* a portion of the arms it had captured in the civil war in China, and also agreed to help train Viet Minh regular units. In the summer of 1950 the Chinese installed three camps at Ching-hsi, each with a capacity for 10,000 trainees. It is believed that 24,000 Viet Minh regulars were trained here in 1950, with a total of about 40,000 through the course of the Franco-Vietnamese war. Most of the additional trainees must then have been personnel for the 351st Heavy Division. Given Viet Minh losses over 1950–54 and the size to which Giap's army nevertheless grew, Chinese training for the Viet Minh cannot have been the critical factor in their success.

As for reports of Chinese in Viet-Nam, there were too few to be consistent with a very large military presence. There were allegations from Colonel Roger Trinquier of French military intelligence that the Chinese committed an infantry battalion across the border between the Red and Black rivers against a French partisan group in 1951, and repeated this operation with the 302nd Rifle Division in the summer of 1952. There are also 1952 reports from the French Air Force that the border town of Cao Bang was defended by six batteries of Chinese medium anti-aircraft guns. But Associated States Minister Marc Jacquet told the Laniel Cabinet in early April 1954 that French troops had never run into Chinese soldiers inside Viet-Nam.

Other reports amounted to mere rumors. In late 1952 there were supposed sightings of tanks with red and yellow insignia accompanying Viet Minh supply convoys. But no Viet Minh or Chinese tank was ever encountered during the Franco-Vietnamese war, and an American intelligence estimate in 1951 put total Chinese armored strength in the Chinese provinces near Viet-Nam at a single battalion—less than forty tanks for provinces with a total area of about 250,000 square miles. Bernard Fall also reports rumors that aircraft with Viet Minh markings had been sighted on fields in southeast China. However, Radford was told in 1954 by the chief of his Joint Intelligence Group, Rear Admiral Edwin T. Layton, that "US intelligence has no evidence that Viet Minh personnel are being trained as pilots of piston or jet aircraft, or that the Viet Minh is organizing an air force."[6]

It is clear the Viet Minh did receive material assistance from the People's Republic of China and the Soviet Union. There are no agreed figures on the total aid, although the monthly tonnage rose over time from an average of 10 to 20 tons in 1950 to 400 to 600 tons in 1953 and 1,500 tons in March 1954, rising to a peak at 4,000 tons in June 1954. There are higher figures from Nationalist Chinese sources. Calculations from the available data show a range of 20,000 to 80,000 tons of aid to the Viet Minh over the entire period of the war, with the actual total probably approximating 25,000 tons. Compilations of arms transfers show that the Viet Minh acquired about half its imported small arms for cash. The evidence also suggests that local production and capture from the French accounted for about a third of Viet Minh weapons.

The U.S. military assistance program accounted for a greater proportion of French equipment and delivered over 160,000 tons of durable items alone. John Foster Dulles noted in one 1954 conversation that American aid to the French was ten times as great as communist aid to the Viet Minh.

The question of Chinese presence among the Viet Minh is difficult to explore in detail given the lack of authoritative sources. The smallest claim—from the French Press—is only 200. This is consistent with the only explicit report of a Chinese mission, one made in late 1953 that asserted a General Hsiao-Ke had left for Viet-Nam as the head of 228 advisors. More recent research by Chinese-American scholars has confirmed the presence of the Chinese military mission and provided evidence of PLA advisers down to the regimental level in the Viet Minh army. The Chinese manned some of the artillery at Dien Bien Phu and, it is confirmed, not one but two anti-aircraft artillery regiments. It has long been known the Chinese provided and manned a truck regiment helping move supplies to the Viet Minh in the high mountain valley. The reports fit with claims in the French press of the time that 3,000 to 4,000 Chinese were with the Viet Minh besieging the entrenched camp. The American press carried estimates of double that number. French official sources, however, confirmed only fourteen senior advisers and a general with the Viet Minh high command.

It is difficult to escape the conclusion that the Chinese attitude toward the Viet Minh war was cautious and conservative. Aid was limited and involvement was wholly covert. The aid was concentrated in such special areas as providing artillery training (the 351st Heavy Division), battlefield communications, and antiaircraft capability—these specialized programs provided the greatest benefit within a limited aid program. The official foreign policy of the People's Republic of China was to pursue "just and reasonable settlements through negotiations." Indeed, the Chinese looked forward to participation in the Geneva conference of 1954 because this would, in a sense, acknowledge Mao Tse-tung's China to be among the world community of nations.

Top American officials were well informed about the amount of Chinese aid and chances of Chinese intervention. Arthur Radford received repeated reports on Chinese capability from Edwin Layton of the Joint Intelligence Group, who in World War II had done such an excellent job on intelligence for Admiral Chester Nimitz fighting the Japanese. In Tokyo during a Far Eastern trip on December 21, 1953, Radford was also briefed by Air Force Brigadier General Donald Z. Zimmerman on the status of Chinese aircraft and airfields on the mainland. He was thus well aware of Chinese weaknesses and stated to the Senate in February 1954 his impression that no Chinese intervention in Viet-Nam was possible.

Radford's reason for supporting a Vulture operation was that Peking was still weak in southern China. The moment would never again be as good as when the French fought at Dien Bien Phu. American intelligence thought chances of a Chinese response were fifty-fifty. If so, there was a chance Vulture could have been carried out with impunity.

When John Foster Dulles flew on to Paris from London for talks with French officials on the "united action" concept, he had a similar aim to accomplish: The French, even though they were in trouble at Dien Bien Phu, were not enthusiastic about joining an ad hoc coalition. The French could not bear to hand Indochina over to foreign powers, and the Laniel government felt it could not avoid seeking a negotiated settlement at Geneva if it wished to stay in power. The French could not be counted on in any effort to coerce the People's Republic of China.

The Secretary of State's Paris visit began on a bad note indeed. Met at Orly Airport by Ambassador C. Douglas Dillon, the

The arrival ceremony held at Da Nang by the French Air Force on February 5, 1954, for the U.S. Air Force mechanics coming to Indochina, featured French officers in full dress uniform. Half-tracks and other vehicles await to carry the Americans to processing and a reception. Photograph courtesy Russell De Somer

American C-124 "Globemasters," the jumbo aircraft of their time, unloading Americans and their equipment at Da Nang on February 5, 1954. Note the front-opening bay doors that enabled the C-124 to carry vehicles and other large items of equipment. The United States used C-124s regularly on flights from the Philippines (Clark Air Force Base) to Saigon (Tan Son Nhut), on this special lift to Da Nang, and at least a few times to Haiphong (Cat Bi). At the height of the battle of Dien Bien Phu President Eisenhower approved the use of C-124s to carry reinforcements directly from France to Da Nang. Photograph courtesy Russell De Somer

Officers of the 483rd Troop Carrier Wing standing in front of the operations shack at Da Nang later in 1954. Major Ed Yarbrough, half-turned away from the camera, is fourth from the left. At the left is Colonel George Foster, commanding the operational group under Maurice Casey.
Photograph courtesy Thomas A. Julian

Flight line at Haiphong's Cat Bi airfield, where twin-tailed C-119 aircraft wait to take a unit of French paratroops on a practice air drop. The paratroopers listen to instructions as their weapons, helmets, and other gear are stacked on the ground nearby. Note that the C-119s have their rear doors in place, the most common arrangement in Indochina when the planes were carrying troops rather than supplies. Photograph courtesy Thomas A. Julian

A C-119 rigged to carry supplies, with its rear doors removed. Ground crews-could place or remove the doors in a matter of hours. The stripes on the tail surface are United States Air Force markings. Photograph courtesy Jack McDonald

Viet Minh prisoners (prisoniers internees militaires or P.I.M.s) were frequently used by the French as porters or for manual labor. Here P.I.M.s work on the barbed wire barriers at Cat Bi airfield. Photograph courtesy Thomas A. Julian

The defenses at Cat Bi included bunkers, blockhouses, and numerous entrenchments. Among the more elaborate features along the perimeter was this dug-in compound, which included a small barracks, fighting positions, and to the right rear, a gun under tarpulin in a revetment. Photograph courtesy Thomas A. Julian

The French defenses at Cat Bi, strong though they were, were not able to prevent Viet Minh commandos from getting onto the base, where they made several damaging raids during the battle of Dien Bien Phu. Here French airmen pick around among the wreckage of a French B-26 bomber destroyed in April 1954. Undamaged bombers are on the flight line just across the way.
Photograph courtesy Thomas A. Julian

At Cat Bi Major Ed Yarbrough had a young French paratrooper for his interpreter. Bruno Balas, who appears in this picture, accompanied Yarbrough on a flight to Dien Bien Phu made the day the great siege opened. Colonel de Castries would not permit Balas or the French crew of the C-47 that had brought them to leave the entrenched camp. Yarbrough discovered Balas had survived years later when encountering him by chance in Los Angeles. Both a C-119 transport and a B-26 bomber are visible in the background of this picture taken at Cat Bi. Photograph courtesy Thomas A. Julian

Haiphong street as seen from the window of the Hotel de Paris, which housed the officers of the provisional squadron of C-119s that Major Yarbrough led in Indochina. Enlisted men lived on the base at Cat Bi. Americans from both Cat Bi and Do Son were restricted to an area of a few square blocks around the hotel. Photograph courtesy Thomas A. Julian

On the beautiful Baie d'Along, the beach at Do Son was marred by the extensive defenses necessary for the base. This is a section of the barbed wire on the outer perimeter, where the American mechanics of the Far East Air Force Logistics Command were given positions to defend. The hill visible in the background across the water is Do Son village and the French compound. Americans lived at the other end of the base.

Photograph courtesy Jack McDonald

Another view of the beach defenses at Do Son, this picture shows a French 40-millimeter gun in its emplacement on the perimeter. When the Americans arrived in February 1954 the body of a dead Viet Minh commando lay half covered in sand at the waterline nearby. Photograph courtesy Russell De Somer

The maintenance area at Do Son field. Two Dakotas can be seen undergoing servicing under the shed at the left. The flight line is on the right, with the runway visible in the distance at the far right. One C-47 is taxiing into the flight operations area from beyond the flight line. Major Knox's American mechanics lived in the buildings at the south end of the field, here visible in the center distance behind another parked Dakota. Photograph courtesy Jack McDonald

Sergeant Jack McDonald near the beach not far from Do Son base. McDonald was communications chief for Major Knox's detachment at Do Son but set up much of the radio network for the Americans at Cat Bi and Da Nang as well.
Photograph courtesy Jack McDonald

The flight line at Da Nang is captured in this picture by an American pilot, taken from the hill overlooking the airfield. French B-26 bombers are parked on the apron. Some American mechanics at Da Nang felt the French flew few missions with their aircraft based here. Photograph courtesy Thomas A. Julian

China Beach, which became familiar to a later generation of Americans in Viet-Nam, was an important locale for rest and recreation for U.S. airmen in Indochina. Here a group of airmen participated in a June 1954 beer blast on the beach. Major Yarbrough stands in front of the jeep with his baseball cap brim upturned. On a later day, five Americans making an unauthorized outing in that area would be captured by the Viet Minh and held prisoner until after the conclusion of the Geneva Agreements. Photograph courtesy Thomas A. Julian

Secretary expressed himself very optimistically about the results of his meetings with Eden. Dulles claimed the British were prepared for joint meetings to examine an ad hoc coalition before Geneva, and he ordered preparations for such a meeting. At the American Embassy residence that night, where Dillon hosted the visiting Secretary, Dulles claimed the only remaining obstacle was the attitude of the French.

But the qualified nature of British support was again revealed by the debate in the House of Commons of which Dulles learned the next afternoon. American diplomats recall that the Secretary of State was furious at the British.

Meanwhile, as Dulles arrived in Paris the secrecy of the plans for Operation Vautour was already fast eroding. Two days before his arrival the well-connected American journalist and former war correspondent Cyrus L. Sulzberger had been invited to lunch at the home of a senior French general, Pierre Billotte. Also at Billotte's house that afternoon was General Paul Ely. Sulzberger had already learned at NATO headquarters that a French column was secretly assembling in Laos for an overland relief attempt for Dien Bien Phu. Now he had a chance to question the French joint chiefs' head.

Ely told Sulzberger that France could not afford to lose now at Dien Bien Phu, that although the place had no military value, it had become a political symbol of great importance. Ely dismissed the overland relief effort, calling it "a very complicated process" to build up troops at Luang Prabang and then send them to relieve the entrenched camp, a hundred and twenty miles away through dense jungle and virtually trackless mountains. In December 1953 the French had barely been able to achieve a Dien Bien Phu–Laos linkup, and then there had been no Viet Minh soldiers to block the way.

General Billotte also pointed out the critical French manpower situation—only one paratroop battalion by now remained in reserve in Tonkin. Giap was thought to have suffered 12,000 casualties already, but the Viet Minh were still very strong. The only way to save Dien Bien Phu, Ely thought, was by expanding the area of the entrenched camp, initially by reoccupying and reopening the airfield.

Ely paused to sip from his favored mineral water and then told Sulzberger that he was on his way to Joseph Laniel to request that the French government tell the United States it would be prepared to accept American air assistance. Ely remarked that the "assistance" would include both planes and crews. He wanted an agreement with the United States so that "in case of emergency" American carriers and land-based aircraft would be prepared to move immediately.[7]

Ely pointed out that such an agreement would be difficult because the Americans had made air intervention contingent on "united action." The Laniel Cabinet had discussed the ad hoc coalition idea a week before, and its conclusion was that it should await the outcome of Geneva. A threat to internationalize the war might be effective, but it would have to be formulated so as to give the Chinese no grounds for direct intervention in Viet-Nam. Dulles had been informed of these conclusions at the time by French Ambassador Henri Bonnet in Washington.

Dulles now had the task of convincing the French to embrace his formula for "united action." As he put it at his first meeting, held at the Quai d'Orsay on the afternoon of April 14, he sought to explain more fully than possible by cable "the motives which had led the United States government to embark on its present course of action."

Noting his meetings with congressional leaders of both parties, Dulles remarked that the continuation of military aid and the participation of the United States in the Indochina war, which he characterized as the "present policy" of the United States, would be difficult without the participation of allies.

As for Geneva, "United States study concludes that no peace is possible in Indochina unless the Communists give up their intention of conquering all of Southeast Asia."

The Secretary of State next reported on his efforts for the creation of an ad hoc coalition. Mr. Dulles said that on the whole the effect had been satisfactory—he cited "welcome" approval by the Philippines and Thailand, "favorable" reception by Australia and New Zealand. The statement he had issued together with the British "agrees to studying the establishment of a common defense in the area" and "makes clear that the purpose exists before Geneva to shrink the intentions of the Chinese Communists."

Dulles also made clear the urgency with which he viewed matters: the coalition he had in mind was not something like NATO, which would take "18 months" to negotiate. Rather, "we should do something to create an association now . . . before attempting the creation of a series of multilateral treaties."

So, on April 14, Dulles clearly distinguished between a coalition for intervention and the longer-term aim of an alliance. It should further be noted that the Secretary of State was not entirely honest with either the French or the British. To the British, he maintained the U.S. Congress was completely willing to act. To the French, Dulles misrepresented the degree to which "united action" had received foreign, especially British, support.

From the Quai d'Orsay, Bidault and Dulles, accompanied by Ambassador Dillon and U.S. military attaché Lieutenant Colonel Vernon Walters, headed for another meeting, this one with Prime Minister Joseph Laniel. The meeting began at the Matignon at 5:30 P.M. Again, Dulles misrepresented the British, noting that they had "moved in considerable measure" toward the position of the United States. Mr. Laniel commented that "this must have been difficult indeed."

Mr. Dulles then said that President Eisenhower spoke constantly of doing everything possible within the limit of human resources to answer appeals made by France. As a concrete example Dulles referred to the Cabinet meeting of April 9 in Washington, where he had given an exposé of the Indochina situation. Eisenhower, "who was himself a general and who understood these things, had taken over the exposé in a masterly fashion and expressed himself in such a way as would have given great satisfaction to . . . Laniel had he heard it."

The agreed communiqué of the Franco-American discussions noted Dulles's "admiration" for the fight in Indochina, deplored the "new climax" of aggression on the eve of the Geneva conference, and stated that "in close association with other interested nations, we will examine the possibility of establishing . . . a collective defense to assure the peace, security and freedom of this area." There was only a nod toward French concern over the Geneva negotiations—the statement was "convinced" that on Western solidarity depended a successful outcome of the Geneva conference that safeguarded the independence and freedom of the peoples of the Associated States.[8]

There was one last, little-known round in the Franco-American talks. While Dulles briefly relaxed at the American Embassy before taking off for the United States, a senior aide met with Joseph Laniel at the French prime minister's private residence, 15 rue Leroux. The meeting lasted an hour and a half and ended at midnight.

The American envoy was Douglas MacArthur II, a wartime associate of Laniel's in the Resistance. MacArthur recalled the assurances given him by Laniel in July 1953, in connection with funding the Navarre Plan, and informally to President Eisenhower at Bermuda, that France "would take no action which directly or indirectly would turn Indochina over to the communists."

Unstated but clearly implied, French acceptance of a negotiated settlement at Geneva would be such an action. The Americans were cashing in their official pledge.

MacArthur noted that Americans recognized Laniel's own "unshakable" determination "not to turn Indochina over to the Communists."

Monsieur Laniel reaffirmed "that he would not be a party to turning the area over," but the French prime minister noted the acute war-weariness in France, which created a difficult political situation. The Laniel government could fall at any time and no successor Cabinet would be able to avoid a negotiated settlement.[9]

The pledges the Americans thought they had when they agreed to pay for the Navarre Plan had turned out to be worthless.

IX

VULTURE REFUSES TO DIE

While British and French diplomats resisted falling into line with Dulles's formula for "united action," it was French General Henri Navarre who really stood to lose the battle of Dien Bien Phu. Faced with the constantly deteriorating position at the entrenched camp, Navarre's shuttle from Saigon to Hanoi and back became frenzied, and his efforts to command were hampered by failing morale and doubts about his own leadership.

One of Navarre's biggest problems was the Tonkin theater commander, Major General René Cogny. This flamboyant Norman officer turned against Navarre as the Dien Bien Phu battle drained away his elite paratroop reserves from the Red River delta. Cogny was also disturbed that Navarre showed no inclination to halt or reduce his Atlante operation in order to support the Tonkin battle. Navarre in turn was annoyed at how Major General Cogny seemed to curry favor with journalists—taking credit for Dien Bien Phu when it was going well, and now shifting the blame to Navarre's shoulders.

Tensions between Navarre and Cogny virtually burst into the open at the same time that Navarre was faced with the decision about American intervention, Vautour. At French headquarters in

Hanoi, situated in an old building called "the Citadel," Navarre and Cogny had a very abrasive meeting. Never again would the two men visit or speak, except with frigid demeanors and on purely formal occasions. Navarre cabled to General Paul Ely declaring that he had lost confidence in the Tonkin commander, but the French joint chiefs' chairman told Navarre that there could be no question of arranging a replacement in the middle of the big battle, only later, after it was over.

In Hanoi, Navarre met with reporter David Schoenbrun, who asked how the French could have gotten trapped at Dien Bien Phu. Navarre replied that "when we went into Dien Bien Phu the Viets did not have any artillery and there was no danger from the heights. It was only because the diplomats agreed at the Berlin Conference . . . to convene a peace conference . . . that the Chinese began to send the big cannon to Giap. They wanted to go to Geneva in a strong bargaining position. By then it was too late to get out."[1]

Navarre distorted the facts in claiming Giap possessed no artillery, and, as Schoenbrun pointed out in April 1954, France had openly been pressing for a negotiated settlement months before Navarre moved into the entrenched camp. But the idea that he was betrayed by a lack of direction from political leadership became the main theme for Henri Navarre's defense in subsequent years.

The suggestion for an operation *"Vautour"* can only have appeared as a straw to be grasped at in a desperate situation. In fact that interpretation is borne out by General Navarre's reaction to American conditions attached to execution of the airstrike.

On April 6 Navarre and Paul Ely exchanged cables discussing the possibility that the Americans might be induced to "loan" about fifteen B-29 bombers which could then be flown by French crews. Navarre admitted the next day the French had no crews for the bombers and could not train them in time to make a difference. The French nevertheless pursued the request in Washington.

General Nathan F. Twining opposed the appeal on the grounds that French ability to use the planes was limited, their ability to maintain them nonexistent, and Indochina was judged to have no targets suitable for B-29 type bombers. Later the Americans also discovered that only two airfields in Vietnam, Da Nang and Tan Son Nhut, were able to accommodate the big planes and that, due to the lightness of their construction both might be run down in as little as a month if B-29s flew out of them.

The U.S. reply denied the French request for military aid in the form of B-29 bombers.

As for *"Vautour"* itself, on April 7 French Standing Group representative General Jean Valluy called Ely by trans-Atlantic telephone to say that American preparations seemed to be progressing rapidly. But the same day American Admiral Robert Carney informed CINCPAC that for the moment no intervention was being contemplated. The French government soon learned this. The next day General Ely's personal representative, Colonel Brohon, was telling Radford his boss was embarrassed and disappointed at the U.S. refusal to carry out the suggested airstrike upon demand.

In Paris, Paul Ely was a little puzzled at Navarre's suddenly very pessimistic views on Dien Bien Phu reflected in the Expeditionary Corps commander's requests for American intervention. On April 10, Ely cabled Navarre that he was "struck" by the "apparent insecurity" with which the situation was being viewed. He reminded Navarre that a Viet Minh attack on the entrenched camp had been the aim of occupying the mountain valley. Ely pointed out that according to the original strategy a Dien Bien Phu battle would "remain" a military success even if the camp fell, in that Giap's army would suffer heavy casualties. And the casualties were heavy—twelve thousand, Ely told Cyrus Sulzberger at lunch on April 12.

Navarre apparently was not comforted by Ely's encouragement. Rather, his reply from Saigon on April 12 took the form of suggesting an alternative to Operation Vautour, which was taking too long to materialize. In top-secret cable no. 11 the possibility was raised for a "limited action" to consist of nightly raids by fifteen to twenty of the big American bombers. With the number of planes restricted to avoid too great a "mass effect," Navarre thought intervention would be directly proportionate to what the Chinese were doing.

He also thought that for multi-engine aircraft flying at night, at high altitude, there would be practically no risk of damage by the enemy or operational loss of an aircraft. The Americans could fly their B-29s with no insignia and carry no papers, just in case.

The French joint chiefs' chairman replied the same day from Paris. There could be no question of a limited action. Ely claimed Admiral Radford rejected this possibility and wanted all or nothing on the air strike option. Navarre commented in a return cable, again the same day, that Admiral Radford seemed to be thinking in terms only of how to win the Indochina war. Navarre felt the proper objective was to prolong the resistance at Dien Bien Phu.

General Navarre had exhausted his means of prolonging the life of the entrenched camp, aside from the possibility of bringing in the Americans. The paratroop reserves were at a critical level, and Navarre still refused to reconstitute this reserve by bringing in the three airborne battalions engaged in the field in Operation Atlante and in central Laos. There were signs of strain as well in the air bridge to Dien Bien Phu. Supply arrivals at the camp were very uneven. French naval pilots, exerting themselves to the utmost in the air support effort, were dangerously close to exhaustion. Navarre had activated an overland relief effort from Laos, Operation Condor, with four battalions and a partisan group, but this was barely yet in motion and would have slow going in the jungle highlands.

Meanwhile, in Saigon on April 14, Navarre met with another American officer, General Earle E. Partridge, commander of the Far East Air Force. Navarre asked Partridge whether B-29 operations over Indochina were feasible and repeatedly asked whether B-29s were capable of eliminating Viet Minh antiaircraft guns around the entrenched camp. Navarre evidently preferred an air strike targeted at the Viet-Nam People's Army rear base for Dien Bien Phu, which was located at Tuan Giao.

Partridge did not reply directly to Navarre's questions. Feasibility of B-29 operations could only be determined by a specific survey mission for that purpose. Navarre was disappointed and reported to General Paul Ely that Partridge seemed to know nothing about the Vautour project.

"Pat" Partridge knew much more than he was letting on. For one thing since February 1954 the FEAF had been using the possibility of aerial operations in Indochina as a reason to oppose planned redeployment of its B-29 bomber wings, supposed to return stateside for conversion to newer jet B-47 medium bombers (and subsequent reassignment to the Strategic Air Command). Only one unit, the 98th Bombardment Group, was to retain B-29s and it was supposed to withdraw to Guam where it too would revert to the Strategic Air Command. Meanwhile Partridge had had time to order a contingency plan for an Indochina bombardment mission and had been briefed on it just before his departure for Saigon.

In Washington "Nate" Twining learned on the morning of April 19 of Partridge's impression that the situation was deteriorating and the French were unable to reverse that trend with the means at their disposal. He saw Navarre as grasping straws with respect to Dien Bien Phu. Partridge reported he himself had raised the subject of defense against Chinese air forces but that Navarre had not been receptive. Before leaving Partridge left Navarre a note appreciating the better understanding he had received during his visit, but he told Twining the French air force was woefully inadequate and its fields reminded him of the cow pasture bases of the 1930s.

Navarre and Partridge had nevertheless talked over using B-29s, including the need to have accurate radar navigation equipment in place to guide the mission. Navarre had emphasized that it would be shameful if intervention was approved but then had to be delayed because these matters had not been worked out. Partridge agreed to send a B-29 survey mission. While flying back to Tokyo Partridge ordered the chief of his Bomber Command to meet the plane at Haneda airport. Brigadier General Joseph E. Caldara appeared as ordered and was told to take necessary staff and make a feasibility study in Indochina. Years later, at the height of America's Vietnam war, Partridge was interviewed for an oral history for the Air Force Academy. Partridge told his interviewers that he had never heard of Vulture or a B-29 attack oat Dien Bien Phu.

Meanwhile at Saigon, General Navarre now felt so confident intervention was on the way that on April 17 he wrote a personal letter to Colonel de Castries informing the Dien Bien Phu commander of the projected operation, using the name *"Vautour."*

The difficulty of conducting operations at Dien Bien Phu mounted steadily. By Good Friday, April 16, it required ten hours of fighting by two full battalions of the French to resupply position Huguette-6 with some water and a half-dozen boxes of ammunition. Langlais felt he could not afford such heavy losses to maintain Huguette-6 and reluctantly decided to abandon the position. The entrenched camp was growing smaller with every passing day, and every reduction in size made it more difficult for the transport aircraft to drop their loads within the French perimeter.

On Easter Sunday, Pierre Langlais went to the chaplain to confess his sins. When asked about the tactical situation, the short paratrooper rasped, "We are headed for disaster."

Father Heinrich consoled him: "We must accept that in expiation of our sins."[2]

At the entrenched camp they grumbled that the world was celebrating Easter and had forgotten about Dien Bien Phu.

On April 22, Navarre proposed to General Ely another alternative to Vautour. This time he pointed to the success of the CIA-owned air group, Civil Air Transport. Navarre suggested that some B-29 bombers could be incorporated into the French Foreign Legion and flown by American or foreign pilots under contract to France. No doubt the French Air Force would have been happy to see the Army flying planes, while the Foreign Legion would have happily spread its limited resources into the unknown area of flying!

Washington was far away from the impending military disaster. Indeed, for a moment Washington would drop out of the picture altogether, as President Eisenhower was planning a golf vacation at Augusta, Georgia. After a pro forma meeting of the National Security Council on April 13, Ike and Mamie went to the ball park, where the President threw out the first baseball of the 1954 season. The presidential party then proceeded to the airport, arriving in Georgia that evening.

Admiral Radford and Secretary Charles Wilson spent April 14 and 15 on Capitol Hill testifying in favor of the request for the military assistance program. The discussion turned to Dien Bien Phu at the beginning of the second day when the Senate Foreign Relations Committee chairman, Senator William Knowland, immediately went off the record for a two-hour hearing. Press accounts reported that Radford left the impression that the United States government was *not* considering any form of imminent military action in Indochina.

The official testimony in Congress was misleading at the least. While the Joint Chiefs of Staff chairman and the Secretary of Defense met with the Foreign Relations Committee, they continued to move quietly toward a plan for intervention. A memo passed between their offices at the Pentagon, over Radford's signature and no doubt at Army insistence, to the effect that the Army felt it might be capable of maintaining internal security in Indochina against dissidents and bandits but not of all-out operations against the Viet Minh. Despite this warning, orders were issued by Wilson for the armed services to prepare contingency planning, both military and for mobilization, for operations in Indochina.

The Wilson memorandum was top secret, but soon there was a public affirmation that open intervention was indeed under consideration at the highest levels of government.

On April 16, Vice-President Richard M. Nixon spoke for over an hour at a luncheon of the American Society of Newspaper Editors held in the capital.

Nixon said that "the Vietnamese lack the ability to conduct a war by themselves or even to govern themselves. If the French withdrew, Indochina would become Communist-dominated within a month."

The training of "native troops" was slow.

"What is to be done? For one, the problem is not one of materials and wasn't four months ago. More men are needed and the question is where to get them. They will not come from France, for France is tired of the war, as we were tired of Korea."

Nixon specified that as a leader of the Free World the United States "cannot afford further retreat" in Asia. The United States should go to Geneva and take "a positive stand for united action."

The Vice-President clearly referred to a massive American intervention in this passage: "It is hoped that the US will not have to send these troops there, but if the government cannot avoid it, the administration must face up to the situation and dispatch forces.

"This country is the only nation politically strong enough at home to take a position that will save Asia."[3]

By Friday afternoon the Georgia White House at the Augusta golf club was receiving queries about the Nixon speech and the mention of troops, a statement that had been made in answer to a question. Presidential Press Secretary Jim Hagerty noted: "Think it was foolish of Dick to answer as he did but will make the best of it."

Hagerty "played dumb" to all questions and the White House initially refused to comment. So too did Senator William Knowland, who believed the Nixon statement to be a trial balloon. This trial-balloon-for-intervention theory became the major interpretation of Nixon's remarks that day. Jim Hagerty said to interviewer Herbert S. Parmet in 1969: "I don't think he would have made it without at least the knowledge of the President."[4]

California Senator Knowland had been to Indochina, had been given the VIP tour by French officers, and was a stalwart of the China Lobby of Asia-firsters. Knowland believed that Congress was willing to go ahead with U.S. intervention given certain assurances, namely "independence" for the Associated States in the style of a British dominion. However, the Nixon statement was very upsetting for Knowland because it revealed plans for military intervention at a time when such political preconditions had not yet been obtained. So the senator refused to comment on the reports of the Vice-President's speech.

Others were not so reticent. Three senators, Bourke Hickenlooper (R-Iowa), Hubert Humphrey (D-Minnesota), and Everett

Dirksen (R-Illinois), manifestly opposed adventures in Indochina. All three rejected any use of troops or any other kind of intervention in Indochina.

The next morning, in Georgia, the President was confronted by Jim Hagerty with the problem of the Nixon statement. He told Hagerty to get in touch with Walter Bedell Smith and to have State issue a statement without cutting the ground from under the Vice-President. This statement was drafted and cleared with Eisenhower just before dinner.

At the State Department in Washington, Jameson Parker read the administration statement to reporters: "Certain remarks with regard to United States policy toward Indochina have been attributed to a high government official. . . . The speech enunciated no new United States policy. . . . It expressed full agreement and support for the policy . . . enunciated by the President and Secretary of State."[5]

In later years, questioned by oral historians, Dwight Eisenhower professed not to remember the Nixon speech, or he told interviewers they would have to ask Nixon. But at 9:06 A.M. on April 19, 1954, President Eisenhower telephoned Richard Nixon "to tell him not to be disturbed by [the] stories press boys had been cooking up out of his 'perfectly innocent' remarks." Eisenhower declared he might have said the same thing himself.

The press was probably distorting remarks because both he and Dulles were out of town.[6]

Nixon was concerned that Eisenhower would be upset. He claimed that he had thought the remarks to be off the record and the question hypothetical. This may be the case, but it is difficult to believe that Nixon's remarks were made by coincidence the day after orders for military intervention planning were issued by Secretary Wilson.

John Foster Dulles, just completing his European trip, was also engaged in an activity closely related to the intervention

project—setting up a meeting of powers in Washington to examine the ad hoc coalition idea which would provide the Americans with a basis for action.

Dulles made arrangements for a ten-power meeting to be held
on April 20. He was already scheduled to lunch with President
Eisenhower on the nineteenth, which allowed for a final round
of internal consideration before spreading out the "united action"
plan for international agreement. Dulles contacted each of the
embassies individually to request participation. It was here that
the meeting plan went awry.

The British ambassador, Sir Roger Makins, passed along to
London the Americans' invitation to the planned meeting, but
instead of permission to attend, Makins received a pointed refusal. Anthony Eden instructed Makins to tell the Americans that
an ad hoc coalition meeting prior to Geneva would be harmful
and contrary to the "spirit" of the agreement reached in London
between Eden and Foster Dulles. The question of membership in
such a regional alliance had not been settled—particularly in the
cases of India and Formosa. The British were planning to open a
regional conference of Commonwealth nations in Ceylon on April
26, and they could not afford to cooperate with the United States
in a regional grouping that would exclude India, whose cooperation at Ceylon was vital.

The Secretary of State was at home on 32nd Street in Georgetown when the British reply arrived on April 18 in the form of a
telephone call from Makins.

Eleanor Lansing Dulles, the Secretary's sister, happened to be
present with Dulles near the hallway table when the telephone
rang, and she recalled the circumstances in a 1969 article.

Dulles appeared "visibly disturbed." (Other, more dramatic accounts assert that the Secretary of State pounded the innocent
telephone table with his fist.)

"Eden has reversed himself and gone back on our agreement!"[7]

Since Australia and New Zealand hinged their participation on British support, the ad hoc coalition suddenly seemed rather narrow. The State Department had no choice but to cancel the meeting, substituting in its place a sixteen-nation gathering of signatories to the Korea cease-fire agreement. Several weeks later Dulles told a congressional audience that the countries involved in the prospective meeting "had to go along in helping us to cover up." The Secretary's analysis on that occasion was that Indian leader Jawaharlal Nehru put pressure on the British to suspend action.[8]

Meanwhile, the situation in Indochina was so dismal that it was considered good news that day when the Sunday *New York Times* headlined INCREASED RAINS SEEN SLOWING THE FIGHTING.

The following morning Dulles flew to Augusta as arranged, to lunch with Eisenhower. He was received at the airport by Jim Hagerty, who rode with the Secretary of State in a car while the two composed a news release that could be issued by either Eisenhower or Dulles.

Among other things Dulles and Ike discussed the Department of Justice paper on the war powers of the President. Dulles, the lawyer, thought the paper "unduly legalistic" and felt "the heart of the matter was that the Government of the United States must have the power of self-preservation. . . . If the danger was great and imminent and Congress unable to act quickly enough to avert the danger, the President would have to act alone." Eisenhower agreed and added that the President had the responsibility for "carrying out the will of the people" and was subject to impeachment if he made a mistake in this respect. But in view of the congressional debate over the Bricker Amendment, President Eisenhower thought it unwise to "ventilate" the war powers issue at this time.

Dulles agreed but said his views had been expressed only as

matters he "thought should be in the background of NSC thinking and planning."[9]

Secretary Dulles's press release, meanwhile, was put out by Jim Hagerty in Augusta. The statement noted the violent battles in Indochina were "rousing the free nations to measures which we hope will be sufficiently timely and vigorous to preserve these vital areas from Communist domination."

Hagerty had more time to discuss matters with Secretary Dulles while riding him back to the airport for the Washington flight. Dulles told Hagerty that Eisenhower had left the decision of what to do with Geneva up to him.

Dulles said that "we do not want to let the Communists know ahead of time what our plans are, nor do we want to lessen our pressure on Indochina—at present [the] Communists do not know whether we will attack if they move . . . and we want to leave it that way."

Dulles was also bitter about the failure of some Republican senators—William F. Knowland was mentioned specifically—to back up the President on foreign policy.

"We have the greatest President since Washington—a military genius and a statesman who is trying to guide our country through a very delicate situation with war on both sides of the road we are taking. We must not give in to the Communists and we must keep our allies. That is a tough job. Why those people on the Hill cannot understand that and cannot back us up is more than I can understand."[10]

One penciled addition to Dulles's agenda for his meeting with Eisenhower was the matter of the Nixon statement. Foster was actually quite close to the Vice-President and frequently had him over for dinner. At 5:15 P.M. on April 19, shortly after Dulles returned to Washington, Nixon reached him on the telephone.

Dulles observed, "I see you've got your name in the papers."

Nixon replied he had not intended to do so.

Dulles remarked that the question Nixon had addressed hypothetically was not one he himself cared to reply to. But on the whole "the result might be on the plus side," citing a good reaction in the French press.

Both men criticized Knowland and the lack of political support for foreign policy; Dulles repeated his characterization of the President as the "best man" since George Washington "for this kind of situation." Dulles mentioned he had told Ike that a course was necessary that would avoid war, and told Nixon that "one cannot explain everything to our own people, as it also explains things to the enemy."[11]

On April 20 Dulles departed for the NATO meetings in Paris and to attend the opening of the Geneva conference and its sessions on Korea. At the airport the Secretary of State insisted that Geneva did not imply American recognition of the People's Republic of China. At Geneva, Dulles would refuse to shake the hand of Chinese delegate Chou En-lai.

During the days between April 6 and April 19, the possibility of a Vulture operation began to seem more and more unlikely. But armed intervention was by no means a dead issue.

X

"AND IF I GAVE YOU TWO A-BOMBS FOR DIEN BIEN PHU?"

Just before he left again for Paris, John Foster Dulles met with legislators to inform Congress of the results of his first trip to Europe. According to the papers the next day, Mr. Dulles said that intervention in Indochina was neither imminent nor even under consideration by the United States.

Even as the Secretary of State spoke, a mission from the Far East Air Force was arriving at Saigon to determine whether operations by B-29 bombers were feasible under the circumstances.

The mission was the result of General "Pat" Partridge's discussions with Navarre and the French commander's deputy, General Pierre Bodet. "Smokey" Caldara was told to draw no press or other attention to his mission and, to accomplish this, was instructed to use an old B-17 aircraft rather than a B-29 bomber. There were still many World War II-vintage B-17s serving the United States Air Force as reconnaissance and liaison planes, and the presence of one of these planes in Viet-Nam presumably would excite no one's attention. Caldara was told to make no real commitments to the French command.

Bomber Command, or BomCom as it was known, specialized in heavy-bombing techniques and operations. It had been one of the United States' major advantages during the Korean War, when there was no communist bomber force to match it.

Throughout the Korean War BomCom flew 21,328 effective sorties. These included 1,995 reconnaissance missions and 797 for psychological warfare purposes. Some 167,000 tons of ordnance were dropped on targets all over Korea. It was awarded a Korean Presidential Unit Citation by Syngman Rhee. In 1954 the major elements of BomCom were the 19th, 98th, and 307th Bombardment wings and the 91st Strategic Reconnaissance Squadron.

If there was to be any Indochina aerial intervention, these units would carry it out. But such a mission would be incredibly difficult. As the Air Force official history of the Korean campaign notes, B-29s were "inherently unsuited for pinpoint work" from altitudes above 18,000 feet. True, the 19th Wing had been decorated for accuracy at a time before bombing radars were installed in its B-29s. The 307th Wing also held awards for precision. New bombing radar systems aboard the B-29s could help considerably, as could radio and radar navigation beacons, principally shoran (short-range navigation). But Air Force studies showed that at least thirty-five practice bomb runs were necessary with shoran before B-29 crews attained proficiency with the system, and this had not yet been done.

General Caldara arrived at Saigon with a group of eight officers on April 20. There, for security reasons, they were housed at a downtown hotel rather than at one of the several French military compounds nearby.

Caldara spoke with French Air Force officers, inspected airfields, and flew over the critical air routes to Dien Bien Phu, both in daylight and at night. He personally conducted a reconnaissance of the Viet Minh supply route back to the Chinese border and presented the French with photographs and target data.

Caldara made a total of three flights over the entrenched camp, one of them in a French Dakota. He saw that, because the Viet Minh were closely intermixed with the French around the entrenched camp, extreme precision was mandatory for any bombing mission.

In a meeting at the U.S. mission in Saigon with the chargé d'affaires, Robert McClintock, Caldara made known BomCom's need for a shoran unit in Indochina. McClintock was dismayed that BomCom was not an "all-weather" force. The meeting got so heated that Caldara hit the table and insisted that saturation-bombing missions were flown only with the most careful preparation.

Apparently the chargé d'affaires replied with Georges Clemenceau's famous words that "perhaps war is too important to be left to the generals."

Caldara looked McClintock in the eye and said quietly, "If that mission takes place, I'm going to be riding the lead B-29 into the goddam' flak, and you're welcome to the right seat."[1]

Although Caldara remained in Indochina until April 29, and although he had a private interview with Navarre on the twenty-sixth, the operations plan for Vautour was essentially completed by April 24. The plan called for a "maximum effort strike, utilizing 500 lb. conventional bombs with a minimum intervalometer setting (30 ft.) and 1/10 second delay fusing. This was to meet the requirements that enemy forces totalling some 20–30,000 men were dug into a depth of 3 meters on 3 sides of Dien Bien Phu."

"This bombing raid," wrote Caldara, "could have effectively destroyed the entire enemy force."

Caldara's bomber mission would have been executed with the entire BomCom force of ninety-eight B-29s. The planes would fly from Clark, make a landfall over Thailand along the Gulf of Siam, and then fly over Laos to reach the entrenched camp. From Dien Bien Phu the B-29s would fly back to Clark over the South China Sea, exiting through the Gulf of Tonkin and south of the Red River delta. This would minimize exposure to Chinese fighter interceptors. Each plane would carry fourteen tons of bombs. The plan required any damaged plane to ditch at sea rather than make an emergency landing and risk exposure of Vautour. The 2nd Air Rescue Group was available at Clark to search for survivors. There are other accounts, French ones, that hold that General Caldara considered involving as many as three raids of up to eighty bombers each.

It is worth noting that General Caldara's description of the proposed operation omits any mention of the altitude the mission would be flown at. Caldara also fails to mention that the size of the mission was extraordinary for Bomber Command. "Large" bombing raids during Korea had used up to fifty B-29s over a target. BomCom's daily operational average through most of the Korean conflict was twenty-four.

Navarre had speculated on the possibility of smaller air strikes to eliminate the Viet Minh anti-aircraft guns. In this regard Caldara notes that "inasmuch as my understanding was that any Heavy Bomber attack would be in force, no plan was drawn up for this type effort."[2]

Caldara finished his assignment and returned to Japan. In his opinion, the accuracy needed for a precision strike around Dien Bien Phu exceeded the capabilities of on-board radars. "Smokey" sent copies of this report to General Curtis E. LeMay at the Strategic Air Command as well as to "Pat" Partridge.

On June 5 General Partridge recommended use of carrier aircraft in preference to B-29s in any Indochina action. But as a Far East Air Force historical study put it, "B-29 medium bombers using *conventional* weapons could not in FEAF's opinion produce decisive results in Indochina operations."[3]

By the night of April 19–20, strongpoint positions Huguette-1 and Huguette-6 were almost completely surrounded. The Secretary of State met with Paul Ely and Georges Bidault on April 22 at the home of the French foreign minister. Bidault asked Ely to outline the situation at Dien Bien Phu and the possibilities still offered by an air strike. Ely confirmed that Dien Bien Phu had become virtually hopeless. Breakout from the entrenched camp was no solution because it involved abandoning wounded and equipment. Although Bidault had always opposed internationalizing the Indochina war, he was willing to do so now if this would save the entrenched camp.

Dulles denigrated the efficacy of bombing by claiming that the French already had more planes in Indochina than they could use. Ely denied the allegation. Bidault suggested emergency consultations in Indochina between Generals Navarre and O'Daniel. He also dismissed the need for British participation in intervention, saying their contribution would be minimal in any case. Dulles again refused to move unless "united action" was achieved.

That evening American journalist Cyrus Sulzberger had dinner with a highly emotional Assistant Secretary of State for Far Eastern Affairs, Walter S. Robertson. According to Sulzberger's published diary, Robertson "said April 22 had been one of the worst days in United States history." He compared the situation "in a rather illogical way" with that of George Washington at Valley Forge, insisting that the United States could not abandon its position. "Nevertheless—and if these recollections appear confused they are a faithful portrait of Robertson's mind—he feels that the United States must intervene. There is no point in our arguing we will intervene in one way but not in another way. If we are going to intervene, we have to [do so] wholeheartedly. This is a time to tighten our belts."[4]

Later that evening Sulzberger ran into Dulles at the residence of Ambassador Dillon. The Secretary of State appeared to be in a surprisingly good mood, perhaps as a result of several highballs, in the journalist's opinion. Dulles spoke to Sulzberger about nothing much—he bragged about the pike and perch fishing from his place on Duck Island in the St. Lawrence River. But as he walked away Foster remarked that the discussions that day had been unfortunate and that the situation was "awful, awful."

At Dien Bien Phu the situation was worse than awful. On April 23 the French threw in their only fresh unit, the newly arrived 2nd Foreign Legion Parachute Battalion, in a full-scale effort to recapture Huguette-1, without which the drop zone for supplies would become virtually nonexistent. The attack was a failure when the assault troops were pinned down by Viet Minh fire across the airstrip. But Major Hubert Liesenfeldt, the battalion commander in charge of the attack, did not react. When Lieutenant Colonel Bigeard heard the pleas of the pinned troops, he checked up and found Liesenfeldt's radios tuned to the wrong frequency. The attack collapsed.

On April 24 one of the American CAT pilots, Paul R. Holden, was wounded during his transport mission with the result that all the CAT pilots, whose contracts did not provide for combat missions, refused to make further flights to the entrenched camp through the Viet Minh flak.

Talks continued in Paris. Douglas MacArthur II was called in for a meeting with Prime Minister Laniel and French diplomat André Bougenot. Laniel believed that neither Bidault nor any successor would be able to avoid negotiating at Geneva if Dien Bien Phu were to fall.

Laniel emphasized, "Dien Bien Phu has become a symbol in the mind of the French people."

General Ely had told him the previous day, Laniel said, that only the intervention of American naval aircraft could save the entrenched camp now. Bougenot stressed this point to MacArthur—air support would "galvanize" the defenders and "dramatically change" the situation. He drew an analogy to 1940 when France was going down to defeat and Paul Reynaud, the politician who was then prime minister, appealed for American military aid to President Franklin D. Roosevelt.

In the presence of Laniel, Bougenot told MacArthur that the United States could commit its naval aircraft without risking American prestige or engaging in an act of belligerency by painting the planes with French insignia, disguising them as elements of the French Foreign Legion, and placing them under nominal French command for isolated actions.

Laniel reiterated that Dien Bien Phu had become an emotional thing and "people are no longer capable of reasoning about it."

While Laniel spoke to MacArthur, Georges Bidault was handed a cable by General Ely, in the middle of the NATO council session. The cable reported that the entrenched camp had expended its last reserves in the failed counterattack on Huguette. Nothing could now save Dien Bien Phu except an aerial intervention or a cease-fire.

Foreign Minister Bidault silently passed the cable to John Foster Dulles.

Mr. Dulles replied, "B-29 intervention as proposed seems to me out of the question."[5]

The Secretary of State said he would report all this directly to the President and that he would discuss it with Admiral Radford when that officer arrived in Paris. Dulles informed Eisenhower of the emergency, adding that he and Bidault would speak further at dinner; and that "Bidault gives the impression of being a man close to the breaking point. His mental condition at this morning's session was greatly improved over yesterday, but it has been painful to watch him presiding over the Council at this afternoon's long session."[6]

Eisenhower replied immediately to Dulles's message, telephoning the text of the letter to the State Department for transmittal to Paris. He wrote that his first reaction "is to assure you of my full understanding of the feeling of frustration that must consume you." The difficulties were major.

> *There is little I can say now to help you rally the spirits and determination of our allies, but I am so confident of the unity of convictions you and I hold on these and re-lated matters that I do not even feel the need of assuring you again of my complete support. . . . I am thankful, on behalf of America, that we have in you such a skilled and devoted representative to support our interests in these fateful days.[7]*

Dulles received this accolade before attending dinner at the Quai d'Orsay hosted by the French for NATO members. Before sitting down to table, Dulles took aside Anthony Eden, who was also present in Paris. He told the British foreign secretary that a telegram just arrived from Navarre said that only a powerful U.S. air strike in the next seventy-two hours could save Dien Bien Phu.

In "a brief conversation among the expectant diners," Eden found it difficult to believe that intervention at this stage by aircraft carriers could have a decisive effect. Dulles then produced Eisenhower's letter, which said, inter alia, "I do suggest that you make sure the British government fully appreciates the gravity of the situation and the great danger of French collapse. . . . The British must not be able merely to shut their eyes and later plead blindness as an alibi for failing to propose a positive program."[8]

In his memoirs Anthony Eden remarked that the President's letter seemed to imply the United Kingdom was "somewhat in-different" to the situation.

Eden quotes his own reply: "I frankly did not believe that conditions in Indochina can be remedied by outside intervention alone at this hour, even if help were immediately available."[9]

Later, General Alfred Gruenther came up to Eden to say that from his viewpoint at NATO headquarters he had never seen French morale lower. After dinner Eden was subjected to a scene in which Bidault told Douglas Dillon that if the United States participated to aid Dien Bien Phu and the entrenched camp fell anyway, then France would feel honor-bound to continue fighting in Indochina. If there was no intervention, reaction in France would probably be acceptance of defeat and the installation of a left-wing government in coalition with the French Communist Party.

As Dulles reported to President Eisenhower, "the situation here is tragic. France is almost visibly collapsing under our eyes. There is, of course, no military or logical reason why loss of Dien Bien Phu should lead to collapse of French will.... It seems to me that Dien Bien Phu has become a symbol out of all proportion to its military importance."[10]

What did John Foster Dulles do in this crisis? According to Georges Bidault, the Secretary of State said to him while the two were walking down the stairs during a break between the formal meetings, "And if I gave you two A-Bombs for Dien Bien Phu?"[11]

It should be noted that Bidault recalled the comment at a later stage in his career, when he had joined with the extreme right-wing Secret Army Organization (OAS) to oppose French withdrawal from Algeria and the government of President Charles de Gaulle. Bidault was eventually forced to flee France and live in exile in South America. He reiterated Dulles's remark in a memoir published in the United States in 1967, where the former French foreign minister added, "It was I who answered without having to do much thinking on the subject, 'If those bombs are dropped near Dien Bien Phu, our side will suffer as much as the enemy.' "[12]

Whether or not Secretary of State Dulles made a specific offer of two A-bombs on April 23, it is true that the American did say *something* that at least could have been construed as such. Later in 1954, when Bidault was no longer in office and the Americans were compiling a statement to serve as a detailed record of this period, the matter was brought up by other French diplomats. Roland de Margerie, a close assistant to Bidault, commented on the report by Dulles that it seemed accurate as far as it went "but that it omitted all mention of *your* offer of atomic bombs to Bidault." This naturally shocked Douglas Dillon, who asked whether the offer could have merely been a speculation about whether atomic weapons might have been useful. Margerie replied that he himself plus another Quai d'Orsay aide, La Tournelle, had been present when Bidault immediately afterward told them of the offer. The French foreign minister was described as having been extremely upset, feeling "the use of atomic bombs would have done no good tactically and would have lost all support for the west throughout Asia." Bidault was described that day as having been ill, jittery, overwrought, and even incoherent by other top members of his own staff.

Dillon concluded "Our judgment is that Margerie fears that if Bidault should feel that publication of the [U.S.] statement as drafted placed him in an unfavorable light . . . he might respond by publicizing his version of the conversation regarding atomic bombs and might attempt to take credit for preventing their use."[13]

Dulles professed to be "totally mystified" by the claim and to have no recollection of such an offer. The only thing he thought it could have been was a misinterpretation of his statement on atomic weapons policy to the NATO council on April 23, in which he had said, "Such weapons must now be treated in fact as having become conventional."[14]

In August 1954 the diplomats dismissed the incident as a complete misunderstanding due to language difficulties. It is relevant to note in connection with this explanation, however, that

Georges Bidault had made his living before World War II as a professor of English at the Sorbonne and was in England with the Free French during much of the war. Also the U.S. government never released the statement that had been given to the French diplomats for comment.

There is circumstantial evidence for the A-bomb offer. Dulles purportedly offered two possibilities: that two A-bombs could be dropped on territory of the People's Republic of China near the Vietnamese border in order to break the Viet Minh supply line; or, that bombs could be used in the immediate environs of Dien Bien Phu. In one of the meetings that day the French had, in fact, explained that their own conventional bombing had been ineffective against the Viet Minh supply depot at Tuan Giao because this installation was dispersed over an eight-square-mile area—in other words, the French were implying that conventional weapons were not enough.

An overwhelming mass of material indicates U.S. government interest in the use of atomic weapons, but *not* specifically in Indochina. The President told the British and French at Bermuda that atomic weapons were becoming conventional. With congressional leaders in February 1954, Eisenhower said that if war came with China we would "go all the way," there would be no restrictions on either weapons or targets. The "New Look" military strategy was explicitly based on reliance on atomic weapons, and the related "massive retaliation" speech of Dulles also clearly indicated an atomic approach with its "places and means of our choosing" statement.

There is also a body of evidence in the *recommendations*, as distinct from decisions, about atomic weapons. While National Security Council Document 5405 contained a "special weapons annex" providing for atomic weapons use, this was withheld for a time in 1954, so that there was not always a planning *assumption* that atomic weapons *would* be used. National Security Council Action-1074-(a) did contain such an assumption. Indeed, as part of its opposition to Indochina intervention, the U.S. Army chose to argue that atomic weapons would *not* reduce the need for American troops on the ground in Viet-Nam.

With regard to aerial intervention the record shows various recommendations and considerations of atomic weapons use. The position of a Pentagon Joint Advanced Study Group in late March, a position with which Admiral Radford and General Twining agreed, was that atomic weapons were much more effective and should be used. Two months later General Partridge of the Far East Air Force also recommended the use of atomic weapons in Indochina in preference to conventional explosives. General Curtis LeMay at the Strategic Air Command proposed that the way to end brushfire wars, like Indochina, was to "up the ante" for this type of international poker game. But Walter Bedell Smith, a former general, told a group of fourteen journalists on the occasion of his retirement in September 1954 that he had heard nothing about any military discussions of atomic weapons use.

Under arrangements that were current in 1954, the Pacific Command had custody of the tactical nuclear weapons in the Western Pacific at that time. Special Navy liaison officers would accompany the special storage cradles (called "birdcages") which held the elements of the nuclear cores and kept them from attaining critical mass. The high explosive that held the nuclear bombs were aboard ship, but the U.S. still had so few that when carriers rotated duty in the Far East they had to transfer weapons to each other. The liaison officers were housed at Yokosuka naval base, the bomb high explosive components were stored on ammunition ships or aircraft carriers. Armed security personnel would physically move and hand over the components only upon explicit orders. The Mark VII bomb, of the same type as that dropped over Nagasaki in 1945, could be carried by the AD-4 aircraft of Task Group 70.2. A security officer assigned to Yo-kosuka at the time, Lieutenant Junior Grade Larry Paxson, re-members the top liaison man at Yokosuka had been sent back to Hawaii to escort some other shipment when orders came down to be ready for a possible transfer related to Indochina. Paxson was told to keep the alert to himself. Some time later he was told to stand down, but the demand for secrecy was reiterated.

Paxson attended a training course at Coronado at the end of 1954 where one lesson revolved around an atomic strike at Dien Bien Phu. The day prior to the attack the French were supposed to deepen their trenches by a foot and a half. The bombs would be carried by carrier-based attack aircraft. The timetables had been calculated down to the moment, five minutes prior to det-onation, when French troops were to hunker down in their trenches. Three weapons were to be used in a triangular pattern, fuzed for air burst in the hills above the entrenched camp. The lesson had the feel of a retired operational plan.

Admiral Felix Stump, commanding U.S. forces in the Pacific, also recalls in a 1964 oral history, how "some people . . . felt that it would be very simple" to have dropped three atomic weapons around the periphery of Dien Bien Phu. The targets would have been on the far sides of the crests held by the Viet Minh and the attack could have been launched within ten minutes of receiving orders from Washington. Visiting Saigon in 1963, a few months before the overthrow of Ngo Dinh Diem, Stump asked the South Vietnamese leader if it would have been wise to have executed the atomic attack. Diem replied, "Yes, that would have been wise."[15]

Air Force chief of staff General Nathan Twining also recalled the option in later years: "You could take all day to drop a bomb, make sure you put it in the right place . . . and clean those Com-mies out of there and the band could play the *Marseillaise* and the French could come marching out . . . in great shape."[16]

Arthur Radford also referred to the Dien Bien Phu nuclear attack, a few years afterwards as he spoke to a weapons designer working on new enhanced radiation bombs that would minimize blast damage. Radford ruminated that if the U.S. had had weapons like those at Dien Bien Phu something could really have been done. None of these individuals has commented on what the Viet Minh soldiers might have done in the aftermath, for radiation is a slow killer and the Vietnamese would have known they were about to die anyway.

It happens that Dwight D. Eisenhower himself alluded to atomic weapons, when questioned by Walter Cronkite on CBS Television in November 1961. About saving Dien Bien Phu from the air the former president said, "I just can't see how this could have been done unless you were willing to use weapons that could have destroyed the area for miles and that probably would have destroyed Dien Bien Phu, and that would have been the end of that."[17]

But on April 30, 1954, the President met with Robert Cutler of the National Security Council and Vice-President Richard Nixon to consider questions raised by the National Security Council Planning Board, including whether the United States should decide immediately to use "new weapons" in any intervention, whether one "new weapon" dropped on Viet Minh reserves at Tuan Giao could have a decisive effect (Nixon and Eisenhower agreed that an atom bomb could not be used effectively in the immediate vicinity of the entrenched camp), and "could one 'new weapon' be loaned to France for this purpose?"[18]

Nixon recalls Ike's words on the use of atomic weapons in connection with united action: "I certainly do not think that the atom bomb can be used by the United States unilaterally, and . . . I agree with Dick that we do not have to mention it to anybody before we get some agreement on united action."[19]

Robert Cutler's record also notes discussion of "loaning" atomic weapons to France. Although a marginal note warns that a "question of law" was involved, the text demonstrates that Ike was willing to tell the French that if they wanted some "new weapons, we might give them a few."[20]

In defense of Secretary Dulles, certain other material should be noted. First, General Caldara remembers planning a conventional strike only; there is not a word about nuclear weapons. It is also true that NSC-5405 contained language warning of political problems with allies, and of increased risks of war in the event atomic weapons were used in Indochina. There also exists in the files of John Foster Dulles an undated paper written between April and June 1954, possibly for the meeting with Eisenhower on April 19. This paper notes that "any use of atomic weapons will raise very serious problems of Asian opinion and attitude of our allies." Further, "if US intervention results in war expanding to China, and Soviet Union becomes involved, British and NATO opinion might well be split as to support of US in use of any British and NATO bases."[21]

One version, understood to have come from General René Cogny, claims that the Vulture project involved three atomic bombs. This version is refuted in other French sources, but a Pentagon targeting study concluded that precisely three A-bombs properly distributed would be optimal for the destruction of Giap's army around Dien Bien Phu. Richard Nixon in his own memoirs baldly confirms that three nuclear weapons were involved.

Drew Pearson, a well-informed journalist, noted in his diary on April 11 that "the Pentagon is definitely considering the use of small atomic bombs in that area."[22]

The question of atomic weapons in the 1954 Indochina crisis probably cannot be fully resolved. No records were taken of some crucial meetings. Records from some others were extracted from the files in an "Operation Clean Up" performed on the President's papers when Eisenhower left office. Even the conventional air strike option in Vulture was closely held at the time, so closely that the Far East Air Force commander could complain to Washington that he had never received express orders about it. It is not surprising that considerations of atomic weapons use would be more secret still.

On April 24, Mr. Dulles again explained to the French that he was sure of congressional authorization for intervention only *if* the British were going along. The problem was to convince Anthony Eden and, through him, the Churchill government. In these discussions Dulles consistently minimized potential political difficulties in the United States.

Anthony Eden, who probably thought he had already heard too much about Dien Bien Phu, was told a great deal more, by both the French and the Americans. Foreign Secretary Eden met with Dulles and Radford, who had arrived in Paris that morning, at the American Embassy residence at about 3:30 P.M.

Dulles opened the conversation by declaring that it appeared there was no chance to keep the French fighting in Indochina unless they knew that the Americans and British "were going to be in there with them."

He declared that there was little possibility of an air intervention at Dien Bien Phu because the President did not have the authority to act with such rapidity. In any event, Radford doubted an air strike could be successful in the sense of preventing the fall of the entrenched camp.

Dulles then read most of a cable from Saigon that described the poor military situation and made it appear, in Dulles's estimation, that the camp could last only three or four more days. Dulles's next remark was recorded in a memorandum of conversation: "The Secretary concluded by saying that if the British would go along with us the President was then prepared to seek Congressional approval for intervention by the United States with its Armed Forces in Indochina, but that an essential element in securing such approval would be the fact that it was firmly based on joint action."

Eden asked what exactly the United States wanted from his government. Admiral Radford replied to this that some "prompt military contribution" would be suitable. He suggested an aircraft carrier, one of which Sir Anthony confirmed was then sailing Malayan waters, or squadrons of the Royal Air Force.

Eden insisted that the French seemed to be telling the United Kingdom something much different from what they were telling the Americans. British opinion was that the French intended to carry on in Indochina.

Radford thought it likely the whole Indochina situation could get completely out of control after the fall of the entrenched camp. He had in mind the "serious risk of growing defections" from the Vietnamese national army, riots in Saigon and Hanoi with possible danger of attendant massacres of French civilians, plus the danger to isolated French military units throughout the country.

Anthony Eden rose to the occasion, at least rhetorically. The British foreign secretary answered that his country was an "ally," with all that this implied. He would urgently consider what he had been told and was inclined to think in terms of a quick trip back to London to consult with Prime Minister Churchill and the British chiefs of staff. But Eden reiterated that "he did not think that air intervention would alter the situation."

Radford agreed that positive results could not be guaranteed. But he felt it would have a great psychological effect on the Vietnamese and would prevent them from turning against the French: "the very announcement of our intention to intervene would stabilize the situation." It would be a demonstration that France had powerful allies.

Mr. Eden then asked about the effect on world opinion and particularly on the People's Republic of China:

> *Admiral Radford answered that he had never thought that the Chinese Communists would intervene if we went into Indochina. In any event he felt their capability for intervention was very low. He said he doubted that there were any Chinese Communist troops now in Indochina and that it would be difficult to introduce them in large numbers. He said there might be some limited air action by the Chinese Communists over Indochina but that this could be dealt with.*

Indeed, the admiral pointed out that the airfields in southeast China were very vulnerable to bombing, which would eliminate the Chinese air threat.

Dulles declared, "Our military authorities say that if Indochina goes, the only effective deterrent measures open to us would be those directed at Communist China itself." He claimed that "our military were thinking in terms of a blockade of the China coast, the seizure of Hainan and other measures."

The implications of war with China were staggering. Anthony Eden dryly remarked that, after all, there still existed an alliance between the People's Republic of China and the Soviet Union.

It was Radford who answered. He "did not think the Soviets would start a world war now." They would only do so at a time of their choosing and they "could not be provoked into a war." The American admiral conceded that the risk must be taken into account, but "the acceptance of risks is necessary in order to avoid being nibbled to death."[23]

The meeting continued inconclusively, breaking up after little more than half an hour because a discussion among the French, British, and American secretaries of state was due to begin shortly. At the second meeting Dulles again opened the discussion, this time turning to Georges Bidault and saying it was of the utmost importance to know the views of the French government in the event of the fall of Dien Bien Phu. Mr. Dulles had received a cable from Eisenhower that afternoon in which the President furnished the text for a letter to go to Joseph Laniel, asking the French prime minister for a public statement of France's willingness to continue the Indochina war despite the outcome of Dien Bien Phu. Eisenhower told Dulles to use this letter at his discretion, redraft it if necessary, but use it quickly. Instead, Dulles raised the question directly with Bidault.

Bidault emphasized the symbolic importance of Dien Bien Phu and argued that defeat there would have serious consequences for the French military position in Tonkin. Bidault himself and Laniel would certainly wish to continue the fight, and he would do his best, but "in all honesty and frankness" Bidault could not assure the United States of the French government's reaction to defeat.

Next, Dulles returned to the matter of intervention, referring to Navarre's cable of the previous day. Dulles said he had put down in the form of a draft letter the kind of response he would make to the French request. It again stated that "war action under such circumstances as now prevail should be preceded by a Congressional authorization," in no way attainable in a matter of hours, nor attainable at all except within the framework of "united action."

Secretary Dulles's letter went on to point out that his military advice was that intervention at this juncture could not assure lifting the siege at Dien Bien Phu. But, there was no reason why fall of the camp should be regarded as a drastic alteration of the overall military position. Nevertheless, "the issues of the hour are of the utmost gravity. So far as we are concerned, they evoke a determination to combine ever more closely and vigorously with our trusted allies, among whom we include France. . . . We believe that it is the nature of our nations to react vigorously to temporary setbacks and to surmount them."[24]

Eden was concerned about the implication in all this that the United Kingdom was somehow already committed to armed action. He recalls his report to Churchill: "It is now quite clear that we shall have to take a decision of first-class importance, namely whether to tell the Americans that we are prepared to go along with their plan or not."[25]

After a meeting with Prime Minister Laniel, Dulles returned to the American Embassy residence, where there was a buffet dinner for the senior delegates, who would soon be departing for Geneva and the long-awaited conference. Also at the buffet was the ubiquitous Cyrus Sulzberger, who had just met Radford and found him "less sturdy" than expected. The Secretary of State confirmed to the journalist that the French had requested the intervention of American aircraft manned by American crews. Dulles made it sound as if the French did not understand American law very well, but, significantly, Dulles admitted that the request might be regarded differently if there existed actually a Southeast Asian regional alliance.

For Cyrus Sulzberger this was too much. In the past weeks the papers had been full of talk about intervention in Indochina, but the reports had always been vague and without reference to specific projects. Sulzberger had gotten part of the Vulture story from Paul Ely already, and at lunch earlier in the day he was able to correct Dulles's press spokesman, Carl McCardle, who was not sure whether American crews were included in the French aid request. Now he had confirmation directly from John Foster Dulles. Sulzberger went to his typewriter and wrote a story that appeared on the front page of *The New York Times* on Sunday, April 25. In his lead paragraph Sulzberger wrote, "France has asked for direct large-scale intervention in the Indochina war by United States aircraft manned by American crews."[26] Operation Vulture was no longer a secret.

The Churchill Cabinet gathered for an unusual Sunday morning meeting at eleven o'clock on April 25. The Cabinet unanimously adopted an eight-point policy paper by Eden as its position. This paper declared that the United Kingdom had not committed itself to any action in Indochina, that it was "not prepared to give any undertaking now, in advance of the Geneva conference, concerning United Kingdom military action in Indochina" or about action in the event of failure to reach agreement in Geneva. The only concession to the American point of view was agreement to hold military conversations soon on measures that could ensure the defense of Southeast Asia in case Indochina was lost.

Admiral Radford spent April 25 at NATO headquarters in Rocquencourt, officially to attend the beginning of the annual SHAPE wargame. President Eisenhower told Bedell Smith he should cable Radford and tell him to ask the British "baldly" why they seemed to prefer to fight after "they have lost 200,000 French," rather than immediately, while the French were still powerful in Indochina. Radford traveled to London on Monday, April 26 to meet with the British chiefs of staff.

Field Marshal Sir John Harding had a frank exchange of views with Radford. The British military opinion was just what Anthony Eden had been telling Foster Dulles it was. Harding was convinced he could continue to hold Malaya regardless of the Indochina outcome. Since they believed military action could not have a decisive effect, the British chiefs preferred to do nothing even though they agreed that the loss of Indochina would have grave consequences. Harding also emphasized the high risk of expanding the war by intervention at this time.

Radford reported on the meeting through Ambassador Winthrop Aldrich in London. He felt the British chiefs maximized the risks and potential requirements while minimizing "our collective capabilities." He did not think the British were "squarely facing up" to the prospects for Thailand, Burma, Indonesia, "or any part of Indochina that may temporarily be held by a possible Geneva settlement." Arthur Radford felt the British were basing themselves on " 'narrow' local UK interest."

As Admiral Radford reported his plans:

> I am having dinner with Sir Winston tonight and will continue to state the position taken by Secretary Dulles with Mr. Eden, also emphasizing [the] point that a united front including the US and France now might afford the only opportunity to take any positive action to save Southeast Asia from loss to the Communists one way or another.

Radford noted that he had not mentioned to the British chiefs "the adverse effect on the US Congress and US public opinion of their not standing firmly with the United States," but he expected. "I will make this point evident to Mr. Churchill tonight."[27]

At eight o'clock that evening Admiral Radford arrived at Churchill's country home, Chequers. "Raddy" recalls the occasion as one of the most interesting of his career.

Churchill began by referring to the British decision to give up India in 1947, which had occurred while Sir Winston was in opposition. Although Churchill had been angry then that a nation was being given up over which Britain had maintained control for 250 years, the Indochina situation had to be seen against this background. If Britain had given up India, how could she be ex-

pected now to participate in an exercise to preserve French colonialism in Indochina?

Churchill "was not in any position to convince the people of
England that they should make any investment of their limited
resources to hold Indochina."

Radford explained his own analysis. He had grave apprehen-
sions about the future of Indochina and Southeast Asia unless
there were a "united action." Radford had no illusion that air
action could at this point save Dien Bien Phu, but "the action
taken or not taken would certainly have a very important effect
on the future."

Churchill agreed it was quite probable that there would be a
chain reaction of sorts whose effects would be far-reaching, but
the British prime minister was convinced Britain could hold Malaya and this would be its special contribution to the regional
situation. There was a great danger of general war, given Soviet
possession of atomic and hydrogen weapons, and the proper
course was to settle East-West problems at a summit conference
among himself and the American and Soviet leaders. It was folly
to "squander our limited resources around the fringes."[28]

Admiral Radford stated his impressions clearly in a memorandum for the record he wrote the next day:

*It is quite obvious that the Prime Minister is very much con-
cerned over the possibility that by participating in an action to
save Indochina the war would spread to China, then the Soviet
Union might become involved and a major war result. It was clear
to me that his present thinking is to avoid the risk of such a
possibility even at the ultimate cost of other areas of Southeast
Asia with the exception of Malaya . . .*

*I can not escape the conclusion that the Prime Minister, the
British Cabinet, and the British Chiefs of Staff are not adequately
facing up to the problems of collective security except where they
are definitely identified with their own idea of safeguarding some*

British territory.[29] Clearly the British incurred this wrath from "Raddy" because they would not agree to what he wished of them—participation in "united action." Sir Winston Churchill dispelled any doubts on this score on April 27, when the Prime Minister rose in Parliament to declare that the United Kingdom would make no undertakings on Indochina in advance of the Geneva negotiation.

Eisenhower remained at Augusta on a working vacation. Eisenhower's cottage at the National Golf Club there, called the "Little White House," was not set up to conduct the full business of government. The President often thought through issues and occasionally held meetings while golfing, but that spring the President's golf partners were mostly corporate executives, old Army buddies, and, several times, golf pro Sam Snead. But Ike's vacation was fast coming to an end.

On April 22 the President flew to New York for a major speech to the American Newspaper Publishers Association at the Waldorf-Astoria Hotel.

Following the Waldorf speech Eisenhower went back to Washington for the night before flying to Kentucky the next day. The party reached home late, not arriving at the D.C. airport terminal until 11:30 P.M. A tired Press Secretary Hagerty noted in his diary that the universal reaction among the newspaper publishers had been, " 'You have to educate the people more on Indochina.' They contend that the average citizen does not know where Indochina is, does not realize we have to move in eventually."[30] All had urged Hagerty to get Ike to clarify the reasons for the Indochina problem and American interest in it.

President Eisenhower responded to these informal suggestions. In Lexington the President warned that public opinion that was not based upon "fact—fact as seen in its proper perspective"—could go wrong.

Ike declared, "We cannot live alone," and went on to say that "the words 'Dien Bien Phu' are no longer just a funny-sounding name, to be dismissed from the breakfast conversation because we don't know where it is." The conflict had become a "testing ground" between freedom and dictatorship. If the Associated States fell, they would be "mere additional pawns in the machinations of a power-hungry group in the Kremlin and in China."

The core of the President's message lay in a reiteration of the domino theory so recently publicized. Ike said that "when we begin to picture the possibility of more hundreds of millions, starting with this neck in the bottle in Indochina, spread all over Southeast Asia and through the great islands of the Pacific, then we begin to get an understanding of what your representatives in international conferences are striving to preserve for you: basically the same freedom that your Founders brought to this spot."[31]

Jim Hagerty's diary entry for April 24 deserves to be quoted in full:

Staff on an hour's call to return to Washington because of Indochina. Situation getting very grave and it may be necessary to support French troops at Dien Bien Phu with two aircraft carriers we have off the coast. French would like us to send in these planes for a quick strike. Of course, if we do use them we will probably never admit it, but decision to assist the French by use of American planes will be a very calculated risk and could lead to war.[32]

On April 23 Admiral "Sol" Phillip's Task Force 70 was ordered to prepare for sea. In Japan, at the naval base at Yokosuka, Rear Admiral Harry D. Felt was at the officer's club when the Far East naval forces chief of staff came over and told him to get back to his ship for a message. That dispatch directed Felt to give up his anti-submarine warfare group and get down to the Philippines overnight, where he would take over Carrier Division 3 in Phillips's task force. Admiral Felt flew to Subic Bay, and ordered the skippers of his new ships to assemble ashore for a conference. Before Felt could talk to his captains they were addressed by Pacific commander Admiral Felix Stump, who not coincidentally happened to be at Subic Bay for this encounter. Shortly after going aboard his new flagship Admiral Felt received sealed orders marked "open when ready." They were for the Gulf of Tonkin cruise under Sol Phillips.

Felt at first took *Essex* out en route for Japan while carriers *Boxer* and *Philippine Sea*, which now formed the core of the group steamed into the South China Sea, first from April 26 to 28, then again from May 3 to 7. On May 8 Phillips returned to Manila, but left again for the South China Sea from the 11th to the 15th. The next few days were spent back at Manila, where the *Essex* rejoined. Significantly, the *Essex* had carried out a special communications exercise of a type possibly associated with atomic weapons, had landed sixteen AD-4 aircraft capable of carrying these weapons, and had conducted flight training off Okinawa while on the way south. During the cruise Felt's staff prepared and presented briefings on the situation in Indochina and on Soviet submarine developments. The special weapons officer, who responsible for tactical nuclear weapons, organized a weapons and communications exercise. Intelligence officers briefed on Chinese air, naval, and ground forces, while the photo interpretation section prepared target mosaics and pilots were given general target briefings. Phillips conducted yet another sortie into the South China Sea after the *Essex* rejoined, this time sending home the *Boxer,* which had had so many problems. Robert Kirshner, a young pilot aboard the *Philippine Sea*, recalls that like so many others in different parts of these Indochina operations, he and his comrades were sworn to secrecy during these cruises, when the aviators felt like "we were going in any minute." There were "quite interesting events" in the Gulf of Tonkin, Kirshner remembers.[33]

Admiral Phillips continued to steam into the South China Sea right into the summer of 1954 and kept up a high rate of flight activity.

The fleet made several cruises into the Gulf of Tonkin. The carrier *Boxer*'s Air Group 12 averaged over 1,350 flight hours monthly from March to June. Aboard *Philippine Sea* Air Group 5 logged 1,140 sorties in May, only exceeded by *Essex*, which launched 1,367 sorties totaling almost two thousand flight hours. By contrast, Air Group 5 had the highest number of active "service," as opposed to training flight hours, including a large proportion of both reconnaissance and anti-submarine flights.

In three separate instances in the Gulf of Tonkin American aircraft obtained radar sightings of Soviet or Chinese submarines. French naval authorities later reported intercepting Viet Minh radio transmissions referring to six or eight of the undersea craft.

While some French intelligence sources disputed the report as "disinformation," surfaced submarines, possibly Chinese, physically challenged an American freighter inbound to Haiphong on the night of May 5.

It was nine on the night of April 25 before the presidential plane landed at Washington's National Airport after Ike's political swing through Kentucky. When he got back to the White House, however, Eisenhower found new reports from Paris and London awaiting him. Hagerty's impression was that the "British [are] getting weak-kneed on cooperative effort" while the French were "really wilting." The French had "put all their eggs at Dien Bien Phu. . . . Why I'll never know."[34]

On Monday morning, April 26, the President's first activity back in Washington was to meet with a gathering of Republican legislative leaders. Present were Vice-President Richard Nixon and Senators William F. Knowland; Eugene Millikin, and Charles Halleck, among others.

Eisenhower turned to Indochina after a discussion of Guatemala. The French were "weary as hell" and the President did not know what might happen next; it did not look as if Dien Bien Phu could hold out more than another week and it might fall sooner than that. Ike warned that there could be "tremendous consequences" ahead and that the leaders should keep in mind the possibility that some U.S. combat units might become involved in Indochina.

If the United States were to put as much as "one combat soldier" in Indochina, then its entire prestige would be at stake. Ike referred to the French request for an air strike and repeated that there would be no unilateral intervention. "The French go up and down every day—they are very voluble. They thin[k] they are a great power one day and they feel sorry for themselves the next."

As for the British, the President admitted that the Churchill government was not favorably disposed toward intervention. The United States would not go it alone "in a power move against the Russians."

Senator Knowland warned that "they'll say we're not facing up to the situation."

"Well, they've said that before," answered Eisenhower, who went on to relate the current situation with criticism of previous administrations for nonintervention or not going far enough in China in the 1940s and Manchuria in the 1930s.

Richard Nixon and House leader Millikin emphasized that allies' reactions were disappointing. "Eventually there has to be a showdown on this question of whether the US government intends to oppose aggression overseas." If allies did not go along, there must be a review of the situation, then "the sooner we bail out the better."

Eisenhower posed the dilemma of "bailing out": It was no longer possible to fight just a defensive war, "if allies go back on us, then we would have one terrible alternative—we would have to attack with everything we have."

Senator Knowland remarked that it seemed desirable therefore to get a thorough briefing on Soviet atomic potential then and four years into the future.

Representative Millikin then remarked that "the Fortress America idea is a damned foolish one, but the day may come when we will have to resort to it."

"Listen, Gene," the President responded with evident anger, "if the day ever comes we ever come back to Fortress America, then the word 'fortress' will be entirely wrong. . . . Dien Bien Phu is a perfect example of a fortress and the Reds are surrounding it. . . . If we ever came back to the fortress idea for America, we would have, as I said before, one simple dreadful alternative—we would have to explode an attack with everything we have. What a terrible decision that would be to make."[35]

That day at the Washington bureau of *The New York Times*, which had learned that the French planned one more air drop of reinforcements into Dien Bien Phu, reporter Bill Lawrence volunteered to jump into the doomed fortress with the French paratroopers. Bureau chief James Reston responded with a note, "Look, you coward, go on back up to the Hill and cover McCarthy."[36]

XI

GENEVA AND THE FALL OF DIEN BIEN PHU

For the French, collecting supplies dropped from planes had become a critical problem. Viet Minh trenches and bunkers closely invested the French positions; there was no possibility of leaving the camp to retrieve badly dropped supply containers. The People's Army had also captured enough positions to have the entire French position under constant observation, if not direct fire. With this advantage the Viet Minh artillery could break up any daytime move.

Equally important for the troops at Dien Bien Phu was the ability to distribute supplies among the garrison. French capacity to move supplies over the ground had fallen to critical levels. Before the battle then-Colonel de Castries had possessed twenty-six heavy trucks and ninety light vehicles and jeeps for ground mobility. By April 21 the available vehicles were down to three trucks and a few jeeps. The last trucks were destroyed in an artillery barrage that night.

On April 24 the Paris newspapers printed news that the disengagement operation from Laos had begun. But Operation Condor was only a matter of a few battalions that might claw their way up the Laotian river valleys. It was no match for Giap's Viet-Nam People's Army. At the entrenched camp De Castries began in great secrecy to plan for his garrison to break out from Dien Bien Phu. It was a very desperate maneuver that merited its code name, Operation Albatross.

The next day there was a conference of senior officers in the command bunker at Dien Bien Phu. Under naked light bulbs Langlais reviewed the situation with De Castries, Bigeard, and other officers. Intelligence put Giap's combat strength at twenty-eight battalions for certain, probably thirty, with four heavy artillery groups. Effectives were thought to be 35,000 infantry, 15,000 artillery and support troops, and 30,000 porters. Total French strength in the main area of the camp was put at between 4,000 and 5,000—and of these there were only 3,620 infantry (1,300 paratroopers, another 500 Foreign Legion paratroops, 700 regular Legionnaires, 500 tribal Thais, 300 Moroccans, and 200 Algerians).

While the entrenched camp slowly bled to death, the French generals argued about dispatching reinforcements. Henri Navarre and René Cogny exchanged memoranda, no longer able to speak face-to-face. The Tonkin theater commander wrote of the "moral value of sacrifice" and predicted that the entrenched camp might last another three weeks, *if* reinforced by an additional paratroop battalion, and *if* the Viet Minh *did not* step up the level of their attacks. Navarre was irritated at this posturing and in his reply pointed to positive political and military reasons that justified reinforcements for the garrison.

Most significantly, General Navarre now hoped for a solution from the Geneva conference—either a cease-fire or an American intervention. (This phrase in an April 26, 1954, document belies Navarre's defense in his memoirs that he was defeated because France had agreed to negotiate at Geneva.) The Expeditionary Corps could only take advantage of American intervention at Dien Bien Phu if the garrison's resistance were prolonged until that moment. Navarre still believed that Operation Vautour would be carried out by the Americans. In fact he probably expected the implementation of a scenario that called for President Eisenhower to go to Congress with a resolution for use of force on April 28.

The French commander in chief did not know of the political impediments in Washington and London obstructing any intervention.

Brigadier Caldara, at that moment still in Hanoi, insisted a radio navigation beacon would be necessary for any raid. Caldara's B-29s had bombing radars, and in fact an RB-50C flew over Dien Bien Phu the night of April 30 to get a radar photo to enable the B-29s to calibrate their own terrain imaging radars, but the system was far from perfect. The limestone topography around Dien Bien Phu may also have played havoc with radar returns. In any case, Caldara not only insisted on the radio beacon to Navarre, but forwarded those comments to Partridge in Tokyo and General Curtis LeMay at the Strategic Air Command.

"Smokey" Caldara was also under orders to send his 19th Bomb Wing to Guam. This restricted any possible Vulture strike to at most sixty aircraft. The latter was not as bad as it sounds, however, for the smaller flight meant easier coordination. In fact FEAF Bomber Command had never carried out an air attack as large as the 98 B-29s in its force. Caldara wanted to preposition his bombers at Clark Field but the orders never came. Vulture was mired between its political difficulties and operational problems.

On April 28, instead of news of an American congressional resolution on intervention, Navarre received General Paul Ely's top-secret cable no. 21. The cable confirmed that there was no chance of the American air strike being carried out. The same day, Cogny wired from Hanoi that a negotiated settlement in Indochina would now, in his opinion, be better than any other outcome.

The garrison at Dien Bien Phu knew none of this. They knew only of the prowess of Viet Minh flak, which achieved a *coup dur* on April 26 by shooting down four combat aircraft, two B-26s and two fighter-bombers, in one day. Only 161 volunteer replacements arrived at the entrenched camp during the duration of the Civil Air Transport "strike"—French quartermasters had had to choose between Dakota loads of supplies or of men. Yet since Easter the garrison had lost 900 in wounded alone. To improve morale the French command finally determined to send another battalion to Dien Bien Phu.

Meanwhile, in the hills around the camp the Viet Minh held a conference of party cadre and Viet-Nam People's Army field commanders. General Vo Nguyen Giap addressed the assemblage on April 29. Giap obliquely referred to the Viet Minh morale crisis early in April by criticizing party committees for showing "little boldness in promoting and training new cadres," for neglecting to pick out heroes and "model fighters" and cite them as examples. A "heroic fighting spirit" was the best expression of ideological firmness and the essential criterion for promotion of cadres. Viet Minh cadres, Giap charged, had let slip many opportunities for strengthening both the party and the army.[1]

Giap humbled his audience, but he also thrilled them. He did not confine himself to criticism. He told the assembled cadres that he felt the conditions now warranted a general offensive against Dien Bien Phu. He was determined to wrest a decisive victory from the French.

Late in the morning of April 29, Dwight Eisenhower held a crucial meeting of the National Security Council, the 194th reunion of this advisory body. After discussions on rubber, conditions in Iran, internal security, and defense mobilization, the council spent the last hour and three quarters on Indochina.

Walter Bedell Smith read a cable from Foster Dulles in which the Secretary of State was pessimistic but asserted he would hold firm on the U.S. position. Admiral Radford reported on his own talks in Paris and London. Then Allen Dulles of the CIA spoke of the military situation at the entrenched camp: The French garrison had fallen to about 8,500 infantry and 1,200 artillerymen against at least 40,000 troops in the Viet-Nam People's Army. A national intelligence estimate on the consequences within Indochina of a French defeat was being completed at CIA and would shortly be circulated.

Harold Stassen thought the United States should send ground troops if necessary to save Indochina, moving unilaterally if there was no other way.

The rejoinder came from Vice-President Richard Nixon. Nixon judged, he subsequently claimed, that winning the war in Viet-Nam was not necessarily a question "of committing a lot of ground troops to combat."[2] Nixon preferred "an Air Force contingent" and he argued that air strikes would have psychological value, they would demonstrate that the United States had drawn a line to be crossed only at the peril of other nations.

Ike himself then followed with a startling declaration. The President could not visualize a ground-troop operation in Indochina that would not unbalance U.S. defenses in the long run. "Unilateral" intervention was a violation of the principle of "collective defense" (e.g., NATO) espoused by the United States.

Eisenhower conceded that there was "some merit" in the assumption that an air strike would result in temporary psychological improvements in Indochina. Ike had hoped that a regional grouping of Pacific and Asian nations would overcome British opposition to "united action." Unfortunately Australia had declined.

The President said, "If we, without allies, should ever find ourselves fighting at various places all over the region, and if Red Chinese aggressive participations were clearly identified, then we could scarcely avoid . . . considering the necessity of striking directly at the head rather than the tail of the snake."[3]

This meeting was the first time there is any record of the policy of threat being taken to its logical conclusion, the "head of the snake," China and ultimately the Soviet Union.

But the President could not choose atomic war with Russia to settle the Indochina crisis. Nor could he really choose war with China. The NSC meeting on April 29 listened as Allen Dulles briefed on the characteristics of the new all-jet Russian bomber, the Mya-4 BISON, similar to SAC's B-52. If China were attacked by the U.S. the Russians could retaliate. BISON became a reminder that Russia's rapidly rising strength could not be ignored.

On April 28/29 a British air crew working with the Air Force and CIA on dangerous overflights of the Soviet Union made a deep penetration mission and came back with pictures of Russian bomber bases in the Ukraine. On May 8 the U.S. Air Force sent RB-47 jet reconnaissance planes over the Russian forward bases in the Kola Peninsula that would have been used in any bomber attack on the Unite States. The Russians had not concentrated, but they could. At any time.

Thus in some respects the National Security Council decision was predetermined. Ike and Foster could rail at the British, but confronted with the military realities, Eisenhower's decision was no different than Sir Winston Churchill's and for the same reasons.

Hitting golf balls on the White House lawn that afternoon, Ike told Jim Hagerty that the NSC meeting had been "quite controversial."

*   *   *

Late on Saturday afternoon, May 1, Giap began his general offensive with a massive artillery barrage at the center of resistance of Dien Bien Phu.

The battle began that night when the "Iron Division," the oldest formation of the People's Army, made an attack upon Huguette-5, held by the composite Foreign Legion paratroopers. An immediate counterattack by the French unit regained its positions by morning. There were other assaults on the support strongpoint Isabelle. The next night the attack shifted to the Five Hills sector, where there were strong Viet Minh drives on all the major French hill positions.

Unbeknownst to the assault troops this action was observed by the crew of an American RB-50 photo plane that had come from Hawaii to scout Dien Bien Phu. Briefed at Clark Field to maintain radio silence unless he saw major naval forces in the Gulf of Tonkin, aircraft commander Albert J. Lauer did that, in spite of the pyrotechnics of the battle 10,000 feet below his plane, which made it clear the Viets had amassed huge firepower. The scout plane actually blundered into China, although that would not be known until its radar imagery was analyzed back home. What broke his resolve, however, was seeing big warships in the dark in the South China Sea. Lauer got on the radio and reported the flotilla as he saw it, sending the transmission in the clear, unencoded. He had reported Admiral Phillips's Task Group 70.2. Lauer felt chagrin afterwards that he had, in effect, informed the enemy of the position of the U.S. fleet.

At last some reinforcements were sent from the Red River delta. But no mass drops were made. Instead the 1st Colonial Paratroop Battalion was dribbled in piecemeal over several nights. The first men parachuted in on the night of May 2–3.

One could sense the impending disaster in Hanoi, where fewer French soldiers strolled the shores of the Petit Lac with their Vietnamese girl friends. There were more armed convoys than ever and also a steady stream of couriers and staff cars crossing the Doumer Bridge en route to the Citadel. It was little more than a block from the Petit Lac to the Hotel Metropole, where many Americans stayed while in Hanoi and where one could often meet senior officers of the French Army. The atmosphere at the Metropole was decidedly downbeat.

Two Americans, Marty Reisman and Doug Cartland, were in Hanoi to play Ping-Pong—in a tournament arranged by a Chinese promoter. Reisman saw a good deal of the city during the early days of May, though he had to be inside before the 8:00 P.M. curfew.

At dinner with a French officer Reisman saw the iron grillworks erected at many restaurants to fend off guerrilla grenades, while he was told of how Dien Bien Phu was at the bottom of a valley and trapped by the Viet Minh on the heights around it. French soldiers in Hanoi showed genuine concern for their comrades at Dien Bien Phu but "true Gallic indifference" to the inevitable outcome. Walking back to the Metropole, Reisman decided, "war-weariness sauntered the city like an aging streetwalker."⁴

At Dien Bien Phu the French could not afford to be weary, even though many men were past exhaustion. Giap continued the Viet Minh attacks every night. In the daytime the monsoon rained down on soldiers in waterlogged trenches. Lieutenant Colonel Pierre Langlais had run out of resources for the defense; on May 2, Dien Bien Phu reported it had no reserves left. That night the French parachuted in 107 men of the 2nd Company, 1st Colonial Paratroops under Lieutenant Marcel Edmé. Langlais's losses that day stood at about 420 troops. At a command conference in Navarre's Hanoi office the next day, and despite the opposition of Cogny, the commander in chief personally decided to reinforce the entrenched camp with the remainder of the 1st Colonial Paratroop Battalion, in order that the garrison could hold out at least until a cease-fire was reached at Geneva. Navarre hoped some troops could break out from the camp, but he reportedly ordered that no formal surrender of the garrison could be allowed.

While the French generals met and first spoke the dreaded word *surrender*, at Dien Bien Phu the Viet Minh renewed their assault on Huguette. During the night of May 3–4 they mounted the largest ground attack against a single position of the battle—seven battalions from the 308th and 312th divisions, containing over 3,000 men, against Huguette-4, which was defended by an 80-man "company" of mixed Moroccan and Foreign Legion troops. The French managed to assemble barely 100 soldiers plus their tank "Auerstadt" for a counterattack in the early hours of May 4, but against such odds no attack could possibly succeed. The Viet Minh retained control of Huguette-4, while the only result of the counterattack was French expenditure of 3,800 artillery shells. If the French continued to use this much artillery, they could expect to run out of ammunition the following day.

The French garrison checked its fire on May 5, but this did not stop either the Viet Minh or the rain. Virtually every battalion now was reporting to Langlais that water was turning their bunkers to mud and that these were collapsing. Some of the worst ground was in the Five Hills sector where the positions of Dominique and Eliane had repeatedly been barraged by Vu Hien's 351st Heavy Division artillery. In particular on Eliane-2 the French had discovered that the Viet Minh were tunneling into the hill *underneath* the defenses. Giap's engineers had concocted a plan to blow up the crest of Eliane-2 with a mine stuffed with explosives. Now the mine was nearly finished.

Meanwhile there were problems in the air, not only with the French but among the American CAT crews. The CIA proprietary pilots had pitched in initially as daredevils. In March they had been dropping from altitudes of less than five thousand feet over Dien Bien Phu. A couple of the C-119s had been hit but there were no loses during the 87 missions flown that month. With an additional regiment of Viet-Minh (Chinese?) anti-aircraft guns, drop altitudes increased. At six thousand five hundred feet in April CAT continued to drop from more dangerous altitudes than French transport pilots, who were soon above ten thousand feet. The Americans were unhappy with the support they got from the French air force. Pilot Stuart E. Dew, who logged thirteen missions to Dien Bien Phu, typified the feelings of many of the Americans when he said that "the fighters were supposed to go in and shoot up the anti-aircraft installations, but they never flew as low as we did to drop. They didn't have their hearts in it." In early April the pilots began a work slowdown that critically affected the supply situation at the entrenched camp. Civil Air Transport officials came from Taiwan to talk the CAT crews into keeping up the pace. On the night of April 19–20 both the CAT and French pilots refused to descend to an altitude low enough for accurate parachute drops even though told there was no anti-aircraft fire at all. Eventually CAT plans would complete 428 flights during April. Americans were flying twenty-four of the twenty-nine C-119s in the French air force inventory. Al Judkins led the CAT team with 64 Dien Bien Phu missions, Steve Kusak was second with 59, and nine CAT pilots logged more than fifty flights to the besieged fortress. Allen Pope had 57. Sixteen more pilots had between thirty and fifty Dien Bien Phu missions under their belts.

Nevertheless the dangers were real. American-flown C-119s suffered more than sixty hits over Dien Bien Phu in April. Then on April 24 CAT chief pilot Paul R. Holden was severely wounded as his plane approached the entrenched camp. His right arm was saved by U.S. surgeons at Clark Air Force Base. James B. McGovern and another CAT pilot joked about which man was a "magnet" attracting flak fire, especially when McGovern's C-119 lost its elevator controls to flak on a sortie in early May.

McGovern, popularly known as "Earthquake McGoon" after a character in the *li'l Abner* comic strip, was a legend in Civil Air Transport. He had been a member of the Flying Tigers, rising to captain during World War II. McGovern signed on with CAT and flew in the Chinese civil war, including daring escape missions in a light plane, unusual for a man who weighed almost three hundred pounds. When the CAT pilots arrived in Indochina, "McGoon" startled the French by hauling a refrigerator, no doubt for beer, out of his plane. It was McGovern who dropped René Cogny's general's stars to Christian de Castries when De Castries was promoted to brigadier. On May 6, a day when the CAT pilots flew eighteen sorties, "McGoon" drew for copilot the man with whom he had been joking. It was McGovern's forty-sixth flight to Dien Bien Phu.

"Earthquake McGoon" did not come back that day. Of course there had been signs and portents. McGoon had previously had a conversation with Colonel Maurice Casey of the 483rd Troop Carrier Wing, the Air Force's supervisory authority over the CIA proprietary pilots, about what to do if damaged. Casey had told Earthquake not to crash land his airplane under any circumstances. McGovern had rubbed his forehead and replied, "But sir, there isn't a parachute that'll hold me!"[5] On May 6 McGovern's co-pilot was Wallace Buford, one of the Air Force pilots who had switched to CAT. Buford had been Paul Holden's co-pilot on April 24, when the chief pilot suffered his wounds, and was the very man with whom McGoon had joked about being flak magnets.

Leveling off over strongpoint Isabelle, where McGovern was

supposed to drop a 105mm howitzer rigged to a triple canopy parachute, his Packet sustained a direct hit in its left wing, damaging the leading surface and the engine. Wingman Steve Kusak, with whom McGovern had laid plans for a quick trip to Saigon to dine at the Croix du Sud bar, listened over the radio as "Earthquake" described his damage. So did off-duty Air Force and CAT personnel at Cat Bi. Kusak advised Earthquake to bail out and promised to order up a rescue helicopter. McGovern had no desire to be marooned in Viet Minh country and asked for a compass heading to Haiphong over the lowest terrain possible. Leaking oil, McGovern had to shut down his left engine. The plane gradually lost altitude. Finally his wingtip hit the trees atop a hill sending the plane into a cartwheel and crash.

Kusak continued to fly alongside McGovern's plane until the tragedy. *His* co-pilot was the moonlighting Air Force commander, Ed Yarbrough, who photographed the crash of the CIA aircraft. The CAT detachment did not take at all well to the incident. The next day Civil Air Transport was not asked to make any missions at all.

Despite losses in the air, including two more B-26 bombers, by May 6 the French had landed about 400 men of the 1st Colonial Paratroops. The defenders were short or out of almost everything, from mortar shells to gun crews. There was only one tank left. The Viet Minh mine under Eliane-2 was completed. The People's Army stood poised for its final offensive.

The Geneva conference formally opened on April 26 with a plenary session on the Korean situation, which would be the business of its first phase. Except for the Chinese delegation, excited by participation in their first international conference, and the permanent staff of the Palais des Nations, there were few smiling faces in the obligatory photographs taken opening day. The publicly declared American stand was to do nothing to hinder achievement of a Far East modus vivendi, but the government's instructions to the delegation exhorted it to take a "positive and definite" position not to agree to any settlement compromising United States objectives in Southeast Asia.

While official Korean talks proceeded, quiet negotiations arranged the second phase of Geneva—talks on the Indochina question. There was still no movement for "united action." Dulles reported to the President on April 29 that the British attitude was one of "increasing weakness," and that "we do not have anyone on the French side with whom we can make any dependable agreements." The Secretary of State observed some "French discounting" of the effect of the fall of Dien Bien Phu, due to the continued resistance of the camp.

In this cable Dulles even suggested an alternative military strategy: to "end the scattering and exposure of military forces for local political reasons," regroup them all in "defensible enclaves in deltas where they would have US sea and air protection," and use the bases to develop effective Vietnamese forces, perhaps over two years' time.[6]

Dulles admitted he did not know about the military feasibility of this scheme and he noted that his military advisor, Vice Admiral Arthur C. Davis, seemed to think it difficult. Radford commented that the proposal was "certainly not desirable from a military standpoint." He felt the strategy would commit the United States to a defensive concept "at a time when an offensive spirit would be most important to enhance the morale and support of the native populations."[7]

On Friday, April 30, there was another in the series of discussions between Dulles and Anthony Eden. The Secretary of State was indignant at the "invective" heaped on the United States in the plenary sessions of the Korean conference by the

Chinese and North Koreans. Dulles accused the British of standing silently by as the insults flew. This led to an outburst in which the British were also accused of reneging on an agreement to participate in "united action" talks.

Anthony Eden responded that the United Kingdom really had not known what the United States had in mind—whether the proposal implied commitment to military action in Indochina, to which Britain could not agree. Dulles criticized Admiral Radford for remarks that had caused the British government to draw back, and claimed the United States was not seeking large-scale intervention in Indochina or war with China. It was precisely through a common show of strength that Dulles hoped to avert war. Eisenhower later observed that "the conversation did much to clarify to the British government our concern about our common problems in the Far East."[8]

In his diary columnist Drew Pearson wrote, "While the country is absorbed with McCarthy, Dulles is letting the peace of the world go down the drain at Geneva."[9]

Meanwhile, Bidault told the other Western diplomats that he had hardly a card in his hand, "perhaps just a two of clubs and a three of diamonds."[10]

The last important talks between Dulles and Eden occurred during the evening of May 1. Eden recalls the meeting as a prolonged "onslaught upon our attitude." The arguments were well worn by now and had been heard in many previous exchanges. But Foster Dulles went to the length of saying his impression was that the United Kingdom was not prepared to support the United States under any circumstances. Assistant Secretary Walter S. Robertson claimed there were 300,000 Vietnamese, Cambodians, and Laotians in Indochina anxious to fight the Viet Minh if only given support and matériel. Eden asked why, if the Indochinese were so anxious to fight, they did not do so. In the meantime Dulles answered, to a question from Lord Reading, that a bridgehead would have to be held. When Reading pointed out that such a course would keep things "on the boil" for several years, Dulles responded that that would be a very good thing.

One Eden observation also deserves quotation: "If the Americans went into the Indochina war, the Chinese would inevitably step up their participation. The next stage would be that the Americans and the Chinese would be fighting each other and that was in all probability the beginning of the third world war."[11]

Dulles departed for Washington on May 3, 1954. He would not again return to Geneva. He left the American delegation in the hands of Under Secretary "Beetle" Smith. Dulles was still bitter at the English, and some of them may privately have felt sympathy—Dennis Allen, Eden's Far East expert, was saying that "we are getting very near having cheated the Americans on this question of starting talks on SE Asian security."[12]

As for Eden himself, the British foreign secretary bravely continued his efforts at Geneva to prevent the war from turning into an international confrontation. His account of a dinner conversation and declaration to Molotov on May 5 is significant in that it emphasizes points previously made to Dulles. As Eden recounted it, "toward the end of our conversation, I said I would speak very frankly. If the Indochina situation was not handled effectively here at Geneva, there was a real danger that the supporters of each side would go on increasing the degree of their participation, until finally there was a clash between them."[13] Sir Anthony observed that this could be the beginning of a new world war. Molotov was said to be in entire agreement.

In Washington that Wednesday, Dulles reported back to President Eisenhower. He reviewed British opposition to intervention and noted that they were willing to pursue secret talks on the political-military scope of the planned coalition, as detailed in a memorandum on Southeast Asian defense presented by Eden on April 30. In an extensive briefing to twenty-five congressmen that afternoon, Dulles described the British opposition as rooted in the displeasure of Nehru and India, who were working hard to get a peaceful settlement in Indochina, and to an "almost pathological" fear of the hydrogen bomb. Thus, "the British gave a much higher rating than we did to the risk that open Western intervention in Indochina would lead to Chinese intervention and global war."[14]

The next morning Dulles's report was the first item on the agenda at the National Security Council. Foster felt an immediate decision in principle was desirable on the question of whether the United States was willing to commit its combat forces "in the near future, in some form of regional effort if possible," to prevent the partition or loss of Indochina. A related question was whether the United States was willing to "acquiesce" in the "clearly engineered Communist aggression" of the Viet Minh revolution, "even though we evaluate this loss as very serious and even though we have the military means to redeem the situation (The A-Bomb)."[15]

The articulation of these questions and the way they were phrased suggest the answers desired. Indeed, the National Security Council recommended that certain pressures be brought to bear on the French at least. Eisenhower was urged to tell Paris that being party to a Viet Minh "takeover" in Indochina would have consequences for France's status as a great power and for Franco-American relations in North Africa. The consequences in Europe and elsewhere would be without "apparent limitation." If France agreed to an unsatisfactory settlement, U.S. military aid would be halted immediately.

Finally, the United States, it was recommended, should approach the Associated States directly with a view to pursuing the war against the Viet Minh in another form, with unilateral American military involvement if necessary.

That afternoon the Indochina discussions were continued by the National Security Council Planning Board, where some, mainly the military members, thought the United States should not support the cease-fire proposal France was about to present at Geneva. Rather, the Planning Board recommended that "the US should (as a last act to save Indochina) propose to France that if . . . conditions are met, the US will go to Congress for authority to intervene with combat forces."[16]

The Planning Board option was discussed by President Eisenhower in a meeting with Foster Dulles and Robert Cutler on May 7. But by then it was far too late for Dien Bien Phu.

The final attack on the entrenched camp began on the evening of May 6. The People's Army's 316th Division waited until two hours before midnight and then assaulted Eliane-4. The initial attack fell against a thirty-man company of the 5th Vietnamese Parachute Battalion. Within a half hour the battalion commander was forced to call on his 3rd Company, under Captain Pham Van Phu, which had been resting in the rear after defending Eliane-2.

The Viet Minh also attacked Eliane-10, which was defended by Lieutenant Colonel Bigeard's old battalion, the 6th Colonial Paratroops. Here Lieutenant René Le Page bravely told the French commanders not to illuminate his own positions with flares, even though the defenders badly needed the light to use their weapons, so that French transport aircraft could drop more men into the camp. After a five-hour battle the 6th Colonial Paratroop Battalion was down to twenty men and held only the communications bunker of its position.

An hour after the first attacks Vo Nguyen Giap began his carefully prepared action against Eliane-2. For this attack the Viet Minh secretly shifted the 308th "Iron Division" from the eastern face of Dien Bien Phu to a position opposite the Five Hills. One attack early in the evening was beaten off, but at 11:00 P.M. the Viet Minh detonated their mine under the French strongpoint. Bunkers, weapons, men, were thrown into the air by the blast. Eliane-2 was held by the fresh reinforcements of Captain Jean Pouget's company of the 1st Colonial Paratroop Battalion plus a unit of Foreign Legion paras. Both forces were thrown into confusion by the Viet Minh blast, rapidly followed by the assault groups of the 102nd Regiment of the Viet-Nam People's Army's 308th. It was the climactic battle.

From the French command center Lieutenant Colonel Langlais worked to scrape up troops to bolster the defenses on the Five Hills. Four small companies were sent. Artillery support was almost impossible—the single remaining 155mm gun had only eleven shells, 105mm ammunition was down to three hundred rounds, heavy mortar ammunition to one hundred shells. The battalion mortars had no shells left at all.

By the early morning hours of May 7 not much was left of Eliane-2. There was no trace of the Foreign Legion men. Captain Pouget was down to thirty-five paras himself. He asked for permission to evacuate and break out in the direction of Eliane-3. Pouget was told to hold out at least until dawn. He understood the message and reported he would destroy his radio to keep it from the Viet Minh.

A Viet Minh voice interrupted, speaking French and using Pouget's own radio frequency: "Don't destroy your radio set just yet, President Ho Chi Minh offers you a rendition of the *Chant des Partisans*."[17] It was very ironic; the partisan song had been popular among French Resistance fighters in World War II.

The Viet Minh were literally overrunning what was left of Dien Bien Phu. The strongpoints fell one by one; the French guns were destroyed by direct hits. Only one 105mm cannon was left on the support strongpoint Isabelle. On Eliane-4 the end came at nine thirty in the morning. Lieutenant Le Page radioed Bigeard on the command network and reported, "in the same metallic voice which used to announce 'objective reached,'" that Viet Minh fighters were outside his command post.

Five regiments of Giap's army were spearheading the last assault, a total of perhaps 10,000 to 15,000 men. In the Five Hills when the attack began, the garrison had had about 750 paratroopers and a couple of hundred men who were sent in during the night. Another 91 paratroopers had been dropped into the entrenched camp that night.

The steady attack captured two more of the Eliane positions around ten o'clock. By noon the Viet Minh were on the bank of the Nam Youm; soon afterward they were poised to attack Dien Bien Phu's center of resistance, which contained the command headquarters, artillery, and services.

At half past three the French commanders held a last, baleful meeting. Brigadier General de Castries, Langlais, Bigeard, and Hubert de Seguins-Pazzis met to consider a desperate breakout attempt. The men had to agree that all the garrison were too exhausted to make the effort. The commander of the support point Isabelle was given the option to break out on his own, and an attempt was made that failed.

There were other individual and group efforts also; a total of seventy-six men escaped and joined up with French partisan groups or with the relief force in Laos, or were rescued in other ways. One of them was Lieutenant Makowiak. Before Dien Bien Phu, Makowiak had stayed behind with the rear guard to cover the French withdrawal from the entrenched camp at Na San. In the first days of Dien Bien Phu, "Mako" had succeeded in escaping from the beleaguered Beatrice strongpoint, bringing back the largest party of survivors from that position. Now he held out on Eliane-4 until the last moment at the end of the battle. The blond, blue-eyed lieutenant broke out of Dien Bien Phu and made his way to Laos to meet up with some of the partisans. "Mako" thus became the only French officer to *walk* out of both Na San and Dien Bien Phu, a considerable distinction.

In Hanoi, General René Cogny spoke to De Castries on a radiotelephone link early in the morning. It was clear from De Castries's résumé of the available troops that there was not much time left before the end. Around 2:00 P.M. a message from the entrenched camp set the next morning for the time the French would lay down their arms.

Things looked even worse as the day wore on. By late afternoon Brigadier General de Castries apparently had a white flag raised over the Dien Bien Phu headquarters in an effort to save the wounded. At Hanoi, Cogny was concerned lest there be a formal surrender. He rushed to the radiotelephone office in the Citadel and arrived just as General Pierre Bodet was signing off after a last conversation with Dien Bien Phu.

Cogny grabbed the microphone: "Tell me old boy, this has to be finished now, of course, but not in the form of a capitulation. That is forbidden to us. There can be no hoisting of the white flag, the fire has to die of its own, but do not capitulate. . . ."

De Castries paused before answering. "Ah! Very good, General, it was just that I wanted to preserve the wounded."

"Yes," Cogny insisted, "however, I do have a piece of paper. I haven't got the right to authorize you to capitulate. Well, you'll do as best you can—but this must not end with a white flag. What you have done is too fine for that. You understand, old boy?"

"Very good, General."[18]

The flag did not matter. A white one was probably raised despite Cogny's orders, but by 5:30 P.M. it was the Viet-Nam People's Army flag that flew over De Castries's headquarters. At about that time the garrison destroyed its main radio transmitter.

On Friday, May 7, the French commandos of Captain Henri Lousteau, poised to the southwest of Dien Bien Phu, made their radio checks as usual. The commandos listened in on the radio

for ten minutes each hour to receive messages but avoided trans-
mitting so as not to reveal themselves. They heard Dien Bien Phu
go off the air. Over the next few days a few survivors reached
them. First came a Thai soldier and two Foreign Legionnaires, all
from strongpoint Isabelle, who found their way to 31 Commando.
Both the legionnaires were German, veterans of the Russian front
in World War II, where they had similarly escaped the German
pocket at Velikiye Luki in 1942–43. Seventeen other Europeans,
eight Vietnamese, and fifty-one Thai tribesmen also joined up
with the commandos, with the French-Laotian partisans, or with
the regular troops from Operation Condor. It was not much from
the 15,000 or so French Union soldiers who had fought for Dien
Bien Phu.

For the plucky French and Laotians who had clawed their
ways into the mountains in hopes of saving Dien Bien Phu the
outcome proved a disaster. Already in poor shape—the mobile
group had but 250 men left in one of its columns, and the 2nd
Battalion of the 2nd Foreign Legion regiment another 350—the
result at Dien Bien Phu punctured morale. A quarter of the total
strength of the 1st Laotian Paratroops deserted, as did sixty-seven
men from the Laotian 4th Light Infantry. Captain Lousteau's commandos returning from their positions near Dien Bien Phu were
nearly trapped by the Viet Minh 101st Infantry Regiment. The
French were left to descend from the mountains just as they had
gotten in.

The night of May 7 in Paris, *France Soir* was the first newspaper to carry the news, in a special edition. Translated, the head-
line read: DIEN BIEN PHU HAS FALLEN!

Laniel appeared at the National Assembly. The prime minister
was dressed entirely in black and flanked by several of his Cabinet. He presented a stark statement on the fall of Dien Bien Phu
and said there was no information on the survival of Brigadier
General de Castries. Part of Laniel's statement was intended for

foreign ears: "France must remind her allies that for seven years now the Army of the French Union has unceasingly protected a particularly crucial region of Asia and has alone defended the interests of all."[19]

XII

TRUCE OR TERROR?

In Hanoi on May 8 the French held their customary military parade marking the end of World War II in Europe. As Dien Bien Phu perished, Vietnamese workers in Hanoi were putting up the review stand. But only a handful of people showed up to watch. Even these spectators could not have been reassured by the passing ranks, remnants of units whose other elements had been sent to the camp. There was a company of the 1st Colonial Paratroops that had not been transported in time, and the headquarters company and depot section of the 3rd Foreign Legion Regiment, whose third battalion had been the garrison of "Isabelle." It was not a happy occasion.

In Singapore, meanwhile, senior Central Intelligence Agency officers responsible for Southeast Asia were meeting to plan covert operations. On May 8 officers James Fulton and Robert Boynton flew to Bangkok to review the situation with the CIA station chief there. They would do what they could. At Singapore officer Joseph Burkholder Smith organized a "disinformation" campaign whereby a Straits-born Chinese journalist was used to plant a story claiming that *Chinese* naval vessels had been spotted at sea in the Tonkin Gulf, en route from Hainan to Haiphong. The item suggested open Chinese involvement in Indochina, exactly the kind of pretext required to make intervention seem necessary. The news, attributed to British high commissioner Malcolm MacDonald, earned a "well done" from CIA headquarters.

In Geneva the Indochina phase of negotiations began on May 8. Under Secretary Walter Bedell Smith was alarmed by the fall of Dien Bien Phu and requested that the CIA immediately do a national estimate on the situation in Tonkin. Dulles had anticipated the need; a small board had already completed a draft in late April and this was approved by Allen Dulles's inter-agency committee on April 28. It was the unanimous opinion of all the intelligence organizations of the U.S. government that the fall of Dien Bien Phu would not signal the immediate collapse of the French Union position.

But perhaps the key judgment was: ". . . we believe that general collapse of French and native governmental authority during the next two or three months would be prevented by the continued existence of organized French Union forces and the hope among Indochinese that the US might intervene."[1]

The new notion that the Indochina war might not end at Dien Bien Phu was speedily communicated by the Eisenhower administration. John Foster Dulles spoke on a nationwide radio and television hookup on the evening of May 7 to report to the American people on Geneva and comment on events in Viet-Nam.

Foster Dulles began his statement on Indochina by lashing out at the Viet Minh: ". . . in the name of nationalism, the communists aim to deprive the people of Viet-Nam of their independence by subjecting them to the new imperialism of the Soviet bloc." The Secretary of State advocated that "there should be greater free-world assistance." As for Dien Bien Phu, "an epic battle has ended. But great causes have, before now, been won out of lost battles."[2]

On Sunday morning, May 9, another important meeting occurred at Secretary Dulles's Georgetown home. Foster called the meeting to discuss a proposed military staff conference among five western powers to be held in Washington. Originally proposed by Anthony Eden to mollify the Americans for British coolness to American intervention plans, the U.S. had accepted the idea and was now planning the conference. But the discussion at Foster's house turned also to other measures that could be taken in Southeast Asia.

Admiral Radford was at the meeting held by the Secretary of State. In the presence of Foster's assistants Robert Bowie and Douglas MacArthur II, Radford's own aide Captain George W. Anderson, and newly appointed Undersecretary of Defense Robert Anderson, "Raddy" made a statement very revealing about the policy preference that he continued to hold:

> The only military solution was to go to the source of Communist power in the Far East, i.e. China, and destroy that power. The point was made that the true source of the power of the international Communist conspiracy was Russia, to which the Admiral assented, making the point that three or four years from now the balance of military power between the Soviets and the U.S. will have shifted in the former's favor because they will then have a sufficient stockpile of nuclear weapons which, although numerically less than the U.S. stockpile, will give them the necessary capability to initiate and carry on general war on favorable terms. The Admiral indicated that he did not believe we would at any point in the future be confronted with as clear-cut a basis for taking measures directly against China as was the case now in Indochina.[3]

Foster Dulles, who had brought on Radford's tirade with a suggestion for a simple alliance with Thailand that could be expanded later (and which Radford insisted would be ineffective), responded that he was thinking in terms of increasing deterrents to war.

But Admiral Radford was not alone among the military in the opinion he held. The Pentagon member of the NSC Planning Board, Army Brigadier General Charles H. Bonesteel III, one of the most experienced joint planners in the Department of Defense, from continuous Pentagon assignment since World War II, expressed himself in virtually identical terms in a May 9 memorandum to Defense Secretary Charles Wilson. The Bonesteel paper outlined possible U.S. alternatives in the light of the French armistice proposals at Geneva. His option "a" was to intervene in Vietnam "to redeem the situation." Bonesteel's "b" was to pressure the French to avoid all compromise at Geneva, but he thought this possible only in conjunction with option "a." The "c" option was to adopt a "passive policy" at Geneva while "hastily" organizing a regional alliance "to hold what remains of Southeast Asia."

And Bonesteel's analysis of the options? "Decisions *a* plus *b* offer the only way to stop the Communist advance. They involve substantial risk of war with Red China and increased risk of general war. However, recognizing the steadily increasing Soviet capabilities in nuclear warfare and the consequent steady diminution of the present military advantage of the U.S. over the U.S.S.R., these increased risks can more surely and safely be accepted now than ever again."

An American public warning together with a regional alliance could be of some help but would probably entail a delay before the judgment could be made that the warning had been ignored. During such a delay of "months or years" the Chinese and Soviets would become more powerful, to the point where increased Soviet nuclear capability would make it impossible for the United States to carry out its threats. "Asia could thus be lost," declared the paper.[4]

Meanwhile, in Paris, Joseph Laniel made another late-night summons to the American ambassador. This time Douglas Dillon went to the Matignon at 10:00 P.M. on a Sunday and found the prime minister in a strong and courageous mood. He had an apocalyptic vision and made it clear to Dillon that the real enemy France was facing in Indochina was the Chinese. "Obviously," France alone was no match.

Laniel inquired about what conditions the United States would place upon its participation in the war. He requested that an American general officer familiar with the terrain and situation in Indochina be sent to Paris for talks. The most pressing military problem was shortening French lines in the Red River delta and regrouping fifteen French battalions from Laos to the delta.

Dillon reported the new development by a cable that arrived in Washington the next morning. Dulles's reply to Dillon was a heavily reworked cable in which the President himself made substantial alterations. The French would have to request intervention from a variety of nations, these would have to agree, *and* the whole would have to have formal approval from the French National Assembly. There were other conditions too, "makeweights" in the opinion of Robert Bowie, chief of the State Department policy planning staff. A good analysis is that by Townsend Hoopes, a biographer of Foster Dulles: "The seven conditions were a set of interlocking booby traps for the French, and, if by some miracle they had been able to render them harmless and acceptable, it is likely that a now thoroughly disenchanted Eisenhower would have developed further obstacles."[5]

The President had indeed turned against any Indochina intervention, even though he had encouraged talk of "united action" until this moment. It is very likely that the President began to change his mind in the wake of the National Security Council meeting of April 29 with its explicit discussion of general war against the "head of the snake."

In addition, Vulture received little support from the American public. The administration's efforts to create a broad national consensus for intervention were largely unsuccessful. No political pressure groups came forward to support an intervention policy, and organized groups accounted for little of the mail on the subject that was addressed to President Eisenhower. The same was true of the mail to Senator Lyndon Baines Johnson. LBJ received seventy letters on Indochina intervention during the period March–April 1954, not one of them from any organized group. Of these, sixty-three opposed any further degree of U.S. involvement.

Newspaper editorials and columnists largely supportive of the administration during the early days of Dien Bien Phu became more critical by May. After the Sulzberger revelation in late April, reporters began investigating the administration's secret deliberations.

One reporter on the beat for the intervention story was Chalmers Roberts of the *Washington Post–Times Herald*. Roberts was in Geneva covering the conference. At lunch one day with Anthony Eden, Roberts casually asked who had stopped the American intervention project. The British foreign secretary answered, "I guess I did." Roberts got other details in Geneva and then returned to Washington, where he found out more from State Department officials. Later, Roberts got access to notes of the April 3 meeting made by House Democrat John W. McCormack. The result was a "front page block-buster" story on June 7 that contained important details on the Eisenhower administration's considerations of intervention.

There were likewise few in Congress who gave full support to the intervention plans. Administration poll takers on Capitol Hill, the *Christian Science Monitor* reported, were able to find only five men whose support was unequivocal. Similarly, one political scientist's survey of statements on intervention which appeared in the *Congressional Record* from June 1953 through July 1954, revealed only three declarations in favor, fifteen that opposed unilateral intervention, and another seventeen that opposed any intervention at all.[6]

Perhaps the most alarming aspect of the intervention scheme was that even after the President and many others turned against it, it did *not* go away. Vulture had acquired its own momentum among military men like Admiral Radford.

Advocacy of the single air strike waned after the fall of Dien Bien Phu, when Giap's Viet Minh army concentration began to break up for a march to the Red River delta region. The People's Army became too elusive a target for an air strike, and in addition there were 7,000 to 10,000 French, North African, and Vietnamese prisoners interspersed among Giap's men. By mid-May the Joint Intelligence Group reported to Admiral Radford its expectation that Giap would be able to get his 40,000 soldiers to the delta in four to six weeks, while he could call in another 7,000 troops from Annam and central Laos, who could arrive at the delta in two or three weeks. As a result, intervention talks that in April usually envisioned an air strike, by May were focusing on military intervention on the ground.

In May 1954 the National Security Council was already considering a course of action under which a force of six infantry divisions and a parachute division would be committed in Viet-Nam, either as a supplement to the French or in place of them. Including naval and air support, the force would amount to 322,000 men. On May 18, Robert Cutler set parameters for a series of agency "studies with respect to possible US action regarding Indochina."

The United States Army opposed any deployment of an army force. On May 18, Army Secretary Robert T. Stevens told Charles Wilson that "I am becoming increasingly concerned over the frequency of statements by individuals of influence within and without the government that United States air and sea forces alone could solve our problems in Indochina, and equally so over the very evident lack of appreciation of the logistics factors affecting operations in that area."[7] Stevens objected that limitation to naval and air force would be a basically faulty decision and that the logistics factor "explodes the myth" that naval and air alone would be adequate.

The next day Secretary of Defense Charles E. Wilson was told the exact opposite by Admiral Radford in a memorandum on "US Military Participation in Indochina" on behalf of the Joint Chiefs. The Joint Chiefs directed that the Defense Department should determine the size and composition of U.S. force contributions and an Indochina command structure. The paper recommended that participation be limited "primarily" to naval and air units, specifically carriers and air units as required, in fact a force precisely the size of Task Force 70 plus the Bomber Command. A force greater than this, especially in naval forces, would be "maldeployment" and mean "reduced readiness to meet probable Chinese Communist reaction elsewhere."

In a touch that must have come from "Raddy," the paper said that "the principal sources of Viet Minh military supply lie outside Indochina. The destruction or neutralization of those outside sources . . . would materially reduce the French military problems in Indochina."[8]

The following day Radford sent Wilson a second paper, this one on the defense of Southeast Asia in the event Indochina was lost. The memo cited the domino theory, and asserted that "passing of the countries of Southeast Asia into the Communist orbit would be inimical to the security interests of the United States."

On May 26, Radford reiterated these views in a new paper. Strangely enough it began, "With reference to the Far East as a whole, *Indochina is devoid of decisive military objectives and the allocation of more than token US armed forces in Indochina would be a serious diversion of limited US capabilities.*" But again, the "token" force was set at a carrier group plus air units to conduct operations in support of "allied" forces on the ground. Ominously, "the employment of atomic weapons is contemplated in the event that such course appears militarily advantageous."

In case of overt Chinese intervention, an even greater response was planned: destruction of targets in China, support for attacks made by Chiang Kai-shek, and seizure or neutralization of Hainan and other offshore islands. These and other plans were perhaps hinted at in a speech made the next day by Chief of Naval Operations Robert Carney. Carney referred to fateful decisions being made by the administration concerning war and peace and said the U.S. was reaching a fork in the road "from which there [is] no turning back."

If new troops were not to come from the United States they could have to come from France and the Vietnamese. Navarre had asked Paris for 36,000 reinforcements in early May. So far he had been sent only the two parachute battalions airlifted by the U.S. On May 15 the French government agreed to send a mobile group from North Africa along with a number of individual replacements. Two weeks later the French advanced their annual call-up of 80,000 national service draftees who could be used to substitute for thirty- to forty-thousand regulars who could then be sent to Indochina.

France asked the United States for a repeat of the "Blue Star" long range airlift to move the mobile group. Washington had to refuse after Ceylon, this time following the example of India, refused overflight rights. The U.S. then offered to furnish ships to move the soldiers, but this would take too long and France could provide shipping itself. In the end, between May 1 and June 20 some 9,300 French troops went to the Far East, far short of Navarre's requests, and just 3,600 of them were in constituted units.

Making the best of a bad situation, French psychological warfare officers concocted Operation "Germaine" to convince the world and Viet Minh that massive reinforcement was in progress. One of the paratroop battalions flown to Da Nang previously was sent to the Tonkin delta, and the French then leaked reports that this was related to formation of two fresh mobile groups. Similarly the arrival of the French cruisers *Gloire* and *Montcalm* at Saigon was reported as the lead element of a huge naval squadron bringing soldiers to disembark at Haiphong. These measures were no substitute for the massive intervention the Americans were considering.

Deep divisions on the issue persisted in the U.S. government itself, particularly in the Pentagon. No matter what assurances were given, the Army continued to resist calls to arms. General Ridgway reached out for more concrete information showing intervention to be impossible. The Army sent a technical team of seven officers representing the Engineer, Transportation, and Signal Corps to Indochina to make a covert detailed survey. The leader of the group was Colonel David W. Heiman, a career engineer who had managed logistics for the Leyte invasion of World War II.

The Indochina survey turned up just about what Ridgway expected. To support a ground force of the size anticipated (275,000) would require 35 to 55 engineer battalions, probably a construction group larger than available in the entire U.S. Army, because of the lack of facilities. For example, the planners anticipated a need for a port with about the capacity of Pusan during the Korean War. Pusan handled 15,000 to 25,000 tons of freight a day in 1950. There were two major ports in Indochina, Saigon and Haiphong. Their *combined* freight capacity in 1954 stood at 12,100 tons a day. There were also nine minor ports, which together could land 1,900 tons daily.

If the port volume wasn't problem enough, it turned out that the railroad freight-carrying capacity between Haiphong and Hanoi was less than the port capacity of the former. In addition, some U.S. planners felt that, to protect the sea-lanes into Haiphong, it would be necessary to occupy Hainan Island, territory of the People's Republic of China.

The Army engineering study concluded that the job of supply could be done, but only by saturation use of all port facilities, over-the-beach landing wherever possible, and the maximum use of aircraft for transport hauling. Even with the massive engineer commitment contemplated, construction of the crucial port improvements would take at least a year.

As a military man, especially the man who planned and organized the Normandy invasion of World War II, Ike could not fail to note the magnitude of the necessary engineering task.

On June 1 Eisenhower met with Bobby Cutler. According to Cutler's NSC record, the President said that "the United States would not intervene in China on any basis except united action. . . . The United States should in no event undertake alone to support French colonialism. Unilateral action by the United States in cases of this kind would destroy us."[9] Although Ike resisted unilateral action, he agreed in a June 2 meeting that if China made any overt aggression, the administration would ask for authority to use force without further efforts to enlist allies.

Eisenhower raised no objection, on May 28, when Radford indicated that atomic weapons would be automatically used to counter blatant Chinese intervention. Indeed, the President nodded approvingly when told by Radford of the three contingency plans then under preparation: to attack targets in Manchuria and north China in case of Chinese action in Korea; a plan to counter moves in Indochina with attacks on south China; and a plan by the Strategic Air Command to attack targets in both north and south China in the event of wider hostilities.

Since any mainland Chinese aggression would lead the United States to use its full panoply of destructive force, Ike thought he would need "much more than a congressional resolution." Otherwise he could not be certain the public would back war with China. In fact two weeks before, the State Department had put together a draft resolution that could be passed by Congress to give Ike the authority he wanted. The draft met congressional concerns by specifying that it was not to be construed as a declaration of war, but it nevertheless provided that "The President is authorized to employ naval and air forces of the United States to assist friendly governments of Asia as against subversive and revolutionary efforts fomented by Communist regimes." Thus, ten days *after* the fall of Dien Bien Phu, Eisenhower remained prepared to seek war while denying that war was at issue, a stance that became familiar in America's later Vietnam involvement. Eisenhower believed the U.S. *should* intervene if Peking did so, as he told the full NSC on June 3. The President declared that the United States would not and should not shoulder the entire security burden of the free world, but he stood ready to be satisfied with whatever limited assistance might be forthcoming from smaller Asian nations and European powers.

Ike instructed Dulles to try and get commitments from Australia, New Zealand, and the Philippines that, if the U.S. government got authority from Congress to intervene, those countries would do the same with their parliaments. In early June, President Eisenhower was not excluding military action. In fact the policy machinery had begun circulating NSC-5421, a compilation of departmental studies with respect to intervention. As Ike wrote Al Gruenther, "I am even yet spending days and hours trying to get a political climate ... that would make it politically feasible within the United States to render the kind of help that our own interests and those of the free world would seem to require.[10]

Meanwhile, concerned with the military situation in Vietnam, the French made increasingly desperate pleas for help. The latest came when the Laniel government, in its final days in office, asked that a U.S. Marine division be sent to Tonkin. It professed to believe that a single Marine division (perhaps 22,000 men) could be committed to combat without the congressional approval that was seen as such an obstacle. John Foster Dulles's reply, in a May 21 cable to Paris, had been a Marine deployment *was* possible, "within [the] context of [a] coherent and realistic overall plan for [the] conduct of collective military operations."[11]

Building up to Ike's early June meeting there was a flurry of exchanges over this latest intervention possibility. The French were confident that General Ely could demonstrate the military necessity for the marines, and indeed, at a session with U.S. officials on May 26 the French general stated that with one or two divisions of Marines he would have no trouble holding the Red River delta. Ely, suddenly appointed to replace Navarre as commander-in-chief in Indochina, planned to regroup French mobile forces and concentrate on holding the Hanoi-Haiphong corridor. President Eisenhower told a group including the full Joint Chiefs of Staff on May 28 that the U.S. might put a Marine division temporarily into Southeast Asia.

The United States actually put Marine troops on alert for deployment to Indochina. A contingent of the 3rd Marine Division boarded ships at Yokohama. A young marine officer trainee at Quantico in the States, Daniel Ellsberg, was stunned when his drill instructor, a sergeant named DeWeese, told the men to be doubly sure their weapons were clean for they would soon be bound for Indochina. At the headquarters of the commander of naval forces in the Far East, an intelligence staff under Lieutenant

Robert Oakley apparently as a result of informal requests within Marine channels, was put to work assembling a three-volume compendium of all types of basic data the Marines might need about Indochina.

In Washington the U.S. convened a conference among senior military staffs of five powers, including the French, British, Australia, and New Zealand. Ike had told Admiral Carney, who represented the U.S. at the conference, to flatter the French by referring to their great expertise in ground operations and the need for their command experience, but to reserve naval and air command for the United States. Eisenhower also wanted an American deputy commander in any multinational headquarters. In conjunction with the conference Ely's deputy, General Jean Valluy, held a separate meeting on June 3 with Admiral Radford. Valluy asked if France could count on U.S. assistance, including Marines, if the French were forced to evacuate Hanoi and defend a Haiphong redoubt. Radford avoided a direct answer. The Joint Chiefs chairman said the matter was beyond his control; it would be a political decision, united action remained important. Radford's broadest hint was his reiteration that U.S. participation in the event of intervention would consist primarily of naval and air forces. Valluy reported to his government that for political reasons the U.S. would probably not agree to send Marines to Indochina under any circumstances.

Not only the United States, but France also, backed away from the request for sending Marines to Vietnam. French foreign ministry official Maurice Schumann repeatedly told Ambassador Dillon that the French troop request was intended for the contingency of the failure of the Geneva conference. However, the five-power staff talks went on to conclude that saving the French position in northern Vietnam would require the dispatch of three more divisions of troops plus about 300 aircraft, in all over 50,000 soldiers and airmen. The specter of intervention remained.

The ambiguity proved too much for Matt Ridgway. On Saturday evening, the 5th of June, Ridgway called a group of reporters into his Pentagon office. The Army chief of staff quietly told the group that if the Army were forced to intervene in Indochina he would resign. By now the official Joint Chiefs position specified only naval and air forces for Indochina plus a larger military advisory group to train the Vietnamese army. The Marine option evaporated as suddenly as it had appeared. At Far East naval headquarters in Yokosuka Lieutenant Oakley's people were forced to destroy all those intelligence manuals they had put together so hurriedly. Burning them took several days.

On June 10, Air Force Chief of Staff Nate Twining became a defector from the intervention advocates. With his wife at a dinner at the home of Washington hostess Kay Halle, General Twining now said he agreed with Ridgway that it would be foolhardy to get into Indochina. According to Drew Pearson, who was present, "he was discreet in what he said but I gather that he chafes a bit at Eisenhower's mercurial tendencies."[12]

The intervention issue finally came to a head at the 201st National Security Council meeting, held that day. There, Eisenhower had arranged for General Ridgway to make a presentation of the Army's views to the full council.

Matt Ridgway, prepared with charts, tables, and figures, made a very effective presentation. A sudden disaster hampered the general's presentation when the bulb burned out in his overhead projector and his transparencies became useless. Never the less Ridgway pressed on and began by recalling the sequence in Korea—citing "his own views at the onset of the Korean crisis to the effect that within a very short period the need for American ground forces would be conclusively demonstrated" regardless of whether intervention was first made with naval and air forces.[13]

Then Ridgway ran down the logistics problems: It would take weeks to "squeeze" each arriving Army division through the limited facilities at Haiphong; the supply transport difficulties would be five or six times worse than in Korea. Air cover would be difficult to maintain—it would be perilous for American security to involve any considerable portion of U.S. "air atomic" power, such as Bomber Command, in a jungle war on the Asian mainland, especially since a full-scale Asian war would probably develop.

Ridgway also pointed to the strength of the Army under the "New Look." Manpower reductions were cutting it to fourteen divisions. With some in Europe and the necessity to maintain a strategic reserve, there could be no Indochina action without mobilization at home.

This finally put an end to talk of intervention in Indochina, at least in 1954. Ironically just a few days later the eventuality which President Eisenhower sought to avoid took place:Americans in Vietnam became involved directly in the fighting.

These events took place at Little America in Da Nang. The Americans there had steadily been going about their work of servicing the French B-26 bombers. The days went by, punctuated only by occasional excitements. In early April the base received a series of flights totaling 18 new C-47 transports, flown directly from Japan, which the U.S. was loaning the French to create an additional air group. A week or so later Marine pilots aboard Captain Doyle G. Donaho's escort carrier *Saipan* flew off a deck load of dive bombers intended for the French aircraft carrier *Arromanches*. Both the *Saipan* and Captain Leo's *Arromanches* steamed into Da Nang harbor on April 18, accompanied by a couple of French corvettes. The French carrier returned the American pilots with her helicopters. The *Saipan* also delivered a number of additional helicopters being given to the French forces. *Arromanches* left. Her pilots would be flying the planes on attack missions over Dien Bien Phu before the end of the battle.

Security for the Americans had already been a concern, in particular after the fields at Cat Bi and Do Son in the Tonkin delta were both attacked by the Viet Minh. The maintenance men, aircraft squadrons, and army parachute packers all had different chains of command and communications networks, which did not improve matters any. The Eisenhower administration had also promised originally that the Americans would be out of Vietnam by the middle of June. A few days after the fall of Dien Bien Phu the technicians at Do Son were ordered to move to Da Nang, joining the rest of the 642nd Field Maintenance Squadron (Provisional) there. The C-119s of the 816th Medium Transport Squadron at Cat Bi flew the others south, then were themselves ordered to Da Nang on May 23.

Regrouping did not solve the security problem. At Do Son after the attack there a couple of spare C-46 transports had been permanently parked on one side of the field for the express purpose of emergency airlift of Americans in extremis. With the move to Da Nang one of the C-46s went there for the same reason (the other crashed on landing at Do Son on June 14). One night in late June Viet Minh commandos got onto the base and blew up the airplane. An emergency aerial evacuation was actually carried out that night, but by C-119s flying to Clark Field and to Saigon. The next day they returned to Da Nang. The Americans were then briefed that in case of attack they were to make for the beach below Marble Mountain, paddle out to sea on rubber rafts, and look for a submarine which would be stationed there to rescue them. With 348 Americans at Da Nang by the end of May this plan was not very practical.

Crowding at Little America affected life in other ways as well. Aircrew were not permitted to visit the French bordello and it is not clear whether the facility became off limits for 642nd technicians as well. The *Saipan* had brought more sports equipment so some of the edge could be taken off with intramural leagues, but the Americans remained restless. Offbase activities had been restricted once more. One of the 816th pilots recalls just a single outing to China Beach, under the watchful eye of French security guards. Detachment leader Major Tom Yarbrough carefully briefed his men on restricted areas and times. The French air force was arranging to replace the Americans at a rate of a hundred a month beginning in June, but in the interval time passed slowly.

On the afternoon of June 14 some of the Americans decided they would go swimming come hell or high water. Five men took one of the empty weapons carriers at Da Nang and drove it off the base. The French gate guard had orders to open for Americans and let them off the base. The Americans headed for the beautiful white sand of China Beach, where they frolicked in the surf near the village of My Khe, about a mile and a half south of Da Nang. While they were in the water a Viet Minh patrol chanced upon them, took their clothes, then made them prisoners. The Viet Minh may have been attracted to the scene by the empty truck seemingly on offer, and they may have thought the Americans wanted to surrender because white T-shirts had been draped over the hood of the truck. The Americans were two Army privates: Donald E. Morgan, of Flint, Michigan; and Leonard R. Sroufek, of Chicago; plus three airmen: Ciro Salas, Jr., of Los Angeles; Jerry Schuller, of Cleveland; and Giacomo Appice, from Elizabeth, New Jersey.

The Americans were paraded in their bathing suits before amused Vietnamese villagers. One of them broke down and cried. The Americans were kept at a village near the coast until the evening of June 17, then they were marched inland, eventually to reach Viet Minh Prison Camp No. 3.

At Da Nang the missing Americans were not noticed until roll call the following morning. Soon after 8 A.M., the French base commander, Colonel Grogshillier got patrols out and sent a spotter aircraft to search for the Americans. Villagers near My Khe reported seeing some white men among a group of about twenty prisoners the Viet Minh had marched through their village. The

French tried a rescue attempt, like one of the "Bright Light" missions common to a later war, and CIA's Colonel Edward G. Lansdale came up from Saigon to participate. Lansdale, in Vietnam on a survey mission prior to returning on permanent assignment, thought the rescue effort comical. First it was too heavy—there were several jeeps backed by a tank from the 1st Foreign Legion Cavalry Regiment. Driving up the road the Americans in the lead vehicle encountered a Vietnamese woman who spoke of seeing crying white prisoners. Lansdale recalled, "The bearded Legion sergeant commanding the tank spat on the ground, said he wasn't going to risk his tank trying to rescue such softies, and took his tank back" to Da Nang.[14] That ended the operation.

Airman Giacomo Appice knew nothing of all this. Nor had he counted on being taken prisoner by the Viet Minh. He had lived at home with his sister for many years, then responding to the surge of voluntarism when North Korea invaded South Korea in 1950, joined the Air Force. After three years of stateside service Appice had asked for overseas duty and drawn Japan. Though he liked working in Japan, when the Indochina mission came along he had been selected for the temporary assignment. He had never expected that an innocent trip to the beach could end so badly. Now Appice was a Viet Minh prisoner.

Meanwhile the U.S. military advisory commander, General O'Daniel held an investigation of the disappearance of the Americans. Air attaché Colonel Harold E. Kofahl came to Da Nang to sit on the hearing board with Major J. C. Mitchell, detachment commander, who had first arrived only a few days before the incident, and the French base commander. O'Daniel attended as an observer. An Air Force report maintains the board found that the missing men had often skipped their maintenance assignments. A consequence would be that Colonel Kincaid, the overall Air Force commander, ordered restrictions on Americans at Da Nang increased even more. No one would now be permitted off base without an armed officer escort. A system of bed checks, constant roll calls, and a pass system were instituted.

On June 18, even as the hearing board sat at Da Nang, General Caldara's B-29 groups regrouped on Guam. The FEAF Bomber Command was abolished that day, while on Guam suddenly appeared the Strategic Air Command's 3rd Air Division. Caldara became commander of that unit.

As for Camp No. 3, the American prisoners were well treated. Unlike French prisoners of war in Vietnam, who were subjected to intense political indoctrination, with the Americans Viet Minh were curious and not antagonistic. The Americans got a house to share with a Vietnamese woman. They were allowed to play soccer and volleyball, and though the Viet Minh propagandized them and gave them lectures on the progress of the war, responding to these in the right way (for the Viet Minh) was not made a condition for good treatment as it was for the roughly 150 to 200 Frenchmen at the camp. The Americans were not confined, closely guarded, or made to stand roll call as were the French. Camp No. 3 had no walls. Buried mines kept the prisoners on permitted paths.

But the Viet Minh were not well provisioned and they had practically no medicines. One of the American prisoners lost fifty pounds in captivity. Another contracted malaria. The Franco-Vietnamese war ended on July 21 with signature of agreements at Geneva, Switzerland. The American prisoners regained their freedom on the last day of August.

In the end the non-intervention in Indochina in 1954 still cost Americans life and limb, casualties that were a warning not heeded later. In addition to the five Da Nang prisoners there were two dead Civil Air Transport pilots who worked for the CIA. Another pilot had been wounded. The famous American photographer and movie maker Frank Capa also died during the 1954 campaign, hit by a sniper in late May during an operation in the Tonkin delta.

On the ground in Indochina, defeat at Dien Bien Phu did not end the war. Instead, General René Cogny was faced with the very thing he always had feared, the gathering of Viet Minh armies for a sustained assault on the Red River delta. It was partly to distract Giap from such an attack that a garrison was put at Dien Bien Phu in the first place.

At first the French thought they were safe, predicting that the Viet Minh redeployment would take until the onset of the rainy season in the delta. Had this been so, French observers would subsequently have been able to argue more persuasively that Navarre's objectives in placing the entrenched camp had been met: The French troops lost constituted only a small percentage of the strength of the Expeditionary Corps, while the People's Army had taken heavy losses.

But the Viet Minh were fired by the opportunity to strike at the delta—they could sense coming victory. By May 13 much of the People's Army was already on the road down from the Tonkin highlands. Within four days French intelligence had indications that four of Giap's five divisions were in motion.

The French did what they could to preserve the military situation. Cogny mounted constant sweeps of the Hanoi-Haiphong corridor. But French patrols that tried to move out from the fortified lines of the delta met strong resistance and were driven back to their bases.

Meanwhile the Laniel government had a problem with its Expeditionary Corps commander. During Dien Bien Phu, General Navarre had exchanged cables with Paul Ely expressing an intention to replace René Cogny in Tonkin. But after defeat at the entrenched camp the government lost confidence in Navarre instead. Laniel approached Marshal Alphonse Juin to offer him the command, but Juin was willing to replace Navarre only if American intervention became a reality and he could lead an international expeditionary force. In the end General Paul Ely was appointed to replace Navarre. Ely took charge of the Expeditionary Corps at midnight on June 8.

Every ship that docked in a French port from the Far East bore caskets with bodies, or wounded men being repatriated. General Raoul Salan found that French losses for the first months of 1954 were running at six times the rate of the previous year; and in 1953 the war had already been considered too costly in many quarters in France. There had been a big defeat in 1950, but Dien Bien Phu was even bigger.

In Paris recriminations were just beginning. Marc Jacquet resigned from the Laniel Cabinet at the end of May. The press reported that Jacquet had been at odds since late 1953, when Laniel and Bidault had refused to take up Ho Chi Minh's offer of direct negotiations contained in the *Expressen* interview.

Prime Minister Laniel faced a hurricane of pressure and his Cabinet gave way on June 12. By then the war appeared lost while the Geneva talks seemed stalled. The Viet Minh held 10,000 French prisoners. On the evening of the twelfth, the Laniel Cabinet fell short ten votes on a question of confidence in the National Assembly.

A new French Cabinet was formed four days later by Radical-Socialist Deputy Pierre Mendès-France, who electrified the Assembly with the promise that he would resign if he could not achieve a Geneva settlement within thirty days. Mendès-France took both the post of foreign minister and the task of prime minister in the Cabinet, which won approval by 419 votes to 47 against, with 143 abstentions.

The thirty days of Pierre Mendès-France were a harrowing time for all, as it often seemed that Geneva was deadlocked. But there was no doubt that the French were ready for a ceasefire. Near the end of June they suffered a further substantial defeat in the Central Highlands, where, at Cheo Rheo and Kontum, *Groupe Mobile* 100 was ambushed repeatedly and destroyed by Viet Minh regulars. In Tonkin, General Ely presided over a massive Operation Auvergne, in which the entire southern half of the Red River delta was evacuated. In three breathless days the Viet Minh walked into Phu Ly, Nam Dinh, and Hung Yen. The French also abandoned the traditionally Catholic and pro-French provinces of Phat Diem and Bui Chu.

Even with the regrouping of forces, communication along the Hanoi-Haiphong corridor remained highly tenuous. Highway connection *route coloniale* 5 was sometimes open only two or three hours in a day. Even this required the concentration of four *groupes mobiles* and an armored subgroup on the *route coloniale* 5 with another pair of *groupes mobiles* at Hanoi, the equivalent of two full infantry divisions, or 25,000 men. Naturally this disposition favored the Viet Minh in the rest of the delta. On July 7, General Cogny of the Tonkin theater command reported the Viet Minh to have a two-to-one advantage in battalions surrounding the delta. Given the military situation, Pierre Mendès-France's determination to achieve a settlement at Geneva was hardly surprising.

At the last moment in Geneva, and despite the Viet Minh's favorable military position, there were Viet Minh concessions encouraged by the People's Republic of China: The Viet Minh were now willing to sign an agreement that would partition Viet-Nam. The concession was a key development, and perhaps the new Chinese flexibility stemmed from fear of American atomic weapons. When a senior Chinese delegate spoke of the possibility of United States military bases in Viet-Nam or of an anticommunist regional alliance in Southeast Asia, "his hands shook, and his usually excellent English broke down, forcing him to work through an interpreter."[15]

Once partition became a serious possibility, the other elements of an accord fell into place quickly. Mendès-France actually took a little more than the thirty days he promised, but no

Frenchmen seemed to mind. A Geneva agreement on Indochina was signed on July 21, 1954. It provided for a temporary division of Viet-Nam into "regroupment zones," followed by free elections within two years to lead to reunification. (The elections were never held because the United States had refused to be a party to the Geneva agreement and worked to contravene it in the southern zone, which the United States was soon calling South Viet-Nam.)

Years later, in the midst of a new Viet-Nam war, American journalist James Reston asked Chou En-lai whether China was willing to mediate between the United States and Hanoi. Chou said no: "We don't want to be a mediator in any way. We were very badly taken in during the first Geneva Conference."[16]

In the weeks following the Geneva settlement the prisoners were repatriated. Five American servicemen captured in Annam came home. France was not so fortunate. Less than a third of the men captured at Dien Bien Phu survived the harsh trek through the Tonkin mountains and the conditions in the Viet Minh prison camps. Dien Bien Phu survivors numbered a little over 2,000 among the 10,754 prisoners released by the Viet Minh after Geneva. About 900 more men from the garrison were wounded and evacuated by the French directly from Dien Bien Phu. There is no record of the number of Viet Minh who survived captivity among the French.

By August 11, 1954, the cease-fire was effective throughout Indochina. Under the terms of Geneva, General Ely managed the withdrawal of the Expeditionary Corps: the French pulled out of Hanoi in October 1954 and Haiphong in May 1955. The last 5,000 French troops were repatriated in February 1956. Operation Paper Sack halted U.S. military aid to the French after Geneva, by which time the cumulative amount stood at over $2.9 billion. Aid was later resumed at a much reduced rate designed to encourage the French to withdraw from southern Viet-Nam.

The war cost France 92,000 dead and 114,000 wounded. Another 21,600 French or indigenous persons are still listed as missing, or failed to return from captivity. There are no figures on total Viet Minh losses, but these must have been several times the French total.

President Eisenhower had had enough of the French. American policy henceforth was to cooperate with South Viet-Nam directly. On August 20, 1954, Eisenhower approved a National Security Council document that provided for working with the French in Indochina only insofar as necessary. The Americans did work jointly with the French in the evacuation from Tonkin of all French and South Vietnamese military forces and any civilians who desired to move to the southern regroupment zone. Over a hundred U.S. ships participated in the sea lift and moved 293,000 of over 800,000 Vietnamese who moved south.

It was during this sea lift that the Americans finally achieved the token British military participation for which they worked so hard during the Dien Bien Phu crisis. In September 1954 the Royal Navy sent its aircraft carrier HMS *Warrior* to assist in the evacuation of Tonkin.

General Henri Navarre was not again employed by France in any active field command. He and Laniel disputed each other's accounts in memoirs and the press. René Cogny held the Tonkin command until the north was evacuated and was then transferred to Morocco. The French government inquest into the debacle found plenty of blame to share among them. Perhaps Cogny came out best. Years later, it is reported, Navarre was anonymously sent a boxed dueling pistol, an allusion to a course sometimes chosen by defeated generals.

The veterans of Dien Bien Phu strove to understand how they had been defeated, to make good their errors. Many had the chance to develop and practice their theories in a revolutionary war in Algeria that began in November 1954. The Indochina officers developed and articulated some rather sophisticated counterinsurgency tactics, but they were limited to a military role. Much as in Indochina, the military in Algeria were unable to determine the course of French policy.

General Paul Ely remained commander in chief in Indochina until the last of the Expeditionary Corps was withdrawn. He lost the contest with the Americans for political influence in the new Saigon, and then returned to France, where he resumed the chairmanship of the General Staff for National Defense.

Ely's ubiquitous aide Colonel Raymond Brohon made brigadier soon after Dien Bien Phu. He led the Air Force contribution to the Franco-British attack on Suez in 1956 and there presumably learned just how badly an intervention could fail even when completely successful on the military plane. Brohon's rise in the Air Force was meteoric and he retired in 1960 as a full general. Many other Dien Bien Phu veterans fought at Suez among the paratroops. Among them was Marcel Bigeard, who went on to become chief of staff of the French Army despite having missed out on study at the war college. Lieutenent Colonel Pierre Langlais rose to command of the 11th *Divison Légère d'Intervention*, France's own "Rapid Deployment Force."

Among the American actors in the Vulture operation and the Dien Bien Phu crisis, only one seems to have lost out on the episode. That was General Matthew Ridgway, who had opposed intervention, whose term as Army chief of staff Eisenhower did not renew (another little clue to the administration's attitude in 1954 that has been given insufficient attention by analysts of these events). The other Joint Chiefs of Staff kept their jobs. "Iron Mike" O'Daniel got back his commission as lieutenant general later in 1954 in what Admiral Radford called Operation "Recovery Star." Admiral Herbert Hopwood, who had been sent to confer with Navarre, when on to head the U.S. Pacific Fleet in 1959.

Rear Admiral Harry D. Feldt, who had commanded one of the carrier divisions in Task Force 70.2, would himself lead the Pacific Fleet during the early part of the American war in Vietnam. General Earle E. Partridge, who had had the Far East Air Force, moved up to head the North American Air Defense Command beginning in 1958. President Eisenhower, in very secret orders not revealed until many years afterwards, would delegate in advance to Partridge the authority to use nuclear weapons under certain conditions without the express approval of the President. Brigadier General Caldara retired from the Strategic Air Command to become head of the Flight Safety Foundation of New York.

Admiral Felix B. Stump, erstwhile CINCPAC, left the service to chair the board of the CIA proprietary Civil Air Transport (later Air America). There would be lots more covert operations in Vietnam. Indeed the agency made a start by smuggling eight tons of weapons and ammunition into Haiphong aboard Civil Air Transport flights ostensibly sent to evacuate refugees. America was marching into war in Vietnam.

XIII

EYELESS INTO INDOCHINA?

In a 1958 book Drew Pearson reported that President Eisenhower was "unutterably depressed" for days after the fall of Dien Bien Phu. Eisenhower said as much in a passage finally edited out of his memoir *Mandate for Change*: "It is exasperating and depressing to stand by and watch a free world nation losing a battle to slavery without being able to commit all your resources, including combat troops, to its aid. . . . The conditions which prevented American intervention with military force on behalf of the French Union were surely frustrating to me." But the most important obstacle, indeed the final one, was the tradition of anticolonialism in American foreign policy. As Ike put it, "the moral position of the United States was more to be guarded than the Tonkin delta, indeed than all of Indochina."[1]

Dwight D. Eisenhower learned many lessons from the Dien Bien Phu crisis, one of the first sustained foreign crises of his administration. Among them was the one drawn from the failure of "united action": the need for a preexisting network of regional alliances to support U.S. activities in any given area of operations. Thus, Dulles proceeded with the discussions of a regional coalition begun at the time of Dien Bien Phu. The Manila conference of September 1954 completed work on the Southeast Asia

Treaty Organization (SEATO). This was only the first of a series of alliances that, before the end of the Eisenhower administration, spanned every continent but Africa. Indeed, the word *pactomania* was coined to lampoon the drive for regional pacts that had little substance, which at that time was attributed to the influence of John Foster Dulles.

Eisenhower thought that the "united" character of the intervention would nullify the question of the aims of individual powers. Thus the President failed to recognize "internationalization" as a path leading to assumption of the same neocolonial burden that the French had borne previously.

By their failure to support the Geneva agreement achieved during 1954, and by approaching the Associated States individually, the Americans were most successful in the southern regroupment zone. With a good deal of promoting from the conservative China Lobby and Colonel Edward Lansdale of the CIA, Vietnamese politician Ngo Dinh Diem got Eisenhower's backing as a noncommunist alternative in South Viet-Nam.

The Americans encouraged Diem to violate the Geneva accord provision for nationwide elections, with the result that the Viet-Nam war inevitably rekindled. Before that happened, the Americans had become so strongly committed to Diem that U.S. military advisors were in on the new war from the beginning. Diem frittered away a great deal of his popular support through the corrupt and repressive conduct of his administration. Unlike in 1954 when President Eisenhower vowed no military intervention without congressional approval, when the new guerrilla war started in 1961 (some date it as early as 1959), Congress was not even asked to choose.

Another lesson Eisenhower learned from Dien Bien Phu was the value of a congressional resolution on the use of force. Truman had been criticized for not seeking such approval at the time of intervention in Korea. A congressional resolution offered the convenient way to circumvent the constitutional obstacle of using armed forces in war without a congressional declaration, which would have been debated more seriously and would also have been more difficult to secure under parliamentary procedure. President Eisenhower learned this lesson well, as did many successors. Thus in both the Taiwan Strait crisis of 1955 and the Middle East intervention in 1958, Ike was careful to secure prior passage of joint congressional resolutions. President Lyndon Baines Johnson did the same thing with the Tonkin Gulf resolution of 1964, using it as a justification for the major Viet-Nam intervention of 1965.

The process of authorizing acts of force by means of congressional joint resolutions is an unfortunate one. It is regrettable that the War Powers Act of 1973 continues to allow a role for joint resolutions. The act weakens essential war powers by allowing a president, under certain circumstances, to resort to force prior to any consideration by Congress. It allows a potential accretion of the so-called inherent powers of the presidency that may be exploited at the whim of the incumbent and to the peril of the American citizen. Had joint resolutions been the rule at the time of Operation Vulture, an intervention might have been even more difficult to resist.

An essential military lesson of the Dien Bien Phu crisis lay in the fact that it was the first failure of the new doctrine of "massive retaliation." Under the doctrine the United States was to rely on naval and air power, "air atomic" power in the idiom of that day. But threatening the Viet Minh with atomic war made no sense, nor did dropping nuclear weapons around Dien Bien Phu. China was not the "head of the snake," while general war with Russia over the activities of the Viet Minh was preposterous. Thus the awesome striking power of the Strategic Air Command and the carrier task forces was not convertible into leverage in the actual situation. In addition, although this was not recognized at the time, the attempt to exercise coercive diplomacy helped lock the United States into a policy track that led only into the quagmire of South Viet-Nam.

The failure of "massive retaliation" was noted and commented on at the time. One observer was Bernard Brodie, a perceptive analyst of strategic affairs. Brodie wrote in a November 1954 article: "The conclusion seems inescapable that our government can use the threat of unlimited war to deter only the most outrageous kind of aggression." Nor did Brodie fail to see the undercurrent discussion of preventive war: "Actually there probably never was a time when preventive war would have been technically—not to say politically—feasible. When we had the atomic monopoly, we did not have enough power; and when we had the necessary power, we no longer had the monopoly." Nuclear striking power had reached the point when war meant mutual destruction, and "our present-day diplomacy based on the deterrent value of our great atomic power is in danger of being strait-jacketed by fear of the very power we hold."[2]

Technical military lessons were also drawn about the validity of "massive retaliation." The forces were not available to do all things in all theaters, nor would they be under the "New Look." In view of this the implicit threats, especially to China, contained in the "massive retaliation" speech were hardly realistic. In the words of Paul Y. Hammond, an eminent scholar of the national security function,

> what was perhaps the most important decision made through the NSC machinery during the first term of the Eisenhower Administration did not stand the test either of its first public exposition or its first application. Each test, it should be noted, assayed some aspect of its rationality as well as probed the depths of the Administration's commitment. The least we can conclude from what

*is known about the NSC's role in the Indochina crisis and
in the formulation of the massive retaliation doctrine of
the Eisenhower Administration is that in this case the
freedom from partisan political considerations did not assure it a greater rationality than the more public channels
of government decision-making would permit it.*[3]

Criticism at the time crystallized doubts on the efficacy of
"massive retaliation" and its "New Look." As General Ridgway
said, there could be no intervention without mobilization. Vice
Admiral Arthur C. Davis, Pentagon advisor at Geneva, argued
that "the US should not be self-duped into believing the possibility of partial involvement—such as 'Naval and Air units only.'
One cannot go over Niagara Falls in a barrel only slightly."[4] The
ultimate need for ground forces when viewed against the weakness of the U.S. Army meant that the commitment to intervene
in Operation Vulture lacked credibility. Creating that credibility
in South Viet-Nam was the task of the remainder of the Eisenhower administration and of the Kennedy years.

Because the United States resisted any effort to resolve the
political differences remaining from the 1954 Indochina settlement, challenge to the American presence in South Viet-Nam
became inevitable, regardless of its credibility. Thus the basic
mistake remained the same as it had been in 1953, failure to deal
with all political tendencies in the country. Ultimately the desire
to demonstrate the credibility of the U.S. commitment to South
Viet-Nam—not only to the North Vietnamese, but to our NATO
and SEATO allies as well—required 538,000 combat troops.

John Foster Dulles learned from Dien Bien Phu a lesson in
the manipulation of risk. The juggling act Dulles performed to
keep the French hoping for aid, while at the same time keeping
the U.S. Congress confident of its war powers, marked Dulles as
an able diplomat.

It was true that Dulles's relations with Foreign Secretary Anthony Eden never recovered from Vulture. When the British came to visit Washington at the end of June 1954, President Eisenhower had to ask Dulles to be nicer to the British foreign secretary. On another occasion Dulles expressed himself with such vehemence to a Senate hearing that a Republican member said to him, "You're either a liar or Eden is a double-crosser."[5]

The degree to which Dulles personally favored Indochina intervention is still a matter of dispute. Some of the ambiguity in his position was no doubt intended. As he told an interviewer at the beginning of 1955,

> you have to take chances for peace just as you must take chances in war. Some say that we were brought to the verge of war. The ability to get to the verge without getting into the war is the necessary art. If you cannot master it, you inevitably get into war. If you try to run away from it, if you are scared to go to the brink, you are lost. We've had to look it square in the face. . . . We walked to the brink and we looked it in the face.[6]

When the interview was incorporated into an article about crisis posturing, Dulles critics coined the word *brinkmanship* to characterize the Secretary of State's approach to foreign policy. Both Dulles and Eisenhower tried to reject this description, but it stuck.

The worst aspect of the "brinkmanship crisis" is the inherent danger to world peace and security. As Chalmers Roberts said of the Secretary of State at Dien Bien Phu, "I also have no doubt that this time Dulles was prepared to go over the brink."[7]

President Eisenhower also tested his military advisors in the Dien Bien Phu crisis. It is perhaps significant that in later years Ike exercised closer supervision over the Pentagon across a broad range of military matters. In the missile and space area the President even restrained some of the more ambitious plans of his military chiefs. As for China, historian Robert Donovan, an official during Eisenhower's first term, recalls the President telling a group at one of his "stag dinners" in 1956 that the United States should normalize its relations with that country. Ike came to think it foolish to pretend that so large a nation as the People's Republic did not exist.

However, Eisenhower's general orientation toward the Cold War is evident: Admiral Arthur Radford was in no way sanctioned for any of his views in the Dien Bien Phu crisis. Throughout his tenure as chairman of the Joint Chiefs, which lasted until 1957, Radford continued to work closely with the President. He was replaced by Air Force General Nathan Twining, the man who wanted to march out of Dien Bien Phu playing *La Marseillaise*. The man who did leave the Joint Chiefs of Staff was Matt Ridgway. The "New Look" strategy remained in effect, Army capabilities were further degraded, and General Ridgway retired to dramatize the weakness to American security.

In Ned Lebow's analysis, the motivation for leaders marching to the brink relates mostly to internal politics. There may be weaknesses in the political system; the leader of government may feel vulnerable. Internal political weakness still operates as a motivator of "brinkmanship"—witness Argentine actions over the Falkland Islands in 1982. Eisenhower had broad political support, but present and future American presidents may feel more vulnerable, and more drawn to the sudden act of force.

This brings us back to the original United States objectives in Indochina at the time of Dien Bien Phu. The Eisenhower administration refused to recognize French desire for a settlement; consequently it was bound to do anything necessary to keep the French in the war, with no commitments from the French.

Our inability to gain any leverage with the French military is a lesson that went unlearned. In the aggregate, American aid to the combatant was substantial, but this military assistance did not translate into political influence on the scene. Neither the French command nor its South Vietnamese successors were amenable to dictation or advice from outsiders. Because American leaders could not influence actions in Viet-Nam, the underlying causes of the Vietnamese revolution could not be dealt with even when they were recognized by Washington policy makers.

Of course, the French were swift to react when, by the slightest implication, American advisors questioned French sovereignty or authority in Indochina. South Vietnamese leaders, starting with Ngo Dinh Diem, were no less zealous in guarding their prerogatives. The National Security Council decision documents from the Dien Bien Phu crisis show a wide gap between envisioned policy and the realities of Viet-Nam; in the 1960s the gap would be as wide.

By the 1960s three crucial elements were being used to justify American presence in Viet-Nam: a request for intervention by the South Vietnamese, the maintaining of credibility, and the domino theory. It is disturbing that all three were formed in the crucible of Dien Bien Phu, an occasion in which the country had succeeded—despite itself—in staying out of war.

Watching from the wings as Eisenhower made his decisions about Dien Bien Phu were the men who would be presidents themselves during the years of American involvement in Viet-Nam. All served in the United States Congress and observed Eisenhower from that vantage point, except for Richard Nixon, who sat as Vice-President with the National Security Council.

Jack Kennedy was there, Democratic Senator from Massachusetts. Kennedy had been interested in Indochina from the early stages of his congressional career. He appreciated that only committed Vietnamese would continue a struggle against the committed Vietnamese of Ho Chi Minh. But as President he behaved as if dynamism in *American* action plus a rhetorical flourish or two could substitute for a popular and effective government in Viet-Nam. He moved the nation toward Viet-Nam involvement, not away from it. Before Kennedy's tragic death in Dallas in 1963, the American presence in Viet-Nam had grown to 16,500 men.

Lyndon Baines Johnson had perhaps the best chance to learn the lessons of Dien Bien Phu. Not only was Johnson the top opposition political figure in 1954, he watched the Kennedy years' developments as Vice-President. During his 1964 electoral campaign LBJ promised not to send "American boys" to fight "Asian wars." But apparently what Johnson learned from Dien Bien Phu was something very different: He learned to manage the politics of commitment rather than to question rationales for action.

The American commitment to combat in Viet-Nam in 1964–65 shows careful political fine-tuning, as a glance at the Pentagon Papers will confirm. There was a program for involvement. It involved getting a congressional resolution. The action plan provided for covert activity that would provoke an overt response that could in turn be countered by applications of American force, principally air and naval.

But once the planes were bombing, they needed to be guarded on the ground, and once the American troops were in on the ground, they would be just targets if not used offensively. After he had entered the war in a big way, LBJ insisted on the jargon "Free World Forces" with its awkward acronym, "FWF," to describe the allied expeditionary force in Viet-Nam. Troops were also sent from South Korea, Thailand, Australia, New Zealand, and the Philippines, which sent medical units only. But LBJ's "united action" lacked any European powers or wide Asian support and increasingly seemed to lack that very important ingredient, "credibility."

In 1965, when Johnson was preparing for the major decision to send U.S. ground troops to Viet-Nam in a combat role, McGeorge Bundy at the National Security Council prepared a memo on whether France in 1954 was "a useful analogy" for the United States in Viet-Nam in 1965.

Despite "superficial similarities," Bundy believed the two situations were not "fundamentally analogous." France had been "a colonial power seeking to reimpose its overseas rule, out of tune with Vietnamese nationalism, deeply divided in terms of French domestic opinion, politically unstable at home, the victim of seven years of warfare—the last four of them marked by military engagements on a scale far greater than anything yet encountered by the US."

Bundy did not question whether the United States, particularly the American citizen, was "in tune" with Vietnamese nationalism either. It took only three years of the Viet-Nam War for American opinion to become as deeply divided as had been French opinion at the time of Dien Bien Phu. Bundy's analysis was that the United States remained politically strong and had options that were not available to the French in 1954.[8]

LBJ pushed through the Tonkin Gulf resolution with a unanimous vote in the House of Representatives and the Senate vote of 88 to 2. Even before the resolution there was an intervention plan: In 1964 it was called "Operation 34-A." The plan had as direct an impact on the guerrilla war in South Viet-Nam as the 1954 atomic bombing of China might have had on the Viet Minh. Unlike Vulture, Operation 34-A was indeed implemented by the United States, through 1964, and it led to the first sustained air strikes on the north. The decision to commit ground troops followed soon after. Initially the troops were supposed to protect the air bases from which planes were flying bombing missions over North Viet-Nam.

This was just how Matt Ridgway envisioned it would be in 1954.

Richard Milhous Nixon certainly did not learn from Dien Bien Phu. Having pressed for an intervention, Nixon was disappointed in the events of 1954. The French, once they decided they wanted out of Indochina, went for a quick settlement. As president in his own right Nixon would not do that. In his 1968 campaign he hinted at a secret plan to end the Viet-Nam war. In a campaign speech at Denver that September 25 candidate Nixon had the audacity to declare, "I am proud of the fact that I served in an Administration that ended one war [Korea] and kept the nation out of other wars for eight years."[9] But in office Nixon extended the Viet-Nam conflict for another seven years, indeed beyond his tenure in office. The "secret plan" turned out to be a formula for propping up the Saigon government (which succeeded the French in the southern part of Viet-Nam) for long enough to permit a decent interval that would preserve U.S. prestige through defeat in the war. To attain this goal eventually required a series of military escalations in Indochina of a magnitude not that different from the one Eisenhower had considered at Dien Bien Phu and after.

One of Nixon's most celebrated escalations was the mining of Haiphong harbor in May 1972. Here was an action that certainly qualified as a brinkmanship crisis. The mining occurred during Nixon's reelection campaign and, according to reliable press reports, put the entire campaign staff on "overdrive" for about two weeks—creating a "spontaneous" outpouring of public support for the escalation. This included paying for telegrams to the White House praising the mining, organizing rallies, and bringing people to Washington in buses. There was also a full-page ad in *The New York Times*, costing $4,400 and ostensibly from private citizens, that Nixon's campaign staff managed to get out by May 17, about a week after the Haiphong mining. Was

Nixon's attention to detail in 1972 the result of learning at Dien Bien Phu that thin public support could wreck an intervention plan?

By the time President Gerald Ford took over, U.S. involvement had been reduced once again to the military-advisor level. Within less than a year South Viet-Nam collapsed, finally ending the Viet-Nam War. The American war ended more unfortunately than the French one before it, in the opinion of some Vietnamese. Tran Van Don, who had been one of the senior Vietnamese officers in the Bao Dai army, and who then rose to command the South Vietnamese forces, recalled, "Only one day to get out. Twenty-four hours in 1975 compared to what the French arranged in 1954. Then we had one year to go north or south. In 1975 we had only one day."[10]

After South Viet-Nam collapsed came the final historical refutation of the domino theory. Far from opening the door to an ideological tide that would sweep Southeast Asia, after Viet-Nam was reunited by force, the energies of the communist allies in Indochina were directed against each other, with Viet-Nam fighting Kampuchea, and the Chinese helping Kampuchea and fighting Viet-Nam. The dominos falling were a powerful image but too facile to be true.

There is and will continue to be a great debate over our Viet-Nam involvement. At one level the debate is between those who argue that the United States stumbled into Indochina, step by step, ending in a "quagmire." On the other side of the question are observers who see the process of involvement in Viet-Nam as purposeful in intent and deliberate in action. The system "worked": the military and executive bureaucracies functioned as a "stalemate machine."

It is important to consider the Dien Bien Phu crisis in relation to this great debate on Viet-Nam. The evidence clearly shows that the disastrous outcome of the crisis for the United States was produced by policy machinery functioning smoothly in all respects. There were no breakdowns in communications; there was close coordination among the White House, State, and the Pentagon; and the National Security Council machinery successfully formulated a policy that could be implemented—all with the express approval of the President. The policy had little chance for success because it was not attuned to the realities in Indochina, but the policy was deliberate. The United States did not wander aimlessly into a quagmire, it strode purposefully, "prestige behind the flag," as Dulles put it to General Paul Ely in March 1954.

The image of the "stalemate machine" suggests how difficult it may be to extricate our country from involvements once begun. Under the model, presidents follow certain implicit rules in making decisions: They seek to avoid the "loss" of any ally to an ideological adversary; they do only the minimum necessary to accomplish this, anything to prevent defeat but never the "maximum feasible" to achieve victory; they do this despite advisors' warnings that the minimum will not secure the stated national objectives; and, presidents then pass along the problem to their successors.

President Eisenhower certainly avoided the "maximum feasible" at Dien Bien Phu—Radford's "Vulture." Ike consistently decided in favor of the "minimum necessary": aid for the Navarre Plan; more aircraft for the French; Air Force technicians; CIA pilots; a "regional grouping" for Southeast Asia. Ike considered the "maximum feasible" but then turned against it. Just the initial presidential interest, however, was enough to give the "maximum feasible" an impetus within the bureaucracy, and a momentum that the President himself later had difficulty halting.

After the collapse of the French the "minimum necessary" became the rule. One step followed another on the road to the 1965 intervention. No one questioned the utility of coercive diplomacy, while the "minimum necessary" became more coercive at each step.

There are those who argue that this much wasn't enough, that the U.S. military was not really given its chance in Viet-Nam. A large military commitment very early in the war, runs the analysis, could have defeated Ho Chi Minh. Analysts of this persuasion ignore the logistical factors that existed in 1965 as much as in 1954—before really massive military forces could be introduced and supported, the entire port and transport network of Viet-Nam had to be increased tremendously. This could not be done overnight. The increases in the size of U.S. forces were as great as possible. Further, any president would probably have rejected any military option that required war mobilization for a conflict in the Third World. Both Eisenhower and LBJ did exactly this. In fact the "maximum" was not "feasible."

It did not matter much, the "maximum feasible," for the "minimum necessary" was still enough to make Viet-Nam the most destructive war in American history, in which more than three times as many munitions were expended as had been in all of World War II. The eventual toll for Americans was much higher than in Korea—56,000 dead, over 300,000 wounded, more than 1,800 men still regarded as "missing" three decades after the end of the U.S. combat involvement. If U.S. policy had been changed in 1954, the toll would have been far fewer—only nine men, five of whom returned from the Viet Minh prison camps. In 1945 there had been a chance for the United States to work with Ho Chi Minh; in the post-Geneva realignment of 1954 there was another. Both opportunities were missed. Instead the United States marched into Indochina, seeing but not comprehending.

NOTES

Chapter I. THE IDES OF MARCH

1. *Foreign Relations of the United States: 1945* (Washington: Government Printing Office, 1969), vol. 6, p. 313. For fascinating accounts of American field experience in Indochina at this time, see Archimedes Patti, *Why Viet Nam?* Also, Vice Admiral Milton E. Miles, *A Different Kind of War,* and R. Harris Smith, *OSS.* (Full bibliographic information for the published works cited in the notes is given in the Bibliography.)

2. *The Pentagon Papers: The Senator Gravel Edition,* vol. 1: *The Defense Department History of United States Decisionmaking on Vietnam,* p. 33, (hereafter cited as Gravel Pentagon Papers).

3. *Department of State Bulletin,* August 22, 1950.

4. Gravel Pentagon Papers, vol. 1, p. 362.

5. *Department of State Bulletin,* August 22, 1950.

6. National Security Council, NSC-141, "Reexamination of United States Programs for National Security," January 19, 1953 (declassified September 15, 1978), pp. 38, 50.

7. Eisenhower Diary, entry March 17, 1951. DDEL: Eisenhower Papers; Personal Diaries (Pre-Presidential), box 1/1, folder: "DDE Diary Jan. 1, 1950–Feb. 28, 1952 (2)." Italics in the original.

8. Letter, Eisenhower-Lovett, December 19, 1951 (declassified July 24, 1980). DDEL: Eisenhower Papers; Pre-Presidential Papers, box 72, folder: "Lovett, Robert A. (1)."

9. Letter, Lovett-Eisenhower, January 3, 1952 (declassified September 22, 1980), ibid.

10. Dwight D. Eisenhower, Princeton Oral History, July 28, 1964, p. 24.

Chapter II. THE NAVARRE PLAN

1. Max Olivier, "Un portrait du General Navarre," *Indochine Sudest Asiatique*, no. 22, September 1953, quoted p. 18.

2. Da Nang, a port town and major military base in the United States' war in Viet-Nam (1961–73), was actually called "Tourane" by the French. For the ease of American readers and to avoid the colonial origins of the usage "Tourane," the later Vietnamese name has been used throughout the text. (To provide consistency, the forms "Viet-Nam" and "Indochina" are also used throughout, even in quoted material, in place of "Vietnam" and "Indo-China." However, in quotes where the originator has used such forms as capitalizing words ["Communist," "Red China"], these forms have been retained in the excerpt even though the text consistently uses the lower case.)

3. Jules Roy, *The Battle of Dien Bien Phu*, quoted p. 17. The French edition of this book is considerably more detailed than the English one. For the ease of American readers, however, all references to Roy will be to the English edition except where unavoidable.

4. Pierre Rocolle, *Pourquoi Dien Bien Phu?*, quoted pp. 52–53.

5. Jean Pouget, *Nous étions à Dien Bien Phu*, p. 60.

6. Reprinted in Allan W. Cameron, ed., *Viet-Nam Crisis: A Documentary History*, vol. I: 1940–1956, pp. 198–99.

7. Ibid., p. 75.

8. Department of Defense, *Semi-Annual Report of the Secretary of Defense, January–June 1953*, p. 61.

9. *Public Papers of the President: Dwight D. Eisenhower 1953* (Washington: Government Printing Office, 1960), p. 541.

10. *United States-Vietnam Relations 1945–1967* (hereafter cited as US-VN Relations) (Washington, Government Printing Office, 1972), vol. 9, pp. 134–35.

11. Stephen Jurika, Jr., ed. *From Pearl Harbor to Vietnam*, p. 363.

12. John Lewis Gaddis, *Strategies of Containment*, quoted p. 103.

13. John Foster Dulles, "A Policy of Boldness," p. 151.

14. Dwight D. Eisenhower, Princeton Oral History, op. cit., pp. 39–40.

15. Allan W. Cameron, ed., *Viet-Nam Crisis*, pp. 204–5.

16. The French memo is quoted in item 2 for consideration at the 161st NSC Meeting. US-VN Relations, vol. 9, p. 148.

17. Robert R. Bowie, Columbia University Oral History, August 10, 1967, pp. 24–25.

18. Cameron, ed., *Viet-Nam Crisis*, pp. 206–7.

19. National Security Council, NSC 162/2, "Basic National Security Policy," paragraph 13(b). US-VN Relations, vol. 9, p. 182.

20. Ibid., paragraph 39 on p. 195.

21. *Department of State Bulletin*, January 25, 1954, pp. 107–10.

Chapter III. DIEN BIEN PHU

1. Department of State, "Memorandum of Restricted Meeting of Chiefs of Delegations," December 7, 1953 (declassified January 21, 1976), pp. 4,

2. DDEL: John Foster Dulles Papers (hereafter cited as JFD Papers), Subject Series, box 1, folder: "Memos of President's Conversation at Bermuda."

2. Dwight D. Eisenhower, *Mandate for Change*, p. 307.

3. Allan W. Cameron, ed., *Viet-Nam Crisis*, p. 227.

4. Senate Foreign Relations Committee (*Historical Series*), p. 111.

5. Ibid., p. 230.

6. National Security Council, NSC-177, "United States Objectives and Courses of Action with Respect to Southeast Asia," December 30, 1953 (declassified May 27, 1977), pp. 12–13, 14, 15. DDEL: Eisenhower Papers; White House Office: Office of the Special Assistant for National Security Affairs (hereafter cited as WHO:OS-ANSA); Policy Paper Subseries, box 14, folder: "NSC-177."

7. William Bragg Ewald, Jr., *Eisenhower the President*, quoted p. 107.

8. Department of State, *Foreign Relations of the United States 1952–1954*, vol. 23, pt. 1, p. 969.

9. US-VN Relations, vol. 9, p. 235.

10. Ibid., pp. 240–44.

11. Ibid., p. 239.

12. Hagerty Diary, entry for February 7, 1954. DDEL: James C. Hagerty Papers, box 1, chronological folder.

13. *The New York Times*, February 7, 1954.

14. *Public Papers of the President: Dwight D. Eisenhower: 1954* (hereafter cited as Eisenhower Public Papers 1954) (Washington: Government Printing Office, 1960), pp. 250, 253.

15. Maurice Casey Interview

Chapter IV. HELL IN A VERY SMALL PLACE

1. Bernard Fall, *Hell in a Very Small Place*, pp. 127–28.

2. Joseph and Stewart Alsop, "Where Is Dien Bien Phu?," *New York Herald Tribune*, January 27, 1954, p. 14.

3. Jean Pouget, *Nous étions à Dien Bien Phu*, p. 175.

4. Jules Roy, *The Battle of Dien Bien Phu*, quoted p. 140.

5. Paul Ely, *Mémoires*, vol. 1, p. 51.

6. E. Krieg, et al., *La tragédie indochinoise*, vol. 3, quoted p. 163.

7. Ibid., p. 61.

8. Graham Greene, *Ways of Escape*, p. 189.

9. US-VN Relations, vol. 9, p. 252.

10. Letter, Eisenhower-Dulles, February 10, 1954 (declassified September 14, 1976). DDRS 76–216(c).

11. Dwight D. Eisenhower, *Mandate for Change*, p. 417.

Chapter V. VULTURE CONCEIVED

1. Senate Foreign Relations Committee, *Executive Sessions of the Senate Foreign Relations Committee* (*Historical Series*), vol. 6: 83rd Cong. 2nd Sess., 1954, p. 127.

2. US-VN Relations, vol. 9, pp. 266, 268, 270.

3. Ibid. .

4. Senate Foreign Relations Committee (*Historical Series*), p. 111.

5. Ibid., p. 166.

6. Eisenhower Public Papers 1954, p. 306.

7. Edwin B. Hooper, Dean C. Allard, and Oscar P. Fitzgerald, *The United States Navy and the Viet-Nam Conflict*, Vol. I: *The Setting of the Stage to 1959*, p. 235.

8. *The New York Times*, March 23, 1954, p. 2.

9. Department of State, "John Foster Dulles Press and Radio Conference," March 23, 1954, DOS no. 3 and Press Release no. 154. DDEL: Carl McCardle Papers, box 6, folder: "Mr. Dulles' Press Conferences 1954."

0. Dwight D. Eisenhower, *Mandate for Change*, quoted pp. 417–18.

11. Paul Ely, *Mémoires*, vol. 1, pp. 65–66.

12. Department of State, "United States Policy on Armed Intervention in Indochina," August 1954 (declassified July 3, 1978), p. 5. DDRS 78–406(d).

13. Joint Chiefs of Staff Historical Division, Joint Secretariat, *The History of the Joint Chiefs of Staff: The Joint Chiefs of Staff and*

the War in Vietnam: History of the Indochina Incident 1940–1954, quoted p. 372.

14. Ibid.

15. Hagerty Diary, op. cit., entry for March 24, 1954.

16. Eisenhower Public Papers 1954, pp. 343–44.

17. John Foster Dulles, "Memorandum of Conversation with the President," March 24, 1954 (declassified August 28, 1981). DDEL: JFD Papers; White House Memoranda Series, box 1, folder: "Record of Actions 1954 (1)."

18. National Security Council, Record of Actions at 190th NSC Meeting (declassified September 7, 1978). DDEL: Eisenhower Papers; NSC Series, box 1, folder: "Record of Actions 1954 (1)."

19. CAG-17 Operation Report, Serial 05-54, April 18, 1954. Naval Historical Center.

20. Department of State, *Foreign Relations of the United States 1952–54*, vol. 13: *Indochina*, pt. 1, (hereafter cited as FRUS 1952–54) (Washington: Government Printing Office, 1982), p. 1166.

21. Ely, *Mémoires*, vol. 1, p. 76.

22. Ibid.

23. Hagerty Diary, op. cit., entry for March 26, 1954.

Chapter VI. VULTURE TRANSFORMED

1. *The New York Times*, March 28, 1954; Letter, Eisenhower-Coty, March 27, 1954. DDEL: DDE Diaries, box 6, folder: "March 1954 (1)."

2. Allan W. Cameron, ed., *Viet-Nam Crisis*, pp. 233–36.

3. Telephone notes, Dulles-Knowland, March 29, 1954. DDEL: JFD Papers, loc. eit.

4. *The Times* (London), April 1, 1954, p. 5; April 3, 1954, p. 6.

5. Memorandum, Radford-Wilson, March 31, 1954. FRUS 1952–54, vol. 12, pt. 1, p. 1198.

6. Hagerty Diary, op. cit., entry for April 1, 1954.

7. Telephone notes, Dulles-Radford, April 1, 1954. DDEL:JFD Papers, loc. cit.

8. Anthony Eden, *Full Circle*, p. 102.

9. Anthony Eden, *Full Circle*, pp. 102–3.

10. Henry Brandon, *Anatomy of Error*, quoted pp. 9–10.

11. Charles C. Alexander, *Holding the Line: The Eisenhower Era 1952–61*, quoted p. 79.

12. All the Chiefs' memos went in on April 2, 1954; all were declassified on January 30, 1978. NA:MMB: RG 218; Radford Series, box 9, folder: "091 Indochina (March 1954)."

13. John Foster Dulles, "Memorandum of Conversation with the President," April 2, 1954 (declassified August 28, 1981). DDEL: JFD Papers; White House Memoranda Series, box 1, folder: "Meetings with the President 1954 (4)."

14. The foregoing account of the meeting with congressional leaders has been assembled from the following records and accounts: Chalmers Roberts, "The Day We Didn't Go to War," pp. 31–35. David Halberstam, *The Best and the Brightest*, pp. 140–41. Lyndon Baines Johnson, "Your Senator Reports," April 15, 1954. LBJ Library: Senate Papers, constituent newsletter. John

Foster Dulles, "Memorandum for the Secretary's File," April 5, 1954 (declassified November 1, 1979). DDEL: JFD Papers; Subject Series, box 9, folder: "Indochina 1954 (2)." Cf. "Draft Joint Resolution," April 2, 1954. DDEL: JFD Papers: Subject Series, box 8, folder: "Indochina May 1953–May 1954 (4)."

15. Jean Pouget, *Nous étions à Dien Bien Phu*, quoted p. 280.

16. US-VN Relations, vol. 9, pp. 296–97.

Chapter VII. "THE TIME FOR FORMULATING COALITIONS HAS PASSED"

1. Dwight D. Eisenhower, *Mandate for Change*, pp. 420–21.

2. Eisenhower Oral Histories, loc. cit.

3. Eisenhower, *Mandate for Change*, pp. 419–20.

4. Telephone notes, Dulles-Eisenhower, April 5, 1954. DDEL: DDE Diaries, box 3, folder: "Phone Calls, January–May 1954."

5. Telephone notes, Dulles-Radford, April 5, 1954. DDEL: JFD Papers, loc. cit.

6. Hagerty Diary, op. cit., entry for April 5, 1954.

7. US-VN Relations, vol. 9, p. 359.

8. Matthew Ridgway; *Soldier*, p. 276.

9. US-VN Relations, vol. 9, p. 308.

10. Richard Nixon: *RN: The Memoirs of Richard Nixon*, vol. 1, p. 151.

11. R. Gordon Hoxie, *Command Decision and the Presidency*, quoted p. 285.

12. Memorandum, Radford-Dulles, April 10, 1954 (declassified January 30, 1978). NA:MMB: RG 218; Radford Series, box 10, folder: "091 Indochina (April 1954)." Italics in the original.

13. Minutes of the Cabinet Meeting, April 9, 1954 (declassified April 28, 1977). DDEL: Eisenhower Papers; Cabinet Series, box 3, folder: "Meeting of April 9, 1954."

14. Eisenhower Public Papers 1954, pp. 381–90.

15. *The New York Times*, editorial, April 8, 1954, p. 26.

16. *The Washington Post*, April 8, 1954.

17. Richard Rovere, *Affairs of State: The Eisenhower Years*, p. 191.

18. Stephen Jurika, ed., *From Pearl Harbor to Vietnam: The Memoirs of Admiral Arthur W. Radford.*, pp. 403–5.

19. Telephone notes, Wilson-Eisenhower, April 9, 1954. DDEL: DDE Diaries, box 3, folder: "Phone Calls, January–May 1954."

Chapter VIII. MR. DULLES GOES TO EUROPE

1. *Department of State Bulletin*, April 19, 1954, p. 589. Smith was referring to the continent of Asia, not merely Indochina. Cf. Tyler Abell, ed., *The Drew Pearson Diaries 1949–1959* (hereafter cited as Drew Pearson Diaries), p. 305.

2. Anthony Eden, *Full Circle*, p. 105.

3. Ibid., pp. 107–8.

4. Allan W. Cameron, ed., *Viet-Nam Crisis*, p. 238.

5. Leonard Mosley, *Dulles: A Biography of Eleanor, Allen, and John Foster Dulles and Their Family Network*, quoted p. 355.

6. Memorandum, Layton-Radford, June 3, 1954 (declassified January 30, 1978). NA:MMB:RG 218; Radford Series, box 11, folder: "091 Indochina (May–June 1954)."

7. Cyrus Sulzberger, *A Long Row of Candles*, p. 994.

8. John Foster Dulles, "Memorandum of Conversation," April 14, 1954 (declassified March 3, 1981). DDEL: Eisenhower Papers; Dulles-Herter Series, box 2, folder: "Dulles April 1954 (2)."

9. Douglas MacArthur II, "Memorandum of Conversation," April 14, 1954 (declassified September 11, 1981). DDEL: JFD Papers; White House Memoranda Series, box 1, folder: "Meetings with the President 1954 (4)."

Chapter IX. VULTURE REFUSES TO DIE

1. David Schoenbrun, *As France Goes*, p. 243.

2. Jules Roy, *The Battle of Dien Bien Phu*, quoted p. 239.

3. *The New York Times*, April 17, 1954.

4. Hagerty Diary, op. cit., entry for April 16, 1954. Later opinion from Columbia Oral History.

5. *Department of State Bulletin*, April 26, 1954, p. 623.

6. Telephone notes, Eisenhower-Nixon, April 19, 1954. DDEL: DDE Diaries, box 6, folder: "Phone Calls, January–May 1954."

7. Eleanor Lansing Dulles, "Time and Decisions," p. 277.

8. John Foster Dulles, "Minutes of Congressional Leadership Meeting," May 5, 1954 (declassified March 7, 1978), p. 6. DDRS 78–429(b).

9. John Foster Dulles, "Memorandum of Conference with the President," April 19, 1954 (declassified August 28, 1981). DDEL:

JFD Papers; White House Memoranda Series, box 1, folder: "Meetings with the President 1954 (3)."

10. Hagerty Diary, op. cit., entry for April 19, 1954.

11. Telephone notes, Nixon-Dulles, April 19, 1954. DDEL: JFD Papers: Telephone Calls Series, box 2, folder: "Telephone Memos March-April 1954 (1)."

Chapter X. "AND IF I GAVE YOU TWO A-BOMBS FOR DIEN BIEN PHU?"

1. Bernard Fall, *Hell in a Very Small Place*, quoted pp. 305–6.

2. Joseph D. Caldara, "Memorandum for the Record," March 8, 1966 (declassification date not available), p. 2.

3. Maynard O. Edwards, *Far East Air Force Support of French Indochina Operations*. Vol. 1: *1 July 1952–30 September 1954*, pp. 284–85. Italics in the original.

4. Cyrus Sulzberger, *A Long Row of Candles*, pp. 999–1000.

5. Cable, Dulles-Smith, DULTE 9, April 23, 1954 (declassified March 3, 1981). DDEL: Eisenhower Papers; Dulles-Herter Series, box 2, folder: "Dulles April 1954 (2)."

6. Dwight D. Eisenhower, *Mandate for Change*, pp. 423–24.

7. Ibid.

8. Ibid.

9. Anthony Eden, *Full Circle*, p. 113.

10. Cable, Dulles-Smith, April 24, 1954 (declassified March 3, 1981). DDEL: Eisenhower Papers; Dulles-Herter Series, box 2, folder: "Dulles April 1954 (1)."

11. J. R. Tournoux, *Secrets d'état*, quoted p. 48.

12. Georges Bidault, *Resistance*, p. 196.

13. Cable, Dillon-Dulles, August 9, 1954. US-VN Relations, vol. 10, p. 705.

14. Ibid.

15. Admiral Felix Stump U.S. Naval Institute Oral History, June 25, 1964, p. 292.

16. Charles C. Alexander, *Holding the Line: The Eisenhower Era 1952–1961*, quoted p. 79.

17. Melvin Gurtov, *The First Vietnam Crisis*, quoted p. 134.

18. FRUS 1952–54, vol. 13, pt. 2, p. 1447.

19. Richard Nixon, *RN*, vol. 1, quoted p. 189.

20. FRUS 1952–54, loc. cit.

21. John Foster Dulles, "Points for Discussion," n.d. (April 19, 1954?) (declassified July 8, 1981). DDEL: JFD Papers; White House Memoranda Series, box 1, folder: "Meetings with the President 1954 (3)."

22. Drew Pearson Diaries, p. 305.

23. John Foster Dulles, "Memorandum of Conversation" for April 24, prepared April 26, 1954 (declassified October 15, 1981). DDEL: JFD Papers; Subject Series, box 9, folder: "Mr. Merchant, Top Secret [Indochina] (2)."

24. Cable, Dulles-Smith, DULTE 13, April 24, 1954 (declassified March 3, 1981). DDEL: Eisenhower Papers; Dulles-Herter Series, box 2, folder: "Dulles April 1954 (1)."

25. Eden, *Full Circle*, p. 116.

26. *The New York Times*, April 25, 1954, p. 1.

27. Cable, Aldrich-Dulles, London 4725, April 26, 1954 (declassified March 15, 1982). DDEL: Eisenhower Papers; Dulles-Herter Series, box 2, folder: "Dulles April 1954 (1)."

28. Arthur Radford, "Memorandum for the Record," April 27, 1954 (declassified January 30, 1978). NA: MMB: RG 218, Radford Series, box 10, folder: "091 Indochina (April 1954)."

29. Radford, Memorandum for the Record, April 27, 1954. NA: MMB:RG-218; Radford series, box 10, folder:091 Indochina (April 1954).

30. Hagerty Diary, op. cit., entry for April 22, 1954.

31. Eisenhower Public Papers 1954, pp. 419, 420.

32. Hagerty Diary, op. cit., entry for April 24, 1954.

33. Robert Kirshner Interview, June 26, 1983.

34. Ibid., entry for April 25, 1954.

35. The foregoing account has been assembled from the Hagerty Diary, this date; from Sherman Adams, *Firsthand Report*, pp. 123–24; and from notes by Robert Cutler of the points made by Eisenhower (declassified June 16, 1976). DDEL: Eisenhower Papers; WHO: Project Clean Up, box 19, folder: "Indochina 1954."

36. William Lawrence, *Six Presidents and Too Many Wars*, quoted pp. 198–99.

Chapter XI. GENEVA AND THE FALL OF DIEN BIEN PHU

1. *Contributions to the History of Dien Bien Phu, Vietnam Studies*, no. 3, March 1965. Hanoi: Foreign Languages Publishing House.

2. Richard Nixon, *RN*, vol. 1, p. 189.

3. Dwight D. Eisenhower, *Mandate for Change*, pp. 428–29.

4. Marty Reisman, *The Money Player*, p. 18.

5. Interview with Maurice Casey.

6. US-VN Relations, vol. 9, pp. 397–98.

7. George W. Anderson, "Memorandum for the Record," April 29, 1954 (declassified January 29, 1978). NA:MMB: RG 218; Radford Series, box 10, folder: "091 Indochina (April 1954)."

8. Eisenhower, *Mandate for Change*, p. 429.

9. Drew Pearson Diaries, p. 310.

10. Anthony Eden, *Full Circle*, quoted p. 124.

11. Anthony Eden, *Full Circle*, p. 132.

12. David Carlton, *Anthony Eden: A Biography*, quoted p. 343.

13. Eden, *Full Circle*, p. 132.

14. John Foster Dulles, "Minutes of Congressional Leadership Meeting," May 5, 1954, op. cit., p. 7.

15. US-VN Relations, vol. 9, p. 425.

16. Ibid., p. 437.

17. Bernard Fall, *Hell in a Very Small Place*, p. 389.

18. Jules Roy, *The Battle of Dien Bien Phu*, quoted pp. 282–83; Fall, *Hell in a Very Small Place*, quoted pp. 406–7.

19. Fall, *Hell in a Very Small Place*, quoted p. 417.

Chapter XII. TRUCE OR TERROR?

1. US-VN Relations, vol. 9, pp. 402, 405.

2. "Address by the Honorable John Foster Dulles, Secretary of State," Department of State Press Release no. 238, May 7, 1954, quoted pp. 3, 4, 5.

3. Department of State: "Memorandum of Conversation, Secretary's Residence," May 9, 1954 (declassified January 27, 1982). DDEL:JFD Papers: Subject series, box 8, folder: "Indochina May 1953–May 1954 (2)."

4. Gravell Pentagon Papers, v. I, p. 506.

5. Townsend Hoopes, *The Devil and John Foster Dulles*, p. 229.

6. Melvin Gurtov, *The First Vietnam Crisis*, p. 145n.

7. Gravel Pentagon Papers, vol. 1, p. 508.

8. Memorandum, Cutler-Wilson, May 26, 1954 (declassified June 16, 1976). DDEL: DDE Papers; WHO: Project Clean Up, box 19, folder: "Indochina 1954." Italics in the original. (For continuity the author has substituted "Chinese Communists" and "Communist China" for the abbreviation "CC," which appears twice in the quote.)

9. US-VN Relations, vol. 9, pp. 487–93.

10. Ewald, *Eisenhower, The President*, quoted p. 117–8.

11. Draft Resolution, May 17, 1954. DDSL: John Foster Dulles Papers, Subject Series, b. I, f: "Indochina May 1953-May 1954 (1)."

12. Drew Pearson Diaries, p. 321.

13. Marquis Childs, *The Ragged Edge*, pp. 154–55.

14. Edward Lansdale, *In the Midst of Wars*. New York: Harper & Row, 1972, p. 149.

15. US-VN Relations, vol. 9, p. 663.

16. Seymour Topping, *Journey Between Two Chinas*, quoted p. 152.

Chapter XIII. EYELESS INTO INDOCHINA?

1. William Bragg Ewald, Jr., *Eisenhower the President*, quoted pp. 118, 120.

2. Bernard Brodie, "Unlimited Weapons and Limited War," pp. 16, 17, 18.

3. Hammond's 1960 comment is contained in "The National Security Council: An Interpretation and Appraisal," in Alan Altshuler, ed., *The Politics of the Federal Bureaucracy*, p. 153.

4. Gravel Pentagon Papers, vol. 1, p. 89.

5. Fletcher Knebel, "We Nearly Went to War Three Times," quoted p. 26.

6. J. R. Beal, *John Foster Dulles 1888-1959*, quoted pp. 216–17.

7. Chalmers Roberts, *First Rough Draft*, p. 116.

8. Memorandum, Bundy-Johnson, June 30, 1965 (declassified July 17, 1980). LBJ Library: LBJ Papers; Open McGeorge Bundy Memos on Viet-Nam, unboxed folder, pp. 7–8.

9. Lewis Chester, Godfrey Hodgson, and Bruce Page, *An American Melodrama: The Presidential Campaign of 1968*. New York: Dell Books, 1969, quoted p. 761.

10. Michael Maclear, *The Ten Thousand Day War*, quoted p. 403.

BIBLIOGRAPHY

I. COLLECTIONS

Dwight D. Eisenhower Library (DDEL), National Archives
    Administration Papers
    Ann Whitman Diary
    Ann Whitman File: DDE Diary Series
    Ann Whitman File: Legislative Meetings Series
    Cabinet Series
    Dulles-Herter Series
    National Security Council Series
    Official File
    White House Office: Project Clean Up
    White House Office: Office of the Special Assistant for National Security Affairs: Alphabetical Series
    White House Office: Office of the Special Assistant for National Security Affairs: Policy Paper Subseries
    White House Office: Office of the Special Assistant for National Security Affairs: Special Assistant Series; Presidential Subseries
    Papers Other Than President Eisenhower's:
        John Foster Dulles Papers:

Subject Series
Telephone Calls Series
White House Memoranda Series
James C. Hagerty Papers
Carl McCardle Papers
Walter Bedell Smith Papers

Lyndon Baines Johnson Library, National Archives (LBJ Library)
Senate Papers: Case and Project Files
Senate Papers: Constituent Newsletter
Senate Papers: George E. Reedy Papers
Open McGeorge Bundy Memos on Viet-Nam

National Archives: Modern Military Branch (NA:MMB)
Records Group 218: Records of the Joint Chiefs of Staff
Records Group 218: Records of the Joint Chiefs of Staff: CJCS
Radford 1953–1957

Declassified Documents Reference System (DDRS)
This is a microfiche document collection first issued in 1975. It is organized in a Retrospective (R) series and subsequent annual sets. In citations the series is given, followed by a card number and then an alphabetic document identifier. Example: 76--429(b).

Freedom of Information Act
Documents cited with only the originating agency and a declassification date were obtained directly by the author from the indicated agency under the provisions of 5 USC 552 et seq.

Eisenhower Project Oral Histories (maintained jointly by the Eisenhower Library and Columbia University)

Winthrop Aldrich
Dillion Anderson
Robert R. Bowie
Arleigh A. Burke
C. Douglas Dillon
Dwight D. Eisenhower (Princeton Oral History, 1964)
Dwight D. Eisenhower (Columbia Oral History, 1967)
John S. D. Eisenhower
Gordon Gray
James C. Hagerty (1967–68)
James C. Hagerty (1969)
Karl G. Harr
Walter H. Judd
William F. Knowland
Carl McCardle
Livingston Merchant
Chalmers Roberts
Leverett Saltonstall
James R. Shepley
Robert Thayer

II. OFFICIAL DOCUMENTS AND HISTORIES

Democratic Republic of Viet-Nam. *An Outline History of the Viet Nam Workers' Party 1930–1970.* Hanoi: Foreign Languages Publishing House, 1970.

Department of Defense. *Semi-Annual Report of the Secretary of Defense, January-June 1953.* Washington: Government Printing Office, 1953.

——. *Semi-Annual Report of the Secretary of Defense, July-December 1953.* Washington: Government Printing Office, 1954.

——. *Semi-Annual Report of the Secretary of Defense, January-June 1954*. Washington: Government Printing Office, 1954.

Department of State. *Foreign Relations of the United States 1952–1954*, vol. 13, *Indochina*, 2 parts. Washington: Government Printing Office, 1982.

French Expeditionary Corps

CROIZAT, COLONEL VICTOR J., trans. *A Translation from the French: Lessons of the War in Indochina*. Vol. 2: *Expeditionary Corps*, 1955. RAND Corporation, RM 5271-PR, May 1967.

FOSSY-FRANCOIS, MAJOR A., et al., *La guerre psychologique en Indochine: de 1945 au'cessez le feu*. Expeditionary Corps Report, March 21, 1955 (?).

Joint Chiefs of Staff

Historical Division, Joint Secretariat. *The History of the Joint Chiefs of Staff: The Joint Chiefs of Staff and the War in Vietnam; History of the Indochina incident 1940–1954*. Ms., February 1, 1955.

United States Air Force

EDWARDS, MAYNARD O. *Far East Air Force Support of French Indochina Operations*. Vol. 1; *1 July 1952–30 September 1954*. Historical Section, Headquarters, Far East Air Force. Ms., November 1, 1954 (declassified June 27, 1974).

FEAF Command Historical Report, Vol. II. Historical Section, Headquarters, Far East Air Force. Ms., November 1953 (declassified June 27, 1954).

FUTRELL, ROBERT F., and MOSLEY, GENERAL LAWSON S., USAF. *The United States Air Force in Korea 1950-1953*. New York: Duell, Sloane & Pearce, 1961.

FUTRELL, ROBERT F., with BLUMENSON, MARTIN. *The United States Air Force in Southeast Asia*. Vol. 1: *The Advisory Years to 1965*. Washington: Office of Air Force History, 1981.

MAURER, MAURER, ed. *Air Force Combat Units of World War II*. Air University: USAF Historical Division, 1961.

United States Army
Area Handbook for Vietnam. Washington: Government Printing Office, 1964. *Area Handbook for North Vietnam*. Washington: Government Printing Office, 1967.

United States Congress
Senate. Foreign Relations Committee. 83rd Cong., 2nd Sess. *Hearing on the Mutual Defense Assistance Control Act of 1951*. Washington: Government Printing Office, 1954.

——. 83rd Cong., 2nd Sess. *Hearings on Foreign Policy and its Relation to Military Programs*. Washington: Government Printing Office, 1954.

——. 83rd Cong., 2nd Sess. *Report of Senator H. Alexander Smith: The Far East and South Asia*. January 25, 1954. Washington: Government Printing Office, 1954.

——. *Executive Sessions of the Senate Foreign Relations Committee (Historical Series)*. Vol. 6: 83rd Cong., 2nd Sess., 1954. Washington: Government Printing Office, 1977.

United States Navy

FIELD, JAMES A., JR. *History of United States Naval Operations—Korea.* Washington: Government Printing Office, 1962.

HOOPER, EDWIN B., ALLARD, DEAN C., and FITZGERALD, OSCAR P. *The United States Navy and the Viet-Nam Conlict.* Vol. I: *The Setting of the Stage to 1959.* Washington: Naval History Division, 1976.

III. BOOKS

ABELL, TYLER, ed. *The Drew Pearson Diaries 1949–1959.* New York: Holt, Rinehart & Winston, 1974.

ACHESON, DEAN. *Present at the Creation.* New York: New American Library, 1969.

ADAMS, SHERMAN. *Firsthand Report.* New York: Harper & Row, 1961.

ALEXANDER, CHARLES C. *Holding the Line: The Eisenhower Era 1952–1961.* Bloomington: Indiana University Press, 1975.

ALMOND, GABRIEL. *The American People and Foreign Policy.* New York: Praeger, 1950.

ALTSHULER, ALAN, ed. *The Politics of the Federal Bureaucracy.* New York: Dodd, Mead, 1968.

AMBLER, JOHN. *The French Army in Politics 1945–1962.* Canton: Ohio State University Press, 1966.

BARNETT, A. DOAK. *Communist China and Asia.* New York: Random House, 1960.

BEAL, J....R. *John Foster Dulles 1888–1959.* New York: Harper & Row, 1959.

BERGOT, ERWAN. *2ème Classe à Dien Bien Phu.* Paris: La Table Ronde, 1964.

BIDAULT, GEORGES. *Resistance.* New York: Praeger, 1967.

——. *D'une résistance à l'autre.* Paris: Presses du Siècle, 1965.

BLOND, GEORGES. *La Legion Étrangère.* Ottawa: Le Cercle du Livre de France, 1965.

BOCCA, GEOFFREY. *La Légion.* New York: Thomas Y. Crowell, 1964.

BODARD, LUCIEN. *La guerre d'Indochine.* Vol. 3: *L'Aventure.* Paris: Gallimard, 1967.

BOHLEN, CHARLES E., with assistance of PHELPS, ROBERT H. *Witness to History 1929–1969.* New York: W. W. Norton, 1973.

BONNECARRÈRE, PAUL. *Par le sang versé.* Paris: Fayard, 1968.

BORNERT LUCIEN. *Dien Bien Phu.* Paris: Nouvelles Presses Modernes, 1954.

BOURDENS, HENRI. *Camionneur des nuées.* Paris: Éditions France-Empire, 1957.

BOWLES, CHESTER. *Ambassador's Report.* New York: Harper & Row, 1954.

BRANDON, HENRY. *Anatomy of Error: The Inside Story of the Asian War on the Potomac, 1954–1969.* Boston: Gambit Press, 1969.

BRODIE, BERNARD. *War and Politics.* New York: Macmillan, 1973.

BROPHY, FRANK R. *The Failure of US Policy Toward Viet-Nam 1953–1954.* Columbia University Master's Thesis, 1962.

BUHITE, RUSSELL D. *Soviet-American Relations in Asia 1945–1954*. Norman: University of Oklahoma Press, 1981.

BURCHETT, WILFRED. *North of the 17th Parallel* (2nd ed.). Hanoi: Red River Publishing House, 1957.

BUTTINGER, JOSEPH. *Vietnam: A Dragon Embattled*. New York: Praeger, 1967.

CAMERON, ALLAN W., ed. *Viet-Nam Crisis: A Documentary History*. Vol. I: *1940–1956*. Ithaca, N.Y.: Cornell University Press, 1971.

CAPA, CORNELL, and KARIA, BHUPRENDA, eds. *Robert Capa 1913–1954*. New York: Grossman Publishers, 1974.

CARIDI, RONALD J. *The Korean War and American Politics: The Republican Party as a Case Study*. Philadelphia: University of Pennsylvania Press, 1968.

CARLTON, DAVID. *Anthony Eden: A Biography*. London: Allen Lane, 1981.

CATROUX, GENERAL GEORGES. *Deux actes du drame indochinois*. Paris: Librairie Plon, 1959.

CHASSIN, GENERAL LIONEL MAX. *Aviation Indochine*. Paris: Amiot-Dumont, 1954.

CHEN, KING C. *Chinese Aid to the Viet Minh 1938–1954*. Princeton: Princeton University Press, 1959.

CHILDS, MARQUIS. *The Ragged Edge: The Diary of a Crisis*. New York: Doubleday, 1955.

COLE, ALLAN B., ed. *Conflict in Indochina and International Repercussions: A Documentary History 1945–1955*. Ithaca, N.Y.: Cornell University Press, 1956.

COLLINS, GENERAL J. LAWTON. *War in Peacetime: The History and Lessons of Korea.* Boston: Houghton Mifflin, 1969.

Contributions to the History of Dien Bien Phu. Vietnam Studies, no. 3. Hanoi: Foreign Languages Publishing House, March 1965.

COOPER, CHESTER. *The Lost Crusade: America in Vietnam.* New York: Dodd, Mead, 1970.

CROZIER, BRIAN, with CHOU, ERIC. *The Man Who Lost China.* New York: Scribner's, 1976.

DANNAUD, JEAN P. *Guerre morte.* Paris: Société Asiatic d'Éditions, 1955.

DELPEY, ROGER. *La bataille de Tonkin.* Paris: Éditions de la Pensée Moderne, 1965.

DESPUECH, JACQUES. *Le trafic des piastres.* Paris: Éditions Deux Rives, 1953.

DEUTSCHER, ISAAC. *Russia, China and the West: A Contemporary Chronicle 1953–1966.* London: Oxford University Press, 1970.

DEWEY, THOMAS E. *Journey to the Far Pacific.* New York: Doubleday, 1952.

Dien Bien Phu: Before, During, After. Viet Nam Studies, no. 43. Hanoi: Foreign Languages Publishing House, n.d. (1975).

DIVINE, ROBERT A. *Eisenhower and the Cold War.* New York: Oxford University Press, 1981.

DONOVAN, ROBERT J. *Eisenhower: The Inside Story.* New York: Harper & Row, 1956.

DOUGLAS, WILLIAM O. *North from Malaya.* New York: Doubleday, 1953.

DRUMMOND, ROSCOE, and COBLENZ, GASTON. *Duel at the Brink: John Foster Dulles' Command of American Power.* New York: Doubleday, 1960.

DRURY, ALLEN. *Three Kids in a Court.* New York: Doubleday, 1965.

EDEN, ANTHONY. *Full Circle: Memoirs of Anthony Eden.* Boston: Cassell, 1960.

EISENHOWER, DWIGHT D. *The White House Years.* Vol. I: *Mandate for Change 1953–1956.* New York: New American Library, 1963.

ELLSBERG, DANIEL. *Papers On the War.* New York: Simon and Schuster, 1972.

ELY, GENERAL PAUL. *Mémoires.* Vol. I: *L'Indochine dans la tourmente.* Paris: Librairie Plon, 1964.

EWALD, WILLIAM BRAGG, JR. *Eisenhower the President: Crucial Days 1951–1960.* Englewood Cliffs, N.J.: Prentice-Hall, 1981.

FALL, BERNARD B. *Hell in a Very Small Place.* New York: J. B. Lippincott, 1966.

——. *The Political Development of Viet-Nam: VJ Day to the Geneva Cease Fire.* Ph.D. Thesis, Syracuse University, 1955.

——. *Street Without Joy.* Harrisburg, Pa.: Stackpole Books, 1961.

——. *The Two Vietnams.* New York: Praeger, 1967.

——. *Le Viet Minh.* Paris: Librairie Armand Colin, 1960.

——. *The Vietminh Regime.* New York: Institute of Pacific Relations, 1956.

——. *Vietnam Witness 1953–1966.* New York: Praeger, 1966.

——. ed. *Ho Chi Minh On Revolution: Selected Writings 1920–1966.* New York: New American Library, 1967.

FEHRENBACH, T....R. *This Kind of War: A Study in Unpreparedness.* New York: Pocket Books, 1964.

FERRANDI, JEAN. *Les officiers français face au Vietminh 1945–1954.* Paris: Fayard, 1966.

FERRELL, ROBERT H., ed. *The Eisenhower Diaries.* New York: W. W. Norton, 1981.

FRIANG, BRIGITTE. *Les fleurs du ciel.* Paris: Éditions Robert Lafont, 1955.

GADDIS, JOHN LEWIS. *Strategies of Containment: A Critical Appraisal of Postwar American National Security Policy.* New York: Oxford University Press, 1982.

GALLOIS, GENERAL PIERRE. *The Balance of Terror: Strategy for the Nuclear Age.* Boston: Houghton Mifflin, 1961.

GAVIN, GENERAL JAMES M. *War and Peace in the Space Age.* New York: Harper & Row, 1958.

GEELHOED, E. BRUCE. *Charles E. Wilson and Controversy at the Pentagon 1953–1957.* Detroit: Wayne State University Press, 1979.

GELB, LESLIE H., with BETTS, RICHARD K. *The Irony of Vietnam: The System Worked.* Washington, D.C.: Brookings, 1979.

GEORGE, ALEXANDER L., and SMOKE, RICHARD. *Deterrence in American Foreign Policy: Theory and Practice.* New York: Columbia University Press, 1974.

——, HALL, DAVID K., and SIMONS, WILLIAM E. *The Limits of Coercive Diplomacy: Laos, Cuba, Vietnam.* Boston: Little, Brown, 1971.

GETTLEMAN, MARVIN E. *Viet-Nam.* New York: Fawcett Books, 1965.

GITTINGS, JOHN. *The Role of the Chinese Army.* London: Oxford University Press, 1967.

GOOLD-ADAMS, RICHARD. *John Foster Dulles: A Reappraisal.* New York: Appleton-Century-Crofts, 1962.

GORCE, PAUL-MARIE DE LA. *The French Army.* New York: George Braziller, 1963.

GOULDEN, JOSEPH C. *Korea: The Untold Story of the War.* New York: New York Times Books, 1982.

GRAUWIN, PAUL. *J'étais médecin à Dien Bien Phu.* Paris: Éditions France-Empire, 1954.

GREENE, GRAHAM. *Ways of Escape.* New York: Simon and Schuster, 1980.

GRIFFITH, ROBERT. *The Politics of Fear: Joseph R. McCarthy and the Senate.* Lexington: The University Press of Kentucky, 1970.

GRIFFITH, GENERAL SAMUEL B., II. *The Chinese People's Liberation Army.* New York: McGraw-Hill, 1967.

——. *Mao Tse-tung: On Guerrilla Warfare.* New York: Praeger, 1961.

GUHIN, MICHAEL A. *John Foster Dulles: A Statesman and His Times.* New York: Columbia University Press, 1972.

GUILLAIN, ROBERT L. *La Fin des illusions: notes d'Indochine (Février-Juillet 1954).* Paris: Centre d'Etudes de Politique Étrangère, 1954.

GURTOV, MELVIN. *The First Vietnam Crisis: Chinese Communist Strategy and United States Involvement 1953–1954.* New York: Columbia University Press, 1967.

HALBERSTAM, DAVID. *The Best and the Brightest.* New York: Random House, 1972.

HAMMER, ELLEN J. *The Struggle for Indochina 1940–1955.* Stanford, Calif.: Stanford University Press, 1955.

HINTON, HAROLD C. *China's Turbulent Quest,* Bloomington: Indiana University Press, 1972.

HOANG, VAN CHI. *From Colonialism to Communism: A Case History of North Vietnam.* New York: Praeger, 1964.

HOOPES, TOWNSEND. *The Devil and John Foster Dulles.* Boston: Little, Brown, 1973.

HOXIE, R. GORDON. *Command Decision and the Presidency.* New York: Reader's Digest Press, 1977.

HUBLER, RICHARD G. *SAC: The Strategic Air Command.* Westport, Conn.: Greenwood Press, 1977.

HUGHES, EMMET JOHN. *The Ordeal of Power.* New York: Dell Books, 1962.

IRVING, R.E.M. *The First Indochina War.* London: Croom-Helm, 1975.

JEANDREL, P. PAUL. *Soutane Noire, Béret Rouge.* Paris: Éditions de la Pensée Moderne, 1957.

JEANNERET, COLONEL. *Pages de gloire des parachutistes.* Paris: Société Nouvelle des Éditions Valmont, 1959.

JUIN, MARSHAL ALPHONSE. *Trois Siècles d'obéissance militaire: 1650–1963.* Paris: Librairie Plon, 1964.

JUMPER, ROY, and NGUYEN THI HUE. *Notes on the Political and Administrative History of Vietnam 1802–1962.* Lansing: Michigan State University Press, June 1962.

JURIKA, STEPHEN, JR., ed. *From Pearl Harbor to Vietnam: The Memoirs of Admiral Arthur W. Radford.* Stanford: Hoover Institution Press, 1980.

KALICKI, J. H. *The Pattern of Sino-American Crises.* Cambridge: Cambridge University Press, 1975.

KANITZ, WALTER. *The White Kepi: A Casual History of the French Foreign Legion.* Chicago: Henry Regnery, 1956.

KEEGAN, JOHN. *Dien Bien Phu.* New York: Ballantine, 1974.

KELLEY, GEORGE A. *Lost Soldiers: The French Army and Empire in Crisis 1947–1962.* Cambridge: M.I.T. Press, 1965.

KENNAN, GEORGE F. *Memoirs.* Vol. II: 1950–1963. Boston: Little, Brown, 1972.

KINNARD, DOUGLAS. *The Secretary of Defense.* Lexington: The University Press of Kentucky, 1981.

KRIEG, E., et al. *La tragédie indochinois.* Vol. 3: *Le piège de Dien Bien Phu.* Dijon: Éditions de Saint Clair, 1966.

KRUG, MARK M. *Aneurin Bevan: Cautious Rebel.* New York: Thomas Yoseloff, 1961.

KUNSTADTER, PETER, ed. *Southeast Asian Tribes, Minorities, and Nations,* 2 vols. Princeton, N.J.: Princeton University Press, 1967.

LACOUTURE, JEAN *Between Two Truces.* New York: Random House, 1966.

——. *Cinq hommes et la France.* Paris: Éditions du Seuil, 1961.

——. *The End of a War: Indochina 1954.* New York: Praeger, 1969.

——. *Ho Chi Minh: A Political Biography.* New York: Random House, 1968.

——, and DEVILLERS, PHILIPPE. *La Fin d'une guerre: Indochine 1954.* Paris: Éditions du Seuil, 1960.

LANCASTER, DONALD. *The Emancipation of French Indochina.* New York: Oxford University Press, 1961.

LANGLAIS, COLONEL PIERRE. *Dien Bien Phu.* Paris: Presses Pocket, 1963.

LANIEL, JOSEPH. *Le drame indochinois: de Dien-Bien-Phu au pari de Genève.* Paris: Librairie Plon, 1957.

——. *Jours de gloire, jours cruels 1908–1958.* Paris: Presses de la Cité, 1971.

LANSDALE, GENERAL EDWARD G. *In the Midst of Wars.* New York: Harper & Row, 1972.

LARTÉGUY, JEAN. *The Centurions.* New York: E. P. Dutton, 1961.

LAWRENCE, WILLIAM. *Six Presidents and Too Many Wars.* New York: Saturday Review Press, 1979.

LEBOW, RICHARD NED. *Between Peace and War: The Nature of International Crisis.* Baltimore: Johns Hopkins University Press, 1981.

LECKIE, ROBERT. *Conflict: The History of the Korean War.* New York: Avon Books, 1962.

LEDERER, WILLIAM J., and BURDICK, EUGENE. *The Ugly American.* New York: W. W. Norton, 1958.

LEMAY, GENERAL CURTIS, with KANTOR, MACKINLAY. *Mission With LeMay: My Story.* Garden City, N.Y.: Doubleday, 1965.

LEUTHY, HERBERT. *France Against Herself.* New York: Meridian, 1955.

LINEBARGER, PAUL M. *Psychological Warfare.* Washington, D.C.: Combat Forces Press, 1954.

LOWE, RAYMOND. *The Age of Deterrence.* Boston: Little, Brown, 1964.

✓MACARTHUR, GENERAL DOUGLAS. *Reminiscences.* Greenwich, Conn.: Fawcett, 1965.

MACLEAR, MICHAEL. *The Ten Thousand Day War.* New York: St. Martin's Press, 1981.

MARCHAND, GENERAL JEAN. *L'Indochine en guerre.* Paris: Pouzet, 1955.

MCALISTER, JOHN T. *Vietnam: The Origins of Revolution.* Garden City, N.Y.: Doubleday Anchor, 1971.

——, and MUS, PAUL. *The Vietnamese and Their Revolution.* New York: Harper & Row, 1970.

MCCOY, ALFRED W., READ, CATHLEEN B., and ADAMS, LEONARD P., II. *The Politics of Heroin in Southeast Asia.* New York: Harper & Row, 1972.

MERCER, CHARLES. *Legion of Strangers.* New York: Pyramid Books, 1964.

MERGLEN, ALBERT. *Histoire et avenir des troupes aéroportées.* Paris: Arthaud, 1968.

MILES, ADMIRAL MILTON E. *A Different Kind of War.* Garden City, N.Y.: Doubleday, 1967.

MOSLEY, LEONARD. *Dulles: A Biography of Eleanor, Allen, and John Foster Dulles and Their Family Network.* New York: Dial Press, 1978.

NAVARRE, GENERAL HENRI. *Agonie de l'Indochine 1953–1954.* Paris: Librairie Plon, 1956.

NEWMAN, BERNARD. *Report on Indochina.* New York: Praeger, 1954.

NGHIEM DANG. *Vietnam: Politics and Public Administration.* Honolulu: East-West Center Press, 1966.

NGUYEN KHAC HUYEN. *Vision Accomplished? The Enigma of Ho Chi Minh.* New York: Collier Books, 1971.

NICOLSON, NIGEL. *Alex: The Life of Field Marshal Earl Alexander of Tunis.* London: Pan Books, 1976.

NIXON, RICHARD M. *RN: The Memoirs of Richard Nixon*, Vol. 1. New York: Warner Books, 1978.

O'BALLANCE, EDGAR. *The Indochina War 1945–1954.* London: Faber & Faber, 1964.

——. *The Story of the French Foreign Legion.* London: Faber & Faber, 1961.

O'NEILL, ROBERT J. *General Giap: Politican and Strategist.* New York: Praeger; 1969.

——. *Indochina Tragedy 1945–1954.* Melbourne: F. W. Cheshire, 1968.

OSANKA, FRANKLIN M. *Modern Guerrilla Warfare.* New York: Macmillan, 1962.

OSGOOD, ROBERT E. *Limited War.* Chicago: University of Chicago Press, 1957.

PAILLAT, CLAUDE. *Dossier secret de l'Indochine.* Paris: Presses de la Cité, 1964.

PARET, PETER. *French Revolutionary Warfare in Indochina and Algeria.* New York: Praeger, 1964.

PATTI, ARCHIMEDES L. *Why Viet Nam? Prelude to America's Albatross.* Berkeley: University of California Press, 1980.

PEARSON, DREW, and ANDERSON, JACK. *USA—Second Class Power?* New York: Simon and Schuster, 1958.

PEETERS, PAUL. *Massive Retaliation: The Policy and Its Critics.* Chicago: Henry Regnery, 1959.

The Pentagon Papers: The Senator Gravel Edition. Vol. I: *The Defense Department History of United States Decisionmaking on Vietnam.* Boston: Beacon Press, 1971.

PERRAULT, GILLES. *Les Parachutistes.* Paris: Éditions du Seuil, 1961.

POLMAR, NORMAN. *Strategic Air Command: People, Aircraft and Missiles.* Annapolis, Md.: Nautical and Aviation Publishing Company of America, 1979.

POMEROY, WILLIAM J., ed. *Guerrilla Warfare and Marxism.* New York: International Publishers, 1968.

POUGET, CAPTAIN JEAN. *Nous étions à Dien Bien Phu.* Paris: Presses de la Cité, 1964.

PURCELL, VICTOR. *The Chinese in Southeast Asia.* London: Oxford University Press, 1951.

RANDLE, ROBERT. *Geneva, 1954.* Princeton, N.J.: Princeton University Press, 1969.

REES, DAVID. *Korea: The Limited War.* Baltimore: Penguin Press, 1970.

REINHARDT, COLONEL GEORGE C. *American Strategy in the Atomic Age.* Norman: University of Oklahoma Press, 1955.

REISMAN, MARTY. *The Money Player.* New York: William Morrow, 1974.

RENALD, JEAN. *L'Enfer de Dien Bien Phu.* Paris: Flammarion, 1955.

RIDGWAY, GENERAL MATTHEW B. *The Korean War.* New York: Popular Library, 1967.

——. *Soldier.* New York: Harper & Row, 1956.

RIESEN, RENÉ. *Mission spéciale en forêt mot.* Paris: Editions France-Empire, 1955.

——. *Le Silence du ciel.* Paris: Editions de la Pensée Moderne, 1956.

RIGG, LIEUTENANT COLONEL ROBERT. *Red China's Fighting Hordes.* Westport, Conn.: Greenwood Press, 1951.

ROBBINS, CHRISTOPHER. *Air America: The Story of the CIA's Secret Airlines.* New York: Putnam, 1979.

ROBERTS, CHALMERS. *First Rough Draft.* New York: Praeger, 1973.

ROCOLLE, PIERRE. *Pourquoi Dien Bien Phu?* Paris: Flammarion, 1968.

ROVERE, RICHARD H. *Affairs of State: The Eisenhower Years.* New York: Farrar, Straus & Cudahy, 1956.

Roy, Colonel Jules. *La Bataille dans le rizière*. Paris: Gallimard, 1953.

——. *The Bataille de Dien Bien Phu*. Paris: Julliard, 1963.

——. *The Battle of Dien Bien Phu*, trans. Robert Baldick. New York: Harper & Row, 1965.

Sainteny, Jean. *Ho Chi Minh and His Vietnam*. Chicago: Cowles, 1972.

Salan, General Raoul. *Mémoires: Fin d'un Empire*. Vol. II: *Le Viet Minh mon adversaire*. Paris: Presses de la Cité, 1971.

Schilling, Warner R., ed. *Strategy, Politics and Defense Budgets*. New York: Columbia University Press, 1962.

Schlesinger, Arthur M., Jr. *The Bitter Heritage*. New York: Fawcett, 1967.

Schlesinger, Stephen, and Kinzer, Stephen. *Bitter Fruit: The Untold Story of the American Coup in Guatemala*. Garden City, N.Y.: Doubleday, 1982.

Schoenbrun, David. *As France Goes*. New York: Harper, 1957.

Sheehan, Neil, et al. *The Pentagon Papers* (as published by *The New York Times*). New York: Bantam Books, 1971.

Shepley, James R., and Blair, Clay, Jr. *The Hydrogen Bomb*. New York: David McKay, 1954.

Slessor, Air Marshal Sir John. *Strategy for the West*. London: William Morrow, 1954.

Smith, Joseph Burkholder. *Portrait of a Cold Warrior*. New York: Putnam, 1976.

SMITH, R. HARRIS. OSS: *The Secret History of America's First Central Intelligence Agency*. Berkeley: University of California Press, 1972.

SNOW, EDGAR. *Red Star Over China*, rev. ed. New York: Grove Press, 1968.

STONE, I....F. *The Hidden History of the Korean War*. New York: Monthly Review Press, 1952.

SULLY, FRANÇOIS. *The Age of the Guerrilla*. New York: Avon Books, 1968.

SULZBERGER, CYRUS L. *A Long Row of Candles*. New York: Macmillan, 1969.

TANHAM, GEORGE K. *Communist Revolutionary Warfare*. New York: Praeger, 1967.

TEULIÈRES, ANDRÉ. *La Guerre du Viet Nam 1945–1975*. Paris: Éditions Lavauzelle, 1978.

TOPPING, SEYMOUR. *Journey Between Two Chinas*. New York: Harper & Row, 1972.

TOURNOUX, J. R. *Secrets d'etat*. Paris: Librairie Plon, 1960.

TRINQUIER, COLONEL ROGER. *Les Maquis d'Indochine 1952–1954*. Paris: Éditions Albatross, 1976.

——. *Modern Warfare: A French View of Insurgency*. New York: Praeger, 1963.

TURNBULL, PATRICK. *The Foreign Legion*. London: Heinemann, 1964.

The Vietnam Hearings. New York: Random House, Vintage Books, 1966.

Vo Nguyen Giap. *Dienbienphu*. Hanoi: Foreign Languages Publishing House, 1964.

——. *People's War, People's Army*. New York: Praeger, 1962.

Warner, Denis A. *Out of the Gun*. London: Hutchinson, 1956.

Werner, Dennis. *The Last Confucian*. New York: Macmillan, 1963.

Werth, Alexander. *France 1940–1955*. Boston: Beacon Press, 1966.

Whitson, Colonel William W., with Chen-Hsia Huang. *The Chinese High Command: A History of Communist Military Politics 1927–1971*. New York: Praeger, 1973.

IV. MAJOR PERIODICAL ITEMS

Bodard, Lucien. "Du Grand Na San à la montagne magique de Lai Chau." *Indochine Sud-est Asiatique*, no. 16 (March 1953).

Brodie, Bernard. "Unlimited Weapons and Limited War." *The Reporter* (November 18, 1954).

Chassin, General Lionel Max. "L'Armée Aérienne dans la bataille du Laos." *Indochine Sud-est Asiatique*, no. 22 (September 1953).

Croizat, Colonel Victor J. "Vietnamese Naval Forces: Origin of the Species." *United States Naval Institute Proceedings* (February 1973).

Dalmas, Louis. "En Un Combat Douteux." *Les Temps Modernes* (August-September 1953).

Dejean, Maurice. "The Meaning of Dien Bien Phu," *United States Naval Institute Proceedings* (July 1954).

DERUNES, PIERRE. "L'Essor de la nouvelle armée Lao," *Indochine Sud-est Asiatique*, no. 13 (December 1952).

DULLES, ELEANOR LANSING. "Time and Decisions," *Forensic Quarterly*, August 1969.

DULLES, JOHN FOSTER. "A Policy of Boldness." *Life* (May 19, 1952).

——. "Policy for Security and Peace." *Foreign Affairs* (April 1954).

DUTT, VIDYA PRAKASH, and SINGH, VISHAL. "Indian Policy and Attitudes Towards Indochina and SEATO." Institute for Pacific Relations (1954).

FALL, BERNARD B. "Communist POW Treatment in Indochina." *Military Review* (December 1958).

——. "Indochina: The Last Year of the War." *Military Review* (December 1956).

France-Soir

FRIANG, BRIGITTE. "La Coloniale." *Indochine Sud-est Asiatique*, no. 22 (September 1953).

GAVIN, GENERAL JAMES M. "A Communication on Vietnam." *Harper's* Magazine (February 1966).

GUIGUES, CLAUDE. "Panoplie Vietminh." *Indochine Sud-est Asiatique*, no. 8 (July 1952).

——. "Quang Yen Fabrique les 'Kinh Quan' à la chaîne," *Indochine Sud-est Asiatique*, no. 24 (November 1953).

HESS, GARY R. "The First American Commitment in Indochina: The Acceptance of the 'Bao Dai Solution' 1950." *Diplomatic History* (Fall 1978).

"How Near We Came to War." *U.S. News & World Report* (August 6, 1954).

KNEBEL, FLETCHER. "We Nearly Went to War Three Times." *Look* (February 8, 1955).

LACOUTURE, JEAN. "Les forces en présence." *Le Monde* (November 11 and 12, 1952).

L'Humanité

Le Monde

MARTIN, NORMAN E. "Dienbienphu and the Future of Airborne Operations." *Military Review* (June 1956).

MCCLINTOCK, ROBERT. "The River War in Indochina." *United States Naval Institute Proceedings* (December 1954).

MILLER, D.M.O. "A Handful of Rice: Logistics in the Viet Minh Campaign." *Armed Forces and Defense Quarterly* (Spring 1965).

MURPHY, CHARLES J....V. "The US as a Bombing Target," *Fortune* (November 1953).

New York Herald Tribune

The New York Times

Newsweek

O'BALLANCE, EDGAR. "The Campaign in Indochina: The Fighting in Laos 1953–54." *Army Quarterly* (April 1955).

OLIVIER, MAX. "Un portrait du General Cogny." *Indochine Sud-est Asiatique*, no. 24 (November 1953).

——. "Un portrait du General Navarre." *Indochine Sud-est Asiatique*, no. 22 (September 1953).

ROBERTS, CHALMERS. "The Day We Didn't Go to War." *The Reporter* (September 14, 1954).

ROSENBERG, DAVID A. "A Smoking Radiating Ruin at the End of Two Hours: Documents on American Plans for Nuclear War with the Soviet Union, 1954–55." *International Security* (Winter 1981–82).

SCHLESINGER, ARTHUR M., JR. "Eyeless In Indochina." *The New York Review of Books* (October 27, 1971).

SCHOENBRUN, DAVID. "The Case Against the Absentee Emperor." *Collier's* (September 30, 1955).

SCHREADLEY, COMMANDER R....L. "The Naval War In Vietnam 1950–1970." *United States Naval Institute Proceedings* (May 1971).

SHEPLEY, JAMES R. "How Dulles Averted War." *Life* (January 16, 1956).

Time

TRAN VAN DINH. "The Quan Doi Nhan Dan Vietnam." Ms. (1974).

TURLEY, WILLIAM S. "Origins and Development of Communist Military Leadership in Vietnam." *Armed Forces and Society* (February 1977).

Washington Post-Times Herald

"What Ridgway Told Ike." *U.S. News & World Report* (June 25, 1954).

WILLIAMS, COMMANDER RALPH E., JR. "The Great Debate: 1954." *United States Naval Institute Proceedings* (March 1954).